A
Scottish
Naturalist

The Sketches and Notes of Charles St John
1809–1856

A Scottish Naturalist

The Sketches and Notes of Charles St John
1809—1856

ANDRE DEUTSCH

First published in 1982 by
Andre Deutsch Limited
105 Great Russell Street, London WC1

Designed and produced by
Antony Atha Publishers Ltd,
1 Strafford Road, Twickenham, Middlesex

Printed and bound in the Netherlands by
Comproject BV Holland

ISBN 0 233 97390 7

CONTENTS

COLOUR ILLUSTRATIONS

FOREWORD
by
Robert Dougall

Charles St John's true importance as a naturalist rests with his exceptional gift for intimate, meticulous observation, combined with an ability to write with total accuracy and immense charm about the bird life and other small creatures with which he was so abundantly surrounded. And it is, in a sense, unfortunate that his name is forever associated with the 19th century heyday of the Highland sport of deer stalking. This is the inevitable result of his vivid accounts of many a gory confrontation such as that with "the Muckle Hart of Benmore". Today, few of us have the stomach for a sport which, in those wilder and more spacious days, was generally accepted in Scotland as a normal and praiseworthy pursuit.

Antony Atha has done a great service in distilling for us here the best of St John's work. The author was, of course, living at a time when there were no bird protection laws and all feathered creatures were liable to be mercilessly harried, trapped, shot for sport, or sometimes slain for the purpose of identification.

He was ahead of his time when he wrote "for my own part, I never trust a gun in my gardener's hands, but let the blackbirds and thrushes take as many cherries as they like, in return for which they destroy thousands of grey snails etc. besides giving me many a moment of pleasure by their song".

His account of the daily life of a country gentleman, sportsman and naturalist, in the glory of the Scottish Highlands over a hundred years ago, is enlivened and embellished by his own numerous sketches and watercolours. St John was entirely self-taught in art but his sketches lack nothing in movement and humour. Some of the birds depicted in watercolour seem strangely elongated but nevertheless have a considerable naive charm.

For those unfamiliar with his writings there are rare delights in the pages that follow. There seemed to be birds everywhere—even in the house. One day he found: "A sparrowhawk deliberately standing on a very large pouter-pigeon on the drawing-room floor, and plucking it, having entered in pursuit of the unfortunate bird through an open window, and killed him in the room."

In the company of Charles St John there is certainly not a moment of dullness.

Charles St John was born on the 3rd December, 1809. He went to school in Midhurst in Sussex and then became a clerk in the Treasury in 1828. This occupation was not to the taste of someone whose earliest interests had been in natural history and he was described as 'chafing like a caged eagle at the desk of a Government office'. In 1833 he left the Treasury and went to live in Sutherland where he was lent the place of Rosehall by his cousin Lord Bolingbroke. In November 1834 in an expedition from Rosehall he met and married Miss Anne Gibson the daughter of a Newcastle banker.

Thereafter he lived in various houses in the north of Scotland finally settling in the 'Laigh' of Moray. In the autumn of 1844 he met Mr C. Innes, Sheriff of Moray, shooting partridges, who encouraged his writing and arranged for the sale and publication of *The Wild Sports and Natural History of the Highlands* in 1845. His second book *A Tour of Sutherland* which incorporated *Field Notes of a Naturalist* was published in two volumes in 1849. In 1853 St John suffered a stroke which left him paralysed and he died at Woolston, near Southampton, in 1856

In addition to the two books published in his lifetime Mr Innes edited and arranged St John's journals and these were published in 1863 as *Natural History and Sport in Moray*. In his journals St John wrote, "I have been particularly careful to describe and note down nothing the authenticity of which I am not certain of. Indeed, every bird here mentioned, with one or two exceptions, I have either killed or seen myself during my wanderings in wood and plain for several years in this district. I have carefully avoided the great error of taking things on hearsay."

The text of this book has been taken from the three published works of Charles St John, and arranged to complement the illustrations from his sketchbooks, which are here published for the first time. I have followed the order of the *Natural History of Moray* interspersed with chapters on the main species of birds and animals that St John studied and described. I would recommend anyone who wishes to read a full account of St John's studies to buy a copy of the *Natural History of Moray*.

Some of St John's pen and ink sketches were included in the second edition of that book which was published in 1883 and I have also included in this book some of the etchings which were originally drawn for that edition.

Antony Atha

Basin of the Findhorn. 6th September. 1840.   18 R·81.

INTRODUCTION

I have lived for several years in the northern counties of Scotland, and
during the last four or five in the province of Moray, a part of the
country peculiarly adapted for collecting facts in Natural History, and
for becoming intimate with the habits of many of our British wild birds
and quadrupeds. Having been in the habit of keeping an irregular kind
of journal, and of making notes of any incidents which have fallen under
my observation connected with the zoology of the country, I have now
endeavoured, by dint of cutting and pruning those rough sketches, to
put them into a shape calculated to amuse, and perhaps, in some slight
degree, to instruct some of my fellow-lovers of Nature. From my earliest
childhood I have been more addicted to the investigation of the habits
and manners of every kind of living animal than to any more useful
avocation, and have in consequence made myself tolerably well
acquainted with the domestic economy of most of our British *feræ naturæ*,
from the field-mouse and wheatear, which I stalked and trapped in the
plains and downs of Wiltshire during my boyhood, to the red deer and
eagle, whose territory I have invaded in later years on the mountains of
Scotland.

My present abode in Morayshire is surrounded by as great a variety of
beautiful scenery as can be found in any district in Britain; and no part of
the country can produce a greater variety of objects of interest either to
the naturalist or to the lover of the picturesque. The rapid and glorious
Findhorn, the very perfection of a Highland river, here passes through
one of the most fertile plains in Scotland, or indeed in the world; and
though a few miles higher up it rages through the wildest and most
rugged rocks, and through the romantic and shaded glens of the forests

of Darnaway and Altyre, the stream, as if exhausted, empties itself peaceably and quietly into the Bay of Findhorn, a salt-water loch of some four or five miles in length, entirely shut out by different points of land from the storms which are so frequent in the Moray Firth, of which it forms a kind of creek. At low-water this bay becomes an extent of wet sand, with the river Findhorn and one or two smaller streams winding through it, till they meet in the deeper part of the basin near the town of Findhorn, where there is always a considerable depth of water, and a harbour for shipping.

From its sheltered situation and the quantity of food left on the sands at low-water, the Bay of Findhorn is always a great resort of wild-fowl of all kinds, from the swan to the teal, and also of innumerable waders of every species; while occasionally a seal ventures into the mouth of the river in pursuit of salmon, The bay is separated from the main water of the Firth by that most extraordinary and peculiar range of country called the Sandhills of Moray, a long, low range of hills formed of the purest sand, with scarcely any herbage, excepting here and there patches of bent or broom, which are inhabited by hares, rabbits, and foxes. At the extreme point of this range is a farm of forty or fifty acres of arable land, where the tenant endeavours to grow a scanty crop of grain and turnips, in spite of the rabbits and the drifting sands. From the inland side of the bay stretch the fertile plains of Moray, extending from the Findhorn to near Elgin in a continuous flat of the richest soil, and comprising districts of the very best partridge-shooting that can be found in Scotland, while the streams and swamps that intersect it afford a constant supply of wild-fowl. As we advance inland we are sheltered by the wide-extending woods of Altyre, abounding with roe and game, and beyond these woods again is a very extensive range of a most excellent grouse-shooting country, reaching for many miles over a succession of moderately sized hills which reach as far as the Spey.

On the west of the Findhorn is a country beautifully dotted with woods, principally of oak and birch, and intersected by a dark, winding burn, full of fine trout, and the constant haunt of the otter. Between this part of the country and the sea-coast is a continuation of the Sandhills, interspersed with lakes, swamps, and tracts of fir-wood and heather. On the whole I do not know so varied or interesting a district in Great Britain, or one so well adapted to the amusement and instruction of a naturalist or sportsman. In the space of a morning's walk you may be either in the most fertile or in the most barren spot of the country. In my own garden every kind of wall-fruit ripens to perfection, and yet at the distance of only two hours' walk you may either be in the midst of heather and grouse, or in the sandy deserts beyond the bay, where one wonders how even the rabbits can find their living.

The varieties of the soil and its productions, both animate and inanimate, will, however, be best shown in the extracts from my note-books, with which these pages are filled. My memorandums, having for

the most part been written down at the moment, and describing anecdotes and incidents that fell under my actual observation, will at all events contain correct descriptions of the nature and habits of the animals and birds of the country; though, not being originally intended for publication, they are not arranged in any regular order. Here and there I have quoted some anecdote of animals, which I have heard from others: these I can only offer as I received them, but I can safely assert that I have quoted the words of those persons only upon whose veracity and powers of observation I could depend. My subject, as connected both to natural history and sporting, has led me back to my former wanderings in the more northern and wilder parts of the country, where I had great opportunities of becoming acquainted with the habits of the wilder and rarer birds and beasts, who are natives of those districts; and the pursuit of whom always had greater charms for me than the more commonplace occupations of grouse or partridge shooting.

I hope that my readers will be indulgent enough to make allowances for the unfinished style of these sketches, and the copious use of the first person singular, which I have found it impossible to avoid whilst describing the adventures which I have met with in this wild country, either when toiling up the rocky heights of our most lofty mountains, or cruising in a boat along the shores, where rocks and caves give a chance of finding sea-fowl and otters; at one time wandering over the desert sand-hills of Moray, where, on windy days, the light particles of drifting sand, driven like snow along the surface of the ground, are perpetually changing the outline and appearance of the district; at another, among the swamps, in pursuit of wild ducks, or attacking fish in the rivers, or the grouse on the heather.

JANUARY

Wood-pigeons—Wild Ducks and Potatoes—The Titmouse—Little Auk—Weasels and
Mice—Oyster-catchers—Birds going North—The Water-rail—Greater Titmouse—
Long-tailed and Crested Titmice—Buntings—Habits of the Curlew—Sandpipers—
Trout changing Colour

During the month of January the wood-pigeons commence feeding
greedily on the turnips. They do not, in my opinion, dig into the
roots with their bills, unless rabbits or rooks have been before them to
break the skin of the turnips. In fact the wood-pigeon's bill is not at all
adapted for cutting into a frozen and unbroken turnip. The crops of
those which I kill at this season are full of the leaf of the turnip; and they
appear not to attack the centre or heart of the green leaf, but to eat only
the thin part of it. The wood-pigeon feeds more particularly on the leaf
of the Swedish turnip, which is more succulent.

An agricultural friend of mine pointed out to me the other day
(March 6th) an immense flock of wood-pigeons busily at work on a field
of young clover which had been under barley the last season. "There,"
he said, "you constantly say that every bird does more good than harm;
what good are those birds doing to my young clover?" On this, in
furtherance of my favourite axiom, that *every wild animal is of some service to
us*, I determined to shoot some of the wood-pigeons, that I might see
what they actually were feeding on; for I did not at all fall into my
friend's idea that they were grazing on his clover. By watching in their
line of flight from the field to the woods, and sending a man round to
drive them off the clover, I managed to kill eight of the birds as they flew
over my head.

I took them to his house, and we opened their crops to see what they
contained. Every pigeon's crop was as full as it could possibly be of the

[14]

seeds of two of the worst weeds in the country, the wild mustard and the ragweed, which they had found remaining on the surface of the ground, these plants ripening and dropping their seeds before the corn is cut. Now no amount of human labour and search could have collected on the same ground, at that time of the year, as much of these seeds as was consumed by each of these five or six hundred wood-pigeons daily, for two or three weeks together.

For my own part, I never shoot at a wood-pigeon near my house, nor do I ever kill one without a feeling of regret, so much do I like to hear their note in the spring and summer mornings. The first decisive symptom of the approach of spring and fine weather is the cooing of the wood-pigeon. Where not molested, they are very fond of building their nest in the immediate vicinity of a house. Shy as they are at all other times of the year, no bird sits closer on her eggs or breeds nearer to the abode of man than the wood-pigeon. There are always several nests close to my windows, and frequently immediately over some walk, where the birds sit in conscious security, within five or six feet of the passer-by; and there are generally a pair or two that feed with the chickens, knowing the call of the woman who takes care of the poultry as well as the tame birds do.

In the woods they breed in great numbers, in trees, in ivy sometimes, in a furze bush, and in some few instances I have found the nest on the ground. Frequently they build close to the sparrowhawk, notwithstanding the enmity which exists between these birds; the sparrowhawk frequently killing wood-pigeons, in spite of the superior weight and size of the latter bird. It is to be supposed that when these two so dissimilar birds build so close together, it is for mutual protection against the hooded crow, who is always searching for eggs. The sparrowhawk attacks and drives away every crow which may approach, while the wood-pigeon does good service by giving due notice of the enemy.

I have frequently attempted to tame young wood-pigeons, taking them at a very early age from the nest. They generally become tolerably familiar till the first moult; but as soon as they acquire strength of plumage and wing, they have invariably left me, except in one instance which occurred two years ago. I put some wood-pigeons' eggs under a tame pigeon of my children's taking away the eggs on which she was sitting at the time. Only one of the young birds grew up, and it became perfectly tame. It remained with its foster parents, flying in and out of their house, and coming with them to be fed at the windows. After it had grown up, and the cares of a new nest made the old birds drive it out of their company, the wood-pigeon became still tamer, always coming at breakfast-time or whenever he was called to the window-sill, where he would remain as long as he was noticed, cooing and strutting up and down as if to challenge attention to his beautiful plumage.

However, this poor bird came to an untimely end, being struck down and killed by a hen-harrier. I never on any other occasion saw a wood-

from Dingwall

pigeon remain perfectly tame, if left at liberty; and if they are entirely confined, they seldom acquire their full beauty of feather. The bird seems to have a natural shyness and wildness which prevent its ever becoming domesticated like the common blue rock-pigeon.

About November the wood-pigeons assemble in immense flocks to feed on the stubble and new-sown wheat and it is very difficult to approach wood-pigeons when feeding in the fields. They keep in the most open and exposed places, and allow no enemy to come near them. It is amusing to watch a large flock of these birds while searching the ground for grain. They walk in a compact body, and in order that all may fare alike, the hindmost rank every now and then fly over the heads of their companions to the front, where they keep the best place for a minute or two, till those now in the rear take their place in the same manner. They keep up this kind of fair play during the whole time of feeding.

I have never but once seen a wood-pigeon with any variety of plumage, In this instance a wood-pigeon, almost entirely white, has for three winters, and is still (November 1852), feeding on the same fields near Elgin. I have seen this bird quite distinctly through my telescope and examined its plumage, which is pure white, with a few marks of the natural colour about the neck and tail.

This season (1847) the wild ducks have found out a new kind of food—the remnant of the diseased potatoes which have been left in the fields. My attention was first called to their feeding on them, by observing that my domesticated wild ducks had managed to dig well into a heap of half-rotten potatoes which had been put partly under ground, and then covered over with a good thickness of earth, as being unfit for pigs or any other animal. However, our wild ducks had scented

247   Creeper

them out, and, although well supplied with food, they had dug into the heap in all directions, feeding greedily on the rotten potatoes; in fact, leaving their corn for them. I then found that the wild ducks from the bay flew every evening to the potato-fields to feed on the roots which had been left; and so fond were they of them, that I often saw the ducks rise from the fields in the middle of the day.

In the garden I see the titmice searching for, and feeding on, the nests and eggs of the common garden spider. The little blue tom-tit is of great service to gardeners as a destroyer of many kinds of insects, which would increase to a most injurious extent without the aid of these prying little fellows, who are seen everywhere and at all seasons. Several pairs always breed in my garden wall; they line their nests with a great quantity of feathers and other soft substances, and lay eight to ten eggs; according to some authors twice that number, though I certainly never saw above ten eggs in a nest. When sitting, the old bird is very tame and bold, attacking the hand which is put into her nest, hissing at it like a snake, and frequently refusing to leave her eggs. The young, when first fledged, resemble the parent bird in brightness of colour more than the young of most other birds.

Like the greater titmouse the little bird is quite omnivorous, feeding on everything that comes in its way. It is fond of carrion, and I have frequently seen it feeding on dead mice or rats. It comes boldly to the window, and even into the room, in search of flies. It is, however, very impatient of confinement, and difficult to keep alive in a cage. In the winter it accompanies the golden-crested wren, etc., in their wanderings in the fir-woods in search of insects, though it is always more inclined to the neighbourhood of houses, and it is frequently seen in the midst of large towns. It is a busy meddling little bird, at the head of all attacks on cat or owl that may stray into the gardens or shrubberies, seeming to become quite infuriated against these enemies. The egg is white, spotted not very closely with pale red.

The thrushes begin to sing, and the corn bunting and yellow-hammer to utter their spring note.

January 14th, 1847. Neither widgeon nor teal are yet in full plumage. A great number of the bird called the little auk are found dead along the shore.

This bird, *le petit guillemot* of Buffon, visits us at irregular intervals, and on these occasions it generally comes in great numbers, being found at the mouth of every stream, and not unfrequently in ponds, or even lying disabled and worn out in fields at some distance from the sea. One was brought to me in 1851 which was picked up alive in a ploughed field, where the poor little stranger was found sitting upright, and apparently quite bewildered, by its change of situation from the clear depths of the arctic seas to a muddy ploughed field.

A weasel has eaten a great many of the mice caught in the boys' traps, and was caught itself at last in a rat trap. I don't know a more

courageous little animal; when overtaken by a dog, it flies directly at the dog's head and bites furiously.

January 16th, 1848. I have not seen any swans this winter.

I see the widgeon come regularly now at the ebb of the tide to feed on the grassy banks which are left uncovered by the receding of the water. They first feed as they swim round the edges of the small islands and banks; but when the tide begins to recede, they come out on the banks and graze like geese.

During the present severe frost I am much amused with the long-tailed ducks who at every flow of the tide swim into the bay, and often some way up the river, uttering their most musical and singular cry, which at a distance resembles the bugle note of the wild swan.

As long as these is no collection of floating ice the bay is very full of birds, and the shores are enlivened with large flocks of oyster-catchers and an infinite variety of other waders.

The oyster-catcher remains during the whole year in this district. During the winter it frequents the sea-shore entirely, where it feeds on small shell-fish, and any worms, mollusca, etc., which it can find. In spring many are found in most of the rivers, where they breed on the gravelly banks and ridges. The old birds are very clamorous when the young or eggs are approached, flying and wheeling rapidly round the head of the intruder. At other times they are very shy; at the same time no bird is more easily tamed or lives more contentedly in domestication. Though not web-footed, they dive and swim with great rapidity and strength. Although they pair in the breeding season, I have frequently seen large flocks of these birds collected together in the month of June, when their nesting was in full progress, and when I should have imagined that every bird would be busily employed with eggs or young, instead of sitting in dense masses on the banks and sands of the Bay of Findhorn, with apparently no care on their shoulders. They do not on these occasions appear to be collected for the purpose of feeding, but to be resting and passing their time as they do in the midst of winter.

The redshank begins now to utter the peculiar whistle which indicates the return of spring; early as it is, too, the jack-snipes, redwings, fieldfares, etc., seem to return northwards, as I see great numbers of

these and other birds, which had for the last month or two disappeared, having probably then gone southwards.

The little water-rail seems to be a great wanderer. I find its track, and the bird itself, in the most unlikely places; for instance, I put up one in a dry furze field, and my retriever caught another in a hedge, at some distance from the water. I took the latter bird home alive to show to my children. When I took him out of my pocket, in which most unaccustomed situation he had been for two hours, the strange little creature looked about him with the greatest nonchalance possible, showing fight at every thing that came near him; and when, after having gratified the curiosity of the children, we turned him loose in a ditch of running water, he went away jerking up his tail, and not seeming to hurry himself, or to be in the least disconcerted.

It is, however, seldom seen, in consequence of its very retired and shy habits. Spynie is the only place in which I have succeeded in finding the nest, and then only with the assistance of a good water-dog: so concealed is the nest and so quietly does the old bird leave it.

The greater titmouse is perhaps (with the exception of the crested titmouse) the least common species of the titmouse in this country; at the same time it is by no means rare. It feeds on almost everything—seeds of all kinds, fruit, such as apples and pears, insects, raw meat, indeed nothing comes amiss. I have often seen it caught in mouse-traps baited with toasted cheese. It also eats a great many of my walnuts when they fall from the tree; when it finds one the shell of which is not very hard, it digs into the walnut with its bill till it reaches the kernel, which it feeds on. It also—like the blue tomtit and willow wren—is fond of coming about the windows for the blue-bottle flies, which it seems very fond of.

During the winter, large numbers of long-tailed titmice, in scattered flocks, constantly pass through the woods, flitting from branch to branch, and hanging in all sorts of attitudes to the twigs, as they search for food. They are frequently in company with the golden-crested wren, the other kinds of titmice, and tree-creepers. In summer it is also numerous. The nest is beautifully made, covered at the top, and frequently pendent from a branch, sometimes placed in the heart of a thorn bush, where it is difficult to insert the hand, sometimes fitted into

[19]

the branches of an oak or other tree, and so artfully covered with lichen similar to that on the bark of the tree, that it is very difficult to distinguish the nest. The nest has sometimes two entrances, at other times only one. The long-tailed tomtit has so short a bill, and the head and body are so closely joined, forming together almost one ball, that, with its long slender tail, it has a most singular appearance as it flies, with its dart-like motion, from tree to tree. Constantly in motion, this little bird seems never to be still for an instant.

A pair which built in a yew-tree near my house afforded me much amusement by their constant activity in searching for proper materials, and by the rapidity with which they built. The eggs are eight or nine in number, white, with red spots, though I have heard of many more being found in one nest. The food of this titmouse consists wholly of insects. It is a great mistake to suppose that any titmice are mischievous in a garden. They are accused of picking off the buds of fruit trees. But I am confident that they never touch a bud which does not contain a small grub or caterpillar, and the benefit which they confer by their destruction of insects and caterpillars, and also of the minute eggs of these creatures, exceeds all belief, and can only be known by watching a pair of blue or other titmice feeding their numerous progeny, every one of whose ravenous appetites calls for a constant supply of insect food. Most birds, if not all, repay for the seed which they eat by the insects which they destroy. The titmice do this more than any.

I know no bird so confined to particular spots as the crested-titmouse. Their only regular place of abode, as far as has been ascertained, is the large forest near Grantown on the Spey; there they build tolerably abundantly in the decayed clefts and holes of the old fir-trees, making a smaller nest than most other birds of the same genus. They lay about six eggs, white with dark red spots. Their habits are like those of other titmice; searching the trees for small insects, and flying from branch to branch uttering a loud shrill cry. On the head is a tolerably long and pointed crest of black feathers, the upper parts are pale greenish brown, the lower parts dull white; tail, gray. This is the dullest coloured of all the titmice, but easily distinguished by its remarkable crest, which it erects with great facility. It is little known as a British bird.

The yellow-bunting or yellow-hammer is seen everywhere, though not frequently collecting into flocks. The male is a beautiful bird, the female less brightly marked.

The reed-bunting or black-headed bunting, though common, is not so generally spread as the yellow-bunting, frequenting most commonly rushy, reedy pools, etc. Scarcely two reed-buntings are marked alike, varying also much in different seasons.

Curlews differ very much in size, more so than almost any other bird. As soon as the autumn commences they leave the higher grounds and betake themselves to the sea-shore and the neighbouring fields. When driven to the sea-shore to feed they live on small cockles and other shell-fish, which they can swallow whole; their bills not being hard at the point, like that of the oyster-catcher, they cannot break any hard substance. No bird is more wary and cunning than the curlew. They are almost always the first bird to give an alarm when an enemy approaches. In the breeding season, however, the love of their young overcomes their dread of mankind, and they wheel round and round the head of any intruder, uttering loud and clamorous cries.

In Sutherland once I saw some young curlews on the ground, and got out to examine them; they are curious, long-legged, top-heavy, little fellows, and when pursued seemed to trip themselves up in their hurry, and to tumble head foremost into every hole in their way. The bill of the young bird is as short as that of a golden plover. When I held it in my hand to examine the curious plumage, or rather down which covered it, the little bird looked up at me with its great dark prominent eye with such an expression of confidence and curiosity, that had I been the most determined collector of specimens of birds, I could not have refrained from putting him carefully down on the ground again: when I did so he ran up to the top of a little grassy hillock, and looked round for his screaming parents, who, at a safe distance, were wheeling with a most wonderful outcry round the head of my terrier.

One cannot understand why a curlew's bill should be curved in the curious manner in which it is. The end of the bill is, like that of a woodcock, furnished with a set of delicate nerves to enable it to feel its food under the ground. In those parts of the country where curlews are numerous, the moist turnip fields are generally bored all over by them.

The common sandpiper appears early in spring, and is seen and its note is heard on the bank of every stream. It seems never to rest, but is continually running to and fro on the gravelly shores of rivers and burns searching for insects. This bird frequents not only those streams which are near the coast, but is also seen many miles inland. Though nowhere numerous, it is universally spread over the country during the breeding season. While on wing it may be recognised by its clear shrill note repeatedly uttered, and while running on the ground by the peculiar jerking motion of its tail.

Trout are not nearly so tender a fish as is generally supposed. At the farm-yard here they have two trout, about six inches or more in length, living in the wooden trough out of which the cart horses drink. They were caught in the river in August, and throughout all the severe frost have lived and apparently continued in good condition, although sometimes in passing I have seen the water in the trough so firmly frozen, and the ice apparently reaching so low, that the trout had scarcely room to swim. When fresh water is put in they always come to the place where it is poured, and seem to look for any particles of food, or any insects that may come in with it. They feed on worms which the boys often bring them, and which they take immediately without fear. The change of colour in fish is very remarkable, and takes place with great rapidity. Put

a living *black* burn trout into a *white* bason of water, and it becomes, within half-an-hour, of a light colour. Keep the fish living in a white jar for some days, and it becomes absolutely white; but put it into a dark-coloured or black vessel, and although, on first being placed there, the white-coloured fish shows most conspicuously on the black ground, in a quarter of an hour it becomes as dark coloured as the bottom of the jar, and consequently difficult to be seen. No doubt this facility of adapting its colour to the bottom of the water in which it lives, is of the greatest service to the fish in protecting it from its numerous enemies. All anglers must have observed that in every stream the trout are very much of the same colour as the gravel or sand on which they live. Whether this change of colour is a voluntary or involuntary act on the part of the fish, I leave it for the scientific to determine.

BADGERS, OTTERS & WILD CATS

Badgers, their Food & Habits—Meeting a Badger—The Otter—Fondness for Eels and Flounders—Otters and their Young—Taming an Otter—Hunting Habits—Wild Cats—Scarcity—The Cry of the Wild Cat—Ferocity—Tame Cats going Wild

Amongst the aboriginal inhabitants of our wilder districts, who are likely to be soon extirpated, we may reckon that ancient, peaceable, and respectable quadruped, the badger. Persevering and enduring in his every-day life, he appears to have been equally so in clinging to existence during the numerous changes which have passed over the face of the globe since the first introduction of his family into it.

Notwithstanding the persecutions and indignities that he is unjustly doomed to suffer, I maintain that he is far more respectable in his habits than we generally consider him to be. "Dirty as a badger," "stinking as a badger," are two sayings often repeated, but quite inapplicable to him. As far as we can learn of the domestic economy of this animal when in a state of nature, he is remarkable for his cleanliness—his extensive burrows are always kept perfectly clean, and free from all offensive smell; no filth is ever found about his abode; everything likely to offend his olfactory nerves is carefully removed. I once, in the north of Scotland, fell in with a perfect colony of badgers; they had taken up their abode in an unfrequented range of wooded rocks, and appeared to have been little interrupted in their possession of them. The footpaths to and from their numerous holes were beaten quite hard; and what is remarkable and worthy of note, they had different small pits dug at a certain distance from their abodes, which were evidently used as receptacles for all offensive filth; every other part of their colony was perfectly clean.

Besides coarse grasses, their food consists of various roots; amongst others, I have frequently found about their hole the bulb of the common wild blue hyacinth. Fruit of all kinds and esculent vegetables form his repast, and I fear that he must plead guilty to devouring any small animal that may come in his way, alive or dead; though not being adapted for the chase, or even for any very skilful strategy of war, I do not suppose that he can do much in catching an unwounded bird or beast. Eggs are his delight, and a partridge's nest with seventeen or eighteen eggs must afford him a fine meal, particularly if he can surprise and kill the hen-bird also; snails and worms which he finds above ground during his nocturnal rambles are likewise included in his bill of fare.

I was one summer evening walking home from fishing in Loch Ness, and having occasion to fasten up some part of my tackle, and also expecting to meet my keeper, I sat down on the shore of the loch. I remained some time, enjoying the lovely prospect: the perfectly clear and unruffled loch lay before me, reflecting the northern shore in its quiet water. The opposite banks consisted, in some parts, of bright green sward, sloping to the water's edge, and studded with some of the most beautiful birch-trees in Scotland; several of the trees spreading out like the oak, and with their ragged and ancient-looking bark resembling the cork-tree of Spain—others drooping and weeping over the edge of the water in the most lady-like and elegant manner. Parts of the loch were edged in by old lichen-covered rocks; while farther on a magnificent scaur of red stone rose perpendicularly from the water's edge to a very great height. So clearly was every object on the opposite shore reflected in the lake below, that it was difficult, nay impossible, to distinguish where the water ended and the land commenced—the shadow from the reality.

It is said that from the sublime to the ridiculous there is but one

step;—and I was just then startled from my reverie by a kind a grunt close to me, and the apparition of a small waddling grey animal, which was busily employed in hunting about the grass and stones at the edge of the loch; presently another, and another, appeared in a little grassy glade which ran down to the water's edge, till at last I saw seven of them busily at work within a few yards of me, all coming from one direction. It at first struck me that they were some farmer's pigs taking a distant ramble, but I shortly saw that they were badgers, come from their fastnesses rather earlier than usual, tempted by the quiet evening, and by a heavy summer shower that was just over, and which had brought out an infinity of large black snails and worms, on which the badgers were feeding with good appetite. As I was dressed in grey and sitting on a grey rock, they did not see me, but waddled about, sometimes close to me; only now and then as they crossed my track they showed a slight uneasiness, smelling the ground, and grunting gently. Presently a very large one, which I took to be the mother of the rest, stood motionless for a moment listening with great attention, and then giving a loud grunt, which seemed perfectly understood by the others, she scuttled away, followed by the whole lot. I was soon joined by my attendant, whose approach they had heard long before my less acute ears gave me warning of his coming.

One of his most favourite repasts is the contents of the nest of the wasp or wild bee, great numbers of which he must destroy. However far under ground the hive may be, and in however strong and difficult a situation, he digs them up, and, depending on his rough coat and long hair as a protection from their stings, devours comb, larvæ, honey, and insects. Many a wasps' nest I have found dug up in this way, and often far from the badger's usual abode; but the tracks of the animal always made it evident who had been the robber.

The badger is easily tamed, and will (if taken young and well used) become much attached to his master. When first caught, their efforts to escape show a degree of strength and ingenuity which is quite wonderful, digging and tearing at their prison with the strength of a rhinoceros. When first imprisoned, if looked at, he immediately rolls himself up into a ball and remains quite motionless. As soon as the coast is clear again, he continues his attempts to escape; but if unsuccessful, he soon becomes contented in his confinement.

Though a quiet animal, and generally speaking not much given to wandering, I have occasionally fallen in with his unmistakable track miles from any burrow. His habits are wholly nocturnal, and it is only in the summer evenings, when the darkness lasts but a few hours, that he is ever met with whilst it is light.

During winter he not only keeps entirely within his hole, but fills up the mouth of it to exclude the cold and any troublesome visitor who might intrude on his slumbers. Frequently, however, tempted by mild weather in the winter, he comes out for some good purpose of his own—

either to enjoy the fresh air or to add to his larder; but never does he venture out in frost or snow. Sometimes I have known a badger leave the solitude of the woods and take to some drain in the cultivated country, where he becomes very bold and destructive to the crops, cutting down wheat and ravaging the gardens in a surprising manner. One which I know to be now living in this manner derives great part of his food during the spring from a rookery, under which he nightly hunts, feeding on the young rooks that fall from their nests or on the old ones that are shot.

Though nearly extinct as one of the *feræ naturæ* of England, the extensive woods and tracts of rocks in the north of Scotland will, I hope, prevent the badger's becoming, like the beaver and other animals, wholly a creature of history, and existing only in record. Much should I regret that this respectable representative of so ancient a family, the comrade of mammoths and other wonders of the antediluvian world, should become quite extirpated. Living too, in remote and uncultivated districts, he very seldom commits any depredations deserving of death or persecution, but subsists on the wild succulent grasses and roots, and the snails and reptiles which he finds in the forest glades, or, on rare occasions, makes capture of young game or wounded rabbits or hares, but I do not believe that he does or can hunt down any game that would not otherwise fall a prey to crow or weasel, or which has the full use of its limbs. It is only wounded and injured animals that he can catch.

I am daily more and more convinced that the otter is by no means so great an enemy to salmon as he is supposed to be; his general food being trout, eels, and flounders; although of course when a salmon comes in his way, he is sufficiently an epicure not to refuse taking it.

The otters here are very fond of searching the shallow pools of the sea at the mouth of the river for flounders, and I often find their tracks, where they have evidently been so employed. If surprised by the daylight appearing too soon to admit of their returning to their usual haunts, they will lie up in any broken bank, furze bush, or other place of concealment.

At some of the falls of the Findhorn, where the river runs so rapidly that they cannot stem it, they have to leave the water to go across the ground; and in these places they have regularly-beaten tracks. I was rather amused at an old woman living at Sluie, on the Findhorn, who, complaining of the hardness of the present times, when "a puir body couldna get a drop smuggled whisky, or *shot* a rae without his lordshop's sportsman finding it out," added to her list of grievances that even the otters were nearly all gone, "puir beasties." "Well, but what good could the otters do you?" I asked her. "Good, your honour? why scarcely a morn came but they left a bonny grilse on the scarp down yonder, and the *vennison* was none the waur of the bit the puir beasts eat themselves." The people here call every eatable animal, fish, flesh, or fowl, venison, or as they pronounce it, "vennison." For instance they tell you that the

snipes are "good vennison," or that the trout are not good "vennison" in the winter.

It seems that a few years ago, before the otters had been so much destroyed, the people on particular parts of the river were never at a loss for salmon, as the otters always take them ashore, and generally to the

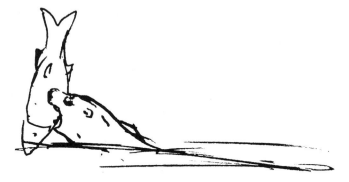

same bank or rock, and when the fish are plentiful, they only eat a small piece out of the shoulder of each, leaving the rest. The cottagers, aware of this, were in the habit of looking every morning for these remains.

When accompanied by her young, the female otter throws aside her usual shyness, and is ready to do stout battle in their behalf. A Highlander of my acquaintance happened to find a couple of young otters in a hollow bank, and having made prisoners of them was carrying them home in triumph in his plaid. The old otter, however, attracted by their cries, left the river, and so determinedly opposed his carrying them away, by placing herself directly in his path, and blowing and hissing like a cat at him, with tail and bristles erect, that the man, although as stout a fellow as ever trod on heather, was glad to give up one of the young ones, and make his escape with the other while the mother was occupied in assuring herself of the safe condition of the one she had rescued.

My keeper tells me that he has seen an old otter feeding her young with fish: the two young ones were sitting on a flat stone at the edge of the burn when their parent brought them a good-sized trout. They immediately both seized the fish, pulling and tearing at it like two bull-dog puppies. At last they came to a pitched battle with each other, biting, squealing, and tugging, and leaving the trout to its fate. On this the old one interfered, and making them quiet, gave the trout to one of them as his own. The other young one, on seeing the parent do this, no longer interfered, but sat quietly looking on, till the old otter (who in the meantime had renewed her fishing) came back with a large trout for it also. When she brings a fish to the shore for her young ones, she calls them by a kind of loud whistling cry.

When caught young no animal is more easily tamed than the otter; and it will soon learn to fish for its master. In educating all wild animals, however, it is absolutely necessary that the pupil should live almost constantly with its teacher, so as to become perfectly familiarised with his voice and presence.

Mr. John Cumming of Altyre caught a young otter at the Findhorn one day in spring, about half grown. He thoroughly tamed him, keeping him constantly by him, and in a short time trained him to catch trout, taking sometimes above a dozen in a forenoon out of the small stream near the house. His general food was porridge and milk, which he devoured quite as freely as fish.

Even when young the otter is a most powerful and severe biter, closing its jaws with the strength of a vice on whatever it seizes. Every courageous dog who has once battled with an otter, retains ever afterwards the most eager and violent animosity against the animal. The scent of an otter renders my otherwise most tractable retriever quite uncontrollable. The remembrance of former bites and wounds seems to drive him frantic, and no sooner does he come across the fresh track of one than he throws aside all control, and is off *ventre à terre* in pursuit.

In hunting down the course of a river the otter always keeps the water, gliding in its quiet ghost-like manner down the deep pools, making scarcely a ripple as he floats down, sometimes diving, and, indeed, rarely showing much of his head above the surface, except when, to listen to some distant sound or to gaze at some doubtful object, he suddenly raises

half his length perpendicularly out of the water. In passing the fords he wades down the shallowest place, or if the stream is there very rapid he comes out of the water and follows the bank of the river, moving along in a curious leaping manner. When in pursuit of fish he seems, as far as can be observed, to try to get below his prey, that he may seize it by the throat.

During the daytime the otter lies quietly in some concealed spot, either in a hole excavated under some overhanging bank or root of a tree, or in some hollow place amongst a cairn of stones. Occasionally, however, when surprised by the light of day in a situation where he deems it imprudent to continue his course towards the usual hiding place, he crawls quietly into some convenient drain, or chooses a dry place in a clump of rushes, and there he will lie during the whole day, till the gloom of evening enables him to continue his journeying, or to commence fishing again. I remember an instance of a groom in Hampshire being startled by an otter jumping from under his wheelbarrow, which he had left leaning against the stable wall close to a stream; into this the otter had crawled in the morning, and there he

would probably have remained till evening, had not the man, having occasion for the barrow, dislodged him by turning it over.

The true wild cat is gradually becoming extirpated, owing to the increasing preservation of game; and though difficult to hold in a trap, in consequence of its great strength and agility, it is by no means difficult to deceive, taking any bait readily, and not seeming to be as cautious in avoiding danger as many other kinds of vermin. Inhabiting the most lonely and inaccessible ranges of rock and mountain, the wild cat is seldom seen during the daytime; at night (like its domestic relative) it prowls far and wide, walking with the same deliberate step, making the same regular and even track, and hunting its game in the same tiger-like manner; and yet the difference between the two animals is perfectly clear, and visible to the commonest observer.

The wild cat has a shorter and more bushy tail, stands higher on her legs in proportion to her size, and has a rounder and coarser look about the head. The strength and ferocity of the wild cat when hemmed in or hard pressed are perfectly astonishing. The body when skinned presents quite a mass of sinew and cartilage.

I have occasionally, though rarely, fallen in with these animals in the forests and mountains of this country; once, I came suddenly, in a rough and rocky part of the ground, upon a family of two old ones and three half-grown young ones. In the hanging birchwoods that border some of the Highland streams and lochs, the wild cat is still not uncommon, and I have heard their wild and unearthly cry echo far in the quiet night as they answer and call to each other.I do not know a more harsh and unpleasant cry than that of the wild cat, or one more likely to be the origin of superstitious fears in the mind of an ignorant Highlander.

These animals have great skill in finding their prey, and the damage they do to the game must be very great, owing to the quantity of food which they require. When caught in a trap, they fly without hesitation at any person who approaches them, not waiting to be assailed. I have heard many stories of their attacking and severely wounding a man, when their escape has been cut off. Indeed, a wild cat once flew at me in

[29]

the most determined manner. I was fishing at a river in Sutherland, and in passing from one pool to another had to climb over some rock and broken kind of ground. In doing so, I sank through some rotten heather and moss up to my knees, almost upon a wild cat, who was concealed under it. I was quite as much startled as the animal herself could be, when I saw the wild-looking beast so unexpectedly rush out from between my feet, with every hair on her body standing on end, making her look twice as large as she really was. I had three small Skye terriers with me, who immediately gave chase, and pursued her till she took refuge in a corner of the rocks, where, perched in a kind of recess out of reach of her enemies, she stood with her hair bristled out, and spitting and growling like a common cat.

Tame cats who have once taken to the woods soon get shy and wild, and then produce their young in rabbit-holes, decayed trees, and other quiet places; thus laying the foundation of a half-wild race. It is worthy of notice, that whatever colour the parents of these semi-wild cats may have been, those bred out of them are almost invariably of the beautiful brindled grey colour, as the wild cats.

COVSEA 1st Sept 1880.

FEBRUARY

Snow and Ice—White Stoats—The Missel-thrush or Storm Cock—Sense of Smell of the
Guinea-pig—A Flock of Wrens—Appearance of the Peewit—Bean Geese—Habits of
Geese—Pink-footed Geese—A Tame Brent Goose—Arrival of the Skylark—Ravens—
The Findhorn Heronry

February 1st., 1848 We are all frozen up here.
February is always with us the most snowy month of the year. I find
that, in my journal for the first week of this month, during several years,
it is generally marked down that the country is clothed in snow. The
quantity of floating snow and ice which comes down the river fills the
bay, and sends the wild-fowl to some less dreary part of the country. In
some places the course of the river is quite altered, being choked up by
the accumulation of ice on the shallows, and the water takes some new
run. What becomes of the fish during this kind of weather? Occasionally
a golden-eye or long-tailed duck pitches in some clear spot of the river,
but is almost immediately driven out again by the floating ice.

The stoats are now pure white in almost every instance, although I
shot one on the 3rd of this month (1848) who had only very partially
acquired his winter colour.

The rooks dig deep into the snow, and plough up the young wheat in
great quantities with their strong bills.

While the river is in this state of confusion with ice, etc., I see that the
otters betake themselves to the unfrozen ditches and springs to hunt for
eels and flounders, which fish they feed on apparently with great
perseverance, if one can judge by the distance they hunt for them in the
snow. The otter, judging from the ground he goes over, must commence
moving as soon as it is dark, and continue hunting till nearly daylight.

February 3rd, 1852. Went to Loch Spynie in the afternoon; a great

many ducks of all kinds, and also large flocks of peewits, the first time that I have seen them this spring. I shot a gull (immature herring gull) with its crop quite full of turnip. I never before knew that any gull ate these plants; the ground was quite free from frost, so the bird apparently might have found plenty of food more suited to it.

February 6th, 1851. Cold and clear. Chaffinches sing; a great number of thrushes, blackbirds, and missel-thrushes in the garden.

The missel-thrush is seen in the autumn in large scattered flocks, feeding either in grass fields on insects and grubs, or collected on patches of juniper, holly, etc., it being a feeder equally on insect food and berries of all sorts. A pair always breed in my garden, but they appear to be quarrelsome birds, driving away all others of the same species during the breeding season The missel-thrush's song is rich-toned and clear, but with no variety. It commences singing earlier in the season than any other bird. In the beginning of January the ear is frequently gladdened by its loud note, resembling more that of the blackbird than the thrush. It sings in the wildest and stormiest days, hence deriving a local name in some districts of "Storm Cock." When singing it usually sits on the highest twig of a tree.

February 7th, 1847. To-day is the hardest frost I ever remember, with a cold north wind. If I dipped my walking-stick in water it was almost instantly covered with ice. Saw a flock of larks for the first time this winter.

February 8th, 1852. The large-headed field-mice do not seem to come out of their holes in the walls much in the wet weather. The best bait for them seems to be pieces of apple, as they appear to be quite vegetable eaters.

No animal seems to have a quicker sense of smell than the guinea-pig. The moment that any apple or other food that they are fond of is put down in the yard, they smell it out at the distance of thirty or forty feet, and all come out of their hiding-places to it. They are very fond of branches of holly, eating both bark and leaves greedily; when fed with winter greens of any kind, they prefer the half-withered leaves to those quite green.

Deer, rabbits, etc., in the same way peel carefully branches of Scotch fir which have been cut for several days, but will not eat the peel of fresh trees of the same kind.

February 9th, 1847. Very severe frost, much snow and drift. The fieldfares come down in great numbers to the fields to feed on the Swedish turnips, and I was much astonished at the great damage done by them to the roots. I watched some of the birds digging at the turnips with their bills, and chipping and scooping out great pieces—thus destroying half the crop at least by letting the frost into the roots

The whole bay and all the streams and springs are so filled up with drift snow, and ice, that there was not a single duck of any sort to be seen, with the exception of one morillon who had found out about six feet

The oyster catcher.

Port Sandhira
March /47

square of open water in the burn. On being flushed from this he flew a long distance up the stream in search of some other opening, but not finding any, came back, and plumped down into the same place close to me, and there I left him.

The widgeons leave the bay, which is nearly covered with ice, and feed on the clover fields, digging under the snow with their bills to get at the herbage. I never saw them do so before in this county; indeed it is very seldom that the snow in Morayshire remains long enough on the ground, at least in the district near the sea, to annoy the wild-fowl to any extent.

While the snow is newly fallen and soft, the rabbits seldom go fifty yards from their seat of the day before, and constantly return to the same bush.

February 11th, 1847. Saw to-day what I never observed before, a flock of eleven wrens together.

February 12th, 1852. Fine and warm. Blackbirds now sing in the garden early in the morning, and the larks all day. I saw two merlins to-day flying round and after each other, and uttering their spring cry. A water-ouzel in the Lossie was singing this morning, and chasing another bird of the same kind, apparently a female, not being so black as the one that was singing. They frequently both dropped into the water, and dived for a short time. The song is very musical and pleasing, though short.

February 13th, 1853. I never saw so severe a snow-storm, everything is covered and quite white; no wheels can move. How the poor birds live, I don't know. The snow will doubtless soon go, and in all probability the

weather will be cleared and fine sunshine after it. To-day, indeed, is the finest and most beautiful day I ever saw, although all is white. The river itself is snowed up.

In the middle of February the peewits begin to appear here. The exact day depends chiefly on the state of the weather: the first break-up of the snow and ice generally brings them. About the same time I hear the coo of the wood-pigeons, who now come near the house for protection. This they do every year as the breeding season approaches.

Three otters are frequenting the mouth of the river, apparently fishing for the flounders left in the pools near the sea. Whilst going *down,* the otter seldom leaves the water at all; but unintermittingly fishes his way to the sea; coming up, he takes the land at all the rapids and strong streams.

The rooks begin to collect on the ash trees at Gordonstoun, where they breed, making a great noise in the morning. I also heard the spring cry of the kestrel hawk.

February 18th, 1847. The widgeon are now in full plumage, excepting a few backward or wounded birds. I saw a peewit to-day, though no flocks have appeared as yet.

19th and 20th. Thrushes and larks begin to sing. Saw a small flock of peewits on the island. Saw also a pair of crested cormorants, at least I consider the birds which I saw to be of their kind. They had the white mark on the hip, and appeared to be different from the cormorants which I usually see here, being both of a darker colour, and of a stouter and heavier shape.

Towards the end of February, whenever the ground is soft, the badgers leave their holes, and wander far and near, digging up the ground like pigs, in the fields as well as in the woods.

Wild cats are brindled gray, and I have observed that domestic cats of that colour are more inclined to take to the woods and hunt for themselves than others. When they do so they grow very large, and are most destructive to game of all kinds. A large cat of this colour found out some tame rabbits belonging to my boys, and killed several of them.

At this season the bean goose and the pink-footed goose feed very much on a coarse reddish-brown grass which grows in swamps and the peat mosses, and which is very succulent. They pull it up and eat the root, which is somewhat bulbous shaped. While feeding on it they become very heavy and fat.

Though these two kinds of geese both feed and fly together, still while on wing and while on the ground they keep somewhat apart. The bean geese are far the most numerous; but there is generally a small company of the pink-footed kind with them, and no one but a close observer would perceive that they do not associate as closely as if they all belonged to one family.

The bean goose visits us both in autumn and spring. Their stay in autumn is very short, stopping only to rest while on their passage from their breeding places in the far North to the more genial shores of the South. They come generally about the beginning of October, but vary according to the weather. The first gales and rough weather about that

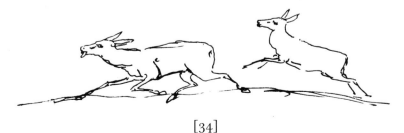

[34]

time generally bring them. They pass over in immense flocks, stopping only for a night or two in some quiet swamp or bay. Their visits in the spring are, however, far more regular. As soon as the first oats are sown in the flat plains of Moray, a squadron of bean geese appear, and seem to reconnoitre the ground as an advance guard. This generally takes place about 10th or 12th March. In a day or two their number increases, and large flocks seem to arrive daily. In the night time they rest in the Bay of Findhorn.

It is a great libel to accuse a goose of being a silly bird. Even a tame goose shows much instinct and attachment; and were its habits more closely observed, the tame goose would be found to be by no means wanting in general cleverness. Its watchfulness at night-time is, and always has been, proverbial; and it certainly is endowed with a strong organ of self-preservation. You may drive over dog, cat, hen, or pig; but I defy you to drive over a tame goose. As for wild geese, I know of no animal, biped or quadruped, that is so difficult to deceive or approach. Their senses of hearing, seeing, and smelling are all extremely acute; independently of which, they appear to act in so organised and cautious a manner when feeding or roosting, as to defy all danger.

When a flock of geese have fixed on a field of new-sown grain to feed on, before alighting they make numerous circling flights round and round it, and the least suspicious object prevents their pitching. Supposing that all is right, and they do alight, the whole flock for the space of a minute or two remain motionless, with erect head and neck reconnoitring the country round. They then, at a given signal from one of the largest birds, disperse into open order, and commence feeding in a tolerably regular line. They now appear to have made up their minds that all is safe, and are contented with leaving one sentry, who either stands on some elevated part of the field, or walks slowly with the rest— never, however, venturing to pick up a single grain of corn, his whole energies being employed in watching. The flock feed across the field; not waddling, like tame geese, but walking quickly, with a firm, active, light-infantry step.

They seldom venture near any ditch or hedge that might conceal a foe. When the sentry thinks that he has performed a fair share of duty, he gives the nearest bird to him a sharp peck. I have seen him sometimes pull out a handful of feathers, if the first hint is not immediately attended to, at the same time uttering a querulous kind of cry. This bird then takes up the watch, with neck perfectly upright, and in due time makes some other bird relieve guard. On the least appearance of an enemy, the sentinel gives an alarm, and the whole flock invariably run up to him, and for a moment or two stand still in a crowd, and then take flight; at first in a confused mass, but this is soon changed into a beautiful wedge-like rank, which they keep till about to alight again. Towards evening, I observe the geese coming from the interior, in numerous small flocks, to the bay; in calm weather, flying at a great height; and their peculiar cry is heard some time before the birds are in sight. As soon as they are above the sands, where every object is plainly visible, and no enemy can well be concealed, flock after flock wheel rapidly downwards, and alight at the edge of the water, where they immediately begin splashing and washing themselves, keeping up an almost incessant clamour. In the morning they again take to the fields. Those flocks that feed at a distance start before sunrise; but those that feed nearer to the bay do not leave their roosting-place so soon. During stormy and misty weather, the geese frequently fly quite low over the heads of the work-people in the fields, but even then have a kind of instinctive dread of any person in the garb of a sportsman.

The pink-footed goose visits us regularly at the same time as the bean goose. The plumage of both birds is very much the same. The pink-footed goose, however, is a finer bird, and more distinctly shaded and marked than the bean goose. The general colour of the plumage is lighter. When a flock of bean geese alight on a field to feed, it may be observed that a small company of birds often separate and feed alone; these will be found to be the pink-footed.

A wounded brent goose which I brought home, very soon became tame, and fed fearlessly close to us; indeed, I have frequently observed this inclination to tameness in this beautiful kind of goose. These birds come in great numbers early in the winter. In the first week in October, or even as early as the end of September, they begin to appear, and their numbers increase apparently till the end of their season here, which is at the end of April, and sometimes the first week of May. During March they are very numerous on the grassy parts of the sea-shore, and as the tide recedes they land in large flocks to feed on the herbage which is left uncovered. There is a kind of short grass in the sheltered bays on parts of this coast, which at high water is covered, but which is bare at low tide, and this seems to commence throwing out young shoots early in March. The brent geese are very fond of this, and leave the Bay of Cromarty and other places where they have fed during the winter on the roots of the long waving sea-grass, in order to feed on this young short herbage which the ebb tide leaves uncovered here. They are, however, very

[36]

wary, and, like the bean geese, always have some of their number on the watch. Their loud peculiar cry is wild and musical, resembling a pack of hounds in full cry. As they pass overhead during a still night it is very striking.

I have frequently seen them feeding on the green wheat towards the spring time; but I never saw them eating grain. They also seem fond of coming to the mouth of any small stream which may run into the bays, and of drinking the fresh water.

February 25th, 1853. There is scarcely a field or piece of open ground which is not frequented by the skylark. They are most numerous during February and March, and in the beginning of winter. During the first snow-storms of the season I have sometimes happened to be on the sea-shore, and all day a constant stream of larks seemed to be coming straight in from the north-east—not coming in compact bodies, but singly and in scattered, yet constant flocks. On these occasions they do not fly high, but drift along not many yards above the water. I observe that the larks generally begin to sing in the first week of February, though no exact rule can be laid down, as this depends much on the weather. The skylark, as Milton knew, is the bird which sings earliest in the morning. Before the sun is up, I often hear the lark singing over my head before there is light enough to distinguish it. Late in the summer evening too, after all is still, and apparently the birds have all retired to their roosting places, I have observed how suddenly every lark rises and sings for a short time, as if their evening hymn, and as suddenly and simultaneously all cease. The nest is placed on the ground. It is carelessly made, fitting into some hollow made by the hoof of a horse or cow, or in some similar inequality.

The raven is now a rare bird in this immediate district. Not many years since it had several breeding places both on the sea-coast and also in some rocky cliffs inland, but traps and increase of population have driven it away to the higher grounds. I occasionally, during the winter season see a pair or single bird pass over my head. Where not much disturbed, the raven will breed in the same spot for many years in succession, adding to and repairing the old nest. Its usual building place is on some lofty cliff, where it fixes on a situation protected by projections of rocks, both from above and below. In England I have found the nest in a lofty tree; and then it fixes on a tree the most difficult to climb in the neighbourhood, and remains constant to the same nest every year. The

[37]

nest is formed of large sticks outwardly, and lined with a great quantity
of wool, hair, soft grass, etc. The principal food of the raven consists of
carrion and dead fish, but it will eat almost anything, animal or
vegetable, which comes in its way. It is easily tamed, and is very amusing
as a pet, owing to its quaint habits and tricks; but its strong and powerful
bill, which it uses on slight provocation, makes it rather a dangerous
inmate where there are children. It breeds very early, the old bird often
sitting on her eggs in the midst of snow and storm. They have eggs
sometimes in February.

There are plenty of herons here (1850), the heron being one of the first
birds to commence breeding in this country. A more curious and
interesting sight than the Findhorn heronry I do not know: from the top
of the high rocks on the east side of the river you look down into every
nest, the herons breeding on the opposite side of the river, which is here
very narrow. The cliffs and rocks are studded with splendid pines and
larch, and fringed with all the more lowly but not less beautiful
underwood which abounds in this country. Conspicuous amongst these
are the bird-cherry and mountain-ash, the holly and the wild rose; while
the golden blossoms of furze and broom enliven every crevice and corner
in the rock. Opposite to you is a wood of larch and oak, on the latter of
which trees are crowded a vast number of the nests of the heron. The
foliage and small branches of the oaks that they breed on seem entirely
destroyed, leaving nothing but the naked arms and branches of the trees
on which the nests are placed. The same nests, slightly repaired, are used
year after year.

Looking down at them from the high banks of the Altyre side of the
river, you can see directly into their nests, and can become acquainted

with the whole of their domestic economy. You can plainly see the green eggs, and also the young herons, who fearlessly, and conscious of the security they are left in, are constantly passing backwards and forwards and alighting on the topmost branches of the larch or oak trees, whilst the still younger birds sit bolt upright in the nest, snapping their beaks together with a curious sound. Occasionally a grave-looking heron is seen balancing himself by some incomprehensible feat of gymnastics on the very topmost twig of a larch-tree, where he swings about in an unsteady manner, quite unbecoming so sage-looking a bird. Occasionally a thievish jackdaw dashes out from the cliffs opposite the heronry and flies straight into some unguarded nest, seizes one of the large green eggs, and flies back to his own side of the river, the rightful owner of the eggs pursuing the active little robber with loud cries and the most awkward attempts at catching him.

The heron is a noble and picturesque-looking bird, as she sails quietly through the air with outstretched wings and slow flight; but nothing is more ridiculous and undignified than her appearance as she vainly chases the jackdaw or hooded crow which is carrying off her egg and darting rapidly round the angles and corners of the rocks. Now and then every heron raises its head and looks on the alert as the peregrine falcon, with rapid and direct flight, passes their crowded dominion; but, intent on his own nest, built on the rock some little way farther on, the hawk takes no notice of his long-legged neighbours, who soon settle down again into their attitudes of rest.

The kestrel-hawk frequents the same part of the river, and lives in amity with the wood-pigeons that breed in every cluster of ivy which clings to the rocks. Even that bold and fearless enemy of all the pigeon race, the sparrowhawk, frequently has her nest within a few yards of the wood-pigeon, and you see these birds (at all other seasons such deadly enemies) passing each other in their way to and fro from their respective nests in perfect peace and amity.

OWLS

The Short-eared Owl—The Long-eared Owl—The Tawny Owl—A Tame Tawny Owl—The White or Barn Owl—The Snowy Owl—A Rare Visitor—An Eagle Owl—Habits of Owls—The Owl's Wings—The Shrew Mouse—The Long-tailed Field-mouse—The Water-rat—The House Rat—Rats and Hen's Eggs

Amongst the migratory birds that pass the winter in this country is the short-eared owl, it arrives in October, sometimes in flights of some number. I have heard from perfectly good authority of sixteen or seventeen of these birds having been found in one turnip-field on the east coast, evidently having just arrived. It is a long-winged bird, and more active in its manner of flight than most of the other owls, nor is it so completely nocturnal. I saw one of this kind hunting a rushy field and regularly beating it for prey at mid-day. The owl was so intent on his pursuit that he flew straight in my direction and nearly close to me before he observed me. When he did so, he darted off with great quickness and with a most hawk-like flight.

I have very frequently flushed this kind of owl in rushes, furze, and other low cover. When put up, instead of being distressed and confused by the light of the sun, he flies boldly and steadily away. Sometimes I have seen one, when put up, rise high in the air and fly straight away until I could no longer distinguish him. Its food consists principally of the field mice which frequent marshy places, though neither snipe nor bunting escape its attacks. Though principally only a visitor, the short-eared owl breeds in the higher districts of the country, building a slight nest in a tuft of long heather on the side of some steep bank.

The other owls that breed here are the long-eared owl, the tawny owl, and the barn-owl: the latter, though so common in England, is by far the rarest in this country.

The long-eared owl is a fine bold bird, and his bright yellow eye gives him a peculiarly handsome appearance: altogether he is of a lighter make and more active than the other owls; they are very common in the shady fir-woods. It is easily distinguished from any other of our owls by its long ears or horns, which are of a dark or black colour edged with white, and by its peculiarly staring eyes of a bright orange colour. The legs and feet are feathered down to the talons, which are remarkably hard and sharp.

Their usual food is mice, but they also prey upon young partridges and other game which they happen to find late in the summer evening. I have also known this owl commit great havoc in the pigeon-house, killing both old and young pigeons in the moonlight nights. I have seen it dash like a sparrowhawk into a hedge or bush to catch the small birds roosting there. Indeed there is every reason to suppose that this owl is the most destructive species that we have, preying more on birds, and on larger kinds of birds, than any other owl that we have.

I often see this bird sitting on a branch close to the stem of the tree, and depending on the exact similitude of his colour to that of the bark, he sits motionless with his bright golden eye watching earnestly every movement I make. If he fancies himself observed, and likely to be molested, down he dashes, flies a hundred yards or so, and then suddenly pitches again. His long ears and bright eyes give him a most unbirdlike appearance as he sits watching one. As soon as evening comes on, the owl issues forth in full life and activity, and in the woods here may be seen and heard in all directions, sitting on the topmost branch of some leafless tree, generally a larch or ash (these two being his favourites), where he hoots incessantly for an hour together, swelling his throat out, and making the eccentric motions of a pouter pigeon.

I do not know why, but I never could succeed in rearing one of these birds—they have invariably died, without any apparent cause, before their first year was over. Not so with the tawny owl which is by no means rare. Its usual abode is in some ivy-covered wall or tree, where it lays its round white eggs. It is marked much like the long-eared owl, but has not the same yellow tinge on its plumage. It is also a rounder and heavier-looking bird, with shorter wings and very large head and eyes. The latter are black. It is a remarkably noisy bird, and in the more solitary woods during the spring time its loud hooting may be heard at all hours of the day. It preys principally on mice, but also on small birds, etc. Altogether, however, I imagine that its good deeds in the way of killing mice far outweigh any mischief it may do amongst young birds during the breeding season.

One of these birds has been in my kitchen-garden for three years. Though his wing is sometimes cut, he can fly sufficiently to get over the wall, but seldom ventures beyond the adjoining flower-garden or

orchard. From habit or tameness this bird seems to pay little regard to sunshine or shade, sitting during the daytime as indifferently in the most open and exposed places as in the more shaded corners: he is quite tame too, and answers to the call of the children. He hoots as vigorously at mid-day as at night, and will take a bird from my hand when offered to him. Although his flight has been impeded by his wing being cut, he seems to have entirely cleared the garden of mice, with which it was much overrun. Though a light bird, and not apparently very strongly built his sharp claws and bill enable him to tear to pieces any crow or sea-gull that is offered to him. When he has had his meal off some large bird of this kind, and has satisfied his appetite he carries away and carefully hides the remainder, returning to it when again hungry. I do not know whether the owl, when at liberty in his native woods, has the same fox-like propensity to hide what he cannot eat.

The white or barn owl though so common in many parts of England, is comparatively rare in this country. I have, however, seen it in the rocks of the Findhorn, and in other places. It frequents buildings and old ruins, but seems, where numerous, particularly to attach itself to church towers; occasionally, however, it takes up its abode in a hollow tree. This bird is of great benefit to the farmer, being a most indefatigable destroyer of mice, which appear to form almost its only food. The numbers they destroy must be very great where they are unmolested and allowed to breed. None indeed but the most ignorant gamekeeper would like to see this owl nailed up amongst his other trophies. Unlike other rapacious birds, the white owl seems sometimes to breed in company, as I have seen more than a dozen young ones of different ages, but all unable to fly, crowded together in the same church tower, being the progeny, as far as I could judge, of several different pairs of owls.

The snowy owl, a magnificent bird, is an occasional, though a rare, visitor here. I have known more than one instance of its being seen and killed on the sea-coast of this country. The breadth of the wings in the female bird is above five feet. The male is considerably smaller. The plumage is white with brown markings. These marks gradually decrease with the age of the bird, and in old specimens the plumage becomes nearly all white. In this country its food appears to consist principally of

rabbits. In Greenland and Iceland this bird is not uncommon, and it preys on the smaller quadrupeds which are found in those regions. Nothing can be more picturesque and startling than the sudden appearance of a snowy owl gliding out of a dark recess or cavern, with its ghost-like appearance and noiseless flight. It is said to be a constant resident on the most northern of the smaller Shetland Islands. One was seen two or three years back on part of the ground rented by me. He was sitting on a high piece of muirland, and at a distance looked, said my informant, "like a milestone."

I have known one instance of the eagle owl being seen in this district, and it was not then captured; but the description given to me could not have applied to any other bird.

A man described to me a large bird, which he called an eagle. The bird was sitting on a fir-tree, and his attention was called to it by the grey crows uttering their cries of alarm and war. He went up to the tree, and close above his head sat a great bird, with large staring yellow eyes, as bright (so he expressed it) as two brass buttons. The man stooped to pick up a stone or stick, and the bird dashed off the tree into the recesses of the wood, and was not seen again. The colour of its eyes, the situation the bird was in on the branch of a tall fir-tree, and its remaining quiet until the man approached so close to it, all convince me that it must have been the great owl, whose loud midnight hootings disturb the solitude of the German forests, giving additional weight to the legends and super-stitions of the peasants of that country, inclined as they are to belief in supernatural sounds and apparitions.

The little owl, called Tengmalm's owl does not exceed eight inches in length. It can scarcely be said to belong to this district, though I have had an owl described to me as being seen in a wood near Elgin which could be scarcely of any other species. I have, however, never known of one being killed here. On the opposite coast of Sutherland I have known of an owl of this kind being killed by Mr. Dunbar in the ruins at Spinnindale. Its appearance in any part of the kingdom is, however, very rare, and when it does visit us, its nocturnal habits and small size prevent its being noticed.

With regard to the mischief done by owls, all the harm they do is amply repaid by their utility in destroying a much more serious nuisance in the shape not only of the different kinds of mice, but of rats also, these animals being their principal food and the prey which they are most adapted for catching.

I knew an instance where the owls having been nearly destroyed by the numerous pole-traps placed about the fields for the destruction of them and the hawks, the rats and mice increased to such an extent on the disappearance of these their worst enemies, and committed such havoc among the nursery-gardens, farm-buildings, etc., that the proprietor was obliged to have all the pole-traps taken down, and the owls having been allowed to increase again, the rats and mice as quickly diminished in number.

The owls have all extremely hard and needle-like claws, and in every respect the bird is singularly well adapted for its manner of feeding, which it does almost wholly at night. Its immensely large ears must enable it to hear the slightest movement of the field-mouse, upon which it chiefly feeds; and its sharply-pointed talons contract with a tenacity and closeness unequalled by those of any of the hawk tribe, excepting perhaps the hen-harrier. Again, the soft downy feathers and rounded wings of the owl enable it to flit as noiselessly as a shadow to and fro, as it searches for the quick-eared mouse, whom the least sound would at once startle and drive into its hole, out of reach of its deadly enemy. As it is, the mouse feeds on in heedless security, with eyes and nose busily occupied in searching for grains of corn or seeds, and depending on its quickly sensitive ear to warn it of the approach of any danger. The foot of man, or even the tread of dog or cat, it is sure to hear; but the owl glides quickly and silently round the corner of the hedge or stack (like Death, "*tacito clam venit illa pede*"), and the first intimation which the mouse has of its danger is being clasped in the talons of its devourer.

The numbers of mice destroyed by a breeding pair of owls must be enormous, and the service they perform by so doing very great to the farmer, the planter, and the gardener. Though neither cats nor owls ever eat the little shrew-mouse, they always strike and kill it when opportunity offers, leaving the animal on the spot. What there is so obnoxious to all animals of prey in this little creature it is impossible to say.

Besides the shrew we have the common house-mouse, the short-eared mouse, and that beautiful bright-eyed kind the long-tailed field-mouse. The last is very destructive to the garden-seeds, and without the assistance of the owls would be kept under with great difficulty. The large-headed, short-eared mouse is not so pretty an animal, but equally destructive, taking great delight in sweet peas and other seeds: they also climb the peach-trees and destroy great quantities of the fruit. A fig-tree this year, when its winter covering of straw was taken off, was found to be entirely barked and all the shoots eaten off by these mice. The shrew-mouse has the same propensity for barking trees. I have known the former kind, indeed, destroy Scotch fir-trees of the height of fifteen or sixteen feet by nibbling and peeling the topmost shoot till the tree gradually withered away.

The proceedings of the common long-tailed field-mouse are amusing, and indicate perfect foresight of the cold and scarcity of winter. They dig deep holes in the stubble-fields, in which they collect large stores of food, such as grain, acorns, nuts, and even cherry-stones. On the approach of cold winds or rain, they shut themselves up in their underground habitations, closing the aperture completely. The quantity of earth which they dig out and leave at the mouth of their hole in a single night is quite astonishing. At the instigation of the gardener my boys wage war against these little pilferers. By pouring water into the holes the poor mouse is obliged, *nolens volens*, to bolt like a rabbit driven out by a ferret.

They seem to produce their young not underground, but in a comfortable, well-built nest, formed in the shape of a ball, with a small entrance on one side. As it is built of the same material as the surrounding herbage, and the entrance is closed up, it is not easily seen.

The poor water-rat is a comparatively harmless animal, feeding principally upon herbage, not refusing, however, fish, or even toads, when they come in its way. The succulent grasses that grow by the sides of ditches, seem to form its chief food during the summer season. Early in the spring, before these grasses are well grown, the water-rat preys much on toads. I have found little piles of the feet, and remains of several of these animals, near the edge of water frequented by these rats, which they seem to have collected together in certain places, and left there. I have known the water-rat do great damage to artificial dams and the heads of ponds, by undermining them, and boring holes in every direction through them, below the water-mark, as well as above it. The water-rat has peculiarly sensitive organs of scent, and it is therefore

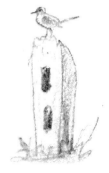

almost impossible to trap him, as he is sure to discover the taint of the human hand. Cunning as the house-rat is, this kind is much more so. Though the former may be in a measure kept down by constant trapping, it is a troublesome method, and there are sure to be some cunning old patriarchs who will not enter any kind of trap. I believe that the best kind of trap in a house is the common gin, laid open and uncovered in their runs. They then do not seem to suspect any danger, but when the trap is covered they are sure to detect its presence, and, like all wild animals, they are much more cautious in avoiding a concealed danger than an open one. Poison is the best means of getting rid of them.

That rats carry off hens' and even turkeys' eggs to some considerable distance is a fact; how they accomplish this feat I should like to know, as they do it without breaking the shell, or leaving any mark upon it. A crow or magpie, Columbus-like, shortens the difficulty by sticking the lower mandible of his bill into a hen's egg when he wants to carry it off, but this is beyond a rat's capabilities; nevertheless, eggs form one of their favourite repasts. The increase of rats, if left to breed in peace, would exceed that of almost any other animal, as they produce broods of six or eight young ones in rapid succession, throughout the greatest part of the year. In building a nest for her young, the female carries off every soft substance which she can find; pieces of lace, cloth, and above all, paper, seem to be her favourite lining.

The natural destroyers in this country of this obnoxious animal seem to be, the hen-harrier, the falcon, the long-eared and the tawny owls, cats, weasels, and stoats; and, *ante omnes*, boys of every age and grade wage war to the knife against rats, wherever and whenever they can find them.

Court of Cats

MARCH

Water-fowl on Loch Spynie—The Hooded Crow—Brent Geese—Iceland Falcon—
Habits of Rooks—Water-fowl on the Water—A Tame Pochard—Wild Swans—
Bewick's Swan—A Tame Crossbill—Arrival of the Dabchick—Nesting Habits—
Arrival of Geese—Pike and Trout

March 1st, 1847. I drove over to Gordonstoun to Spynie. I was
much amused and interested by seeing the immense flocks of
wild-fowl that were congregated on and about the loch. The teal kept up
a constant whistling during the whole day, so did the widgeon; all the
different ducks were pairing, and although on the water they appeared
to be one confused mass, as soon as they rose, I observe they all flew to
and fro in pairs—even in the great flights, as they passed from one end of
the loch to the other, every flock was subdivided into pairs, which had a
very curious effect in the air. I do not know a prettier sight than a vast
number of water-fowl such as I saw to-day, filling the water and the air
above it, and uttering their various cries. The coot's manner of rising is
very peculiar, flapping and running along the water for twenty yards
before he gets well on wing, making a great noise, and sending the water
in all directions around him. Once on wing, the coot has a great
resemblance to a blackcock in manner of flight, etc. On the water this
bird swims very high, giving one the idea of a blackened bladder floating
about. The widgeon, on the contrary, swims very flat and low in the
water, but on wing is quick and sharp in its movements. The teal has a
sudden and rapid, but unsteady flight.

There are a great many marks of otters about the loch. I conclude that
they find plenty of flounders and eels in the muddy ditches and canals.
The otters about Spynie sit in the rushes on the small islands, making
seats like those of a hare.

The keeper caught a beautiful male pochard which had been wounded somewhere in the body, but apparently was not much hurt, although disabled from flying. I took it home with me alive, and turned it into a small enclosure, where it amused us much by its tameness and confidence, beginning to eat worms and porridge immediately, and seeming to enjoy itself in this new situation as much as if it had been always accustomed to it. The eye of this bird is of a very peculiar blood-red colour, and has a very bold and fierce expression.

There are no enemies so destructive to the wild-fowl as the carrion or rather the hooded crow, which is the kind we have here. Though the carrion crow is not supposed to be an inhabitant of this part of the country, it is almost impossible to decide upon the line which divides these two birds, the black carrion crow and the hooded crow. No doubt the hooded crow is the common species here, but I have taken some trouble in examining these birds, and have killed crows of every shade of plumage from pure black to the perfectly marked hooded crow, and this without reference to age or sex. I have also seen a perfect hooded crow paired and breeding with one quite black. There is no internal difference whatsoever in the birds. There is often considerable variety in the size both of the black and of the hooded crow. Though pairs of hooded crows are common enough, I never saw in this country, nor anywhere in the north of Scotland, a pair of perfectly black carrion crows.

The hooded crow is a powerful, active, and very wary bird, feeding on almost everything which comes in its way, but preferring carrion. It often feeds on shell-fish. I have frequently seen it near the sea rise to a considerable height with a mussel, and drop it on a rock in order to crack the shell, an act which amounts to reasoning. It feeds as much on the fresh-water mussels, the shells of which not being so strong as those of the salt-water mussel, the crow is able to break open without making use of the same plan. This bird also kills newly-born lambs, picking out the eyes and tongue while the poor creature is still alive. It preys on young grouse, partridges, hares, etc. etc., and is very destructive to eggs of all sorts. In certain feeding spots in the woods I have seen the remains of eggs of the most extraordinary variety and number. No sooner does a wild duck, pheasant, or any bird leave its nest than the hooded crow is on the look-out, and I have no doubt that a single pair often destroys many hundred eggs in the course of a season. All birds seem aware of this, and peewits, gulls, redshanks, etc., attack most furiously any crow which they see hunting near their nests.

Every day now shows the approach of spring. The swans frequent one particular lake, seldom alighting on any other piece of water. This lake is peculiarly open, and very difficult of approach, which is doubtless one reason for their fixing on it; another is, that in many places it is so shallow that they can reach with their long necks the grassy plants growing at the bottom, on the roots of which plants they feed.

Day by day, at the beginning of March, the brent geese seem to

Wedgeon Oct 18 —

Feb.

Young Scaup Duck —

Feb 1st
Nairn

Pintail Duck —

Loch of Spynie.
March /47

April 17.
/47

Thrush

Blackbird

Hedge Sparrow

Kestrel

Peewit

Moorhen

Robin

Coot

increase in numbers: they feed on the grassy banks on the shores of the neck of land called the "Bar."

I heard of a falcon breeding in Glengarry. The keeper says that a very large light-coloured falcon bred at a certain rock quite different from the common peregrine, being nearly white; that it always came out making a great noise from where it had its nest, and struck at his terriers. This seems very like the Iceland bird, which is a very rare visitor. I have only known of two other instances of its being seen in this part of the kingdom. One of these birds was hunting about the Loch of Spynie and struck down a mallard very near us. This was early in the month of March. The other I saw a year afterwards near Elgin; and a fortnight after the time that I saw her one was killed in Ross-shire, in all probability the same.

The badgers hunt more and more every day at this season if the weather is open, and apparently they wander several miles from their home.

March 2nd, 1847. I see the rooks building; they were very busy to-day carrying up sticks from every direction. This well-known bird is common in all this district, shifting its quarters at different seasons in search of food; and immense must be the supply to feed the tens of thousands which are sometimes seen together. With regard to the mischief done by the rook, the greatest destruction of grain made by it is just as the corn ripens and before it is cut; where the grain is lodged, and at the edges of the fields, it consumes a considerable quantity, and destroys more. It also attacks the potatoes, digging up those roots which are least covered with earth. In severe weather and snow it attacks the turnips, and its powerful bill enables it to break easily into the root. It is mischievous also if allowed to attack the stack-yard, spoiling the stacks by pulling out the straws to get at the grain. The rook is fond of eggs too, and in some rookeries egg-hunting becomes their common habit, when from their great numbers they scarcely allow pheasant or partridge to hatch a brood. This bird is also fond of cherries, strawberries, etc.

To counterbalance this long list of evil, for many months of the year the rooks live wholly on grubs caterpillars, etc., in this way doing an amount of service to the farmer which is quite incalculable, destroying his greatest and most insidious enemy. In districts where rooks have been completely expelled this has been seen by whole crops of wheat and clover being destroyed at the root by the wire worm and other enemies, which can only be effectually attacked by birds. When we consider the short time during which rooks feed on grain, and the far longer season during which they live wholly on grubs and such-like food, it will be believed by all impartial lookers-on that the rook may be set down rather as the farmer's friend than his enemy. On close observation, when the rook appears to be following the harrows for the purpose of feeding on the newly-sown wheat, it will be found that it is picking up a great quantity of large white grubs, leaving the grain untouched. Amongst its misdemeanours I forget to mention one, namely, that in severe weather it often digs up the young wheat just as it begins to sprout above the ground. Where rooks or any other birds increase to an inordinate extent, no doubt they ought to be kept down by destroying part of their eggs or young. Where the farmer is much annoyed by their attacks on any particular field, a few shots at them soon drive them elsewhere. But very bad would be the effect of entirely banishing them from any district.

March 3rd, 1847. When at Loch Spynie yesterday we started several hares, which were lying in perfectly wet seats some distance in the rushes. Saw badger tracks about the loch.

When looking at wild-fowl on the water, it is generally easy to distinguish what kind they are, even from a great distance, Scarcely any two species swim or float in the same manner, and at the same elevation above the surface of the water. Coots, and sea-gulls, float like bladders, with scarcely any of their body immersed: so that it is almost impossible to mistake one of the former at any distance at which a bird can be distinguished. The divers, such as the cormorant, the black-throated diver, and others of the same kind, swim very flat in the water, showing scarcely any part except the top of their back, and their head and neck, which all these birds carry straight and erect, seldom or never bending and arching their throat like ducks or geese. Widgeon swim rather flat and low in the water. Mallards and teal keep more of their bodies above it. Pochards, scaup ducks, and others of that kind, swim higher still.

The live otter's skin never appears to be wet, however long the animal may remain in the water; but, like the plumage of birds, soon becomes soaked through when the animal is dead. Whilst he is alive the water runs off his hair exactly as it does from the back of a bird during a shower. When we find any (live water) bird or animal with its feathers or hair wet and clinging together, it is a sure sign that the creature is either diseased or is suffering from some wound or accident.

When the pools and lochs are frozen, the water-hen takes to any stream or place where the water is open. Though apparently not well suited for so doing, this bird alights readily on trees. They are very familiar, and feed readily with poultry about a house. They eat almost anything, grain, plants, potatoes, etc.

March 4th, 1847. The pochard which I brought home is now perfectly tame. The boys have him in a little yard, and he takes worms from their hand. When he takes a worm from the ground he generally washes it in the water before swallowing it; he has a water trough to himself, in which they have placed a quantity of weeds taken out of the burn.

March 6th. I observe that the herons in the heronry on the Findhorn are now busily employed in sitting on their eggs.

The hooper, or common wild swan is the species most frequently seen on our lochs and coasts. The flocks are now far less numerous and frequent than they were even a few years ago. During a whole winter, only one or two small companies of wild swans are seen to alight and sojourn in any of our lochs. Their first arrival is usually about the middle

of October. In 1852, however, I saw eight pure white swans arrive on the loch of Spynie on the 30th of September. There had been a few days of severe wind, and the higher mountains had already snow on their summits. These birds were gone by the next morning. I never before saw the swans arrive so early; a man told me that he had seen above thirty pass over about the same time. Their coming so very early was, however, a very unusual occurrence. They appear to arrive in this neighbourhood in considerable flocks at the beginning of the season, and immediately afterwards to disperse into smaller companies, each departing to its own favourite wintering-place.

No birds offer so striking and beautiful a sight as a numerous flock of large swans on wing, while their musical cries sound more like the notes produced by some wild-toned musical instrument than the voice of a bird. While they remain with us, they frequent and feed in shallow pieces of water, like Lochlee, Loch Spynie, etc., where the water is of so small a depth that in many places they can reach the bottom with their long necks, and pluck up the water-grasses on which they feed. While employed in tearing up these plants, the swans are generally surrounded by a number of smaller water-fowl, such as widgeon and teal, who snatch at and carry off the pieces detached by their more powerful companions. The rapidity of the flight of a swan is wonderful—one moment they are far from you, the next they have passed you like an arrow. This speed, however, is only attained when at a considerable height from the ground. When first rising from the water they are obliged to flap, or, as it seems, to run, along the surface, before they can get their heavy bodies into the air.

In the flocks of this kind of swan there are generally a few gray birds, the cygnets. These cygnets are smaller and weaker than the old birds. The latter, however, vary much in size and weight. This difference is indeed very perceptible at a distance.

March 13th, 1853. Fine; a great many teal, etc., on Loch Spynie, and two swans appeared—Bewick's swans. These birds usually come in smaller companies than the hooper. I never see above eight of the *Cygnus bewickii* together, usually only four or five. They are easily distinguished, being shorter and more compact-looking birds. They also swim rather higher in the water, and are much tamer. Their plumage is peculiarly white, and the young apparently are not of the same blue gray as those of the hooper swan. I cannot assert this as a fact, but I never saw one of the Bewick's swans that was not of a pure and snow-like whiteness. The wild swan on the water is by no means so picturesque a bird as the tame swan, as it seldom arches its neck, or spreads out its wings to act as sails, as the latter bird does. On wing, however, the wild swan is unrivalled.

The wild swan leaves us about the middle or latter end of April. But the arrivals and departures of water-fowl are by no means so regular as those of some other birds, being more dependent on sudden and perhaps unseasonable changes in the weather.

March 18th, 1847. Walked to-day across the hills as far as the shore. In a kind of loch made by the sea I saw a great number of sheldrakes.

The pochard which I brought home from Spynie remains quite contented, and goes about with the other ducks. He will eat whatever they feed upon, but prefers worms to everything else, showing great activity in diving for them when they are flung into the water. Even when brought into the house he seems quite at home. Many kinds of wild-fowl might, with a little care, be perfectly domesticated, and I have no doubt would breed freely. Care must, however, be taken to prevent their flying away at the migrating seasons, and also to keep them at home when they begin to make their nests, as at that time they seem inclined to wander off in search of concealed and undisturbed places. After two or three generations of any bird have been domesticated, the young ones lose all their wild inclinations, tameness becoming hereditary with them, as skill and the power of benefiting by education become hereditary in dogs to a very striking degree.

The bernacle goose seldom pays us a visit, but I saw a few one day near the bar. This bird is numerous only on the west coast, and is rarely seen here. It is an elegant and beautifully marked bird, smaller than the bean goose. It is easily distinguished, even at a distance, owing to its peculiar pied appearance.

March 19th, 1854. I have a tame crossbill sitting by me now eating the seed out of fir cones. His tongue is very curious, it is like a long red worm. When the cone is open he takes the seed out with his tongue, squeezes the seed off from its "wing" and eats it. He is a fine healthy active bird, quite red. I see, though, that he prefers hempseed to the trouble of opening the cones.

March 20th, 1847. I see a few white-fronted geese feeding in the swamps near the lakes.

On the 22nd the dabchicks come to their breeding places in the smaller lochs, where there are plenty of rushes, and the sheldrakes now come frequently inland.

The dabchick or lesser grebe is a singular bird which visits this country regularly in the spring.

It is difficult to understand how this bird makes out its journey from the region, wherever it may be, where they pass the winter. No bird is less adapted for a long flight, yet they suddenly appear in some rushy loch. Generally a pair take possession of some small pool, where they build their singular nest and rear their young, till the returning autumn warns them that it is time to return to some country less liable than this to have its pools and lochs frozen. In a small rushy pond in Inverness-shire I had frequent opportunities of observing their domestic economy, and the manner in which they build their nest and rear their young. Though there was no stream connecting the pool with any other larger piece of water, a pair, and only a pair, of these little grebes came to it every spring.

After two or three days spent in recruiting their strength and making ·love to each other, the little birds set about making their nest in a tuft of rushes, at a shallow part of the water, a few yards from the shore. They first collected a considerable quantity of dead rushes, which they found in plenty floating about the edges of the water. Both male and female were busily employed in building, swimming to and fro with the greatest activity. After laying a good foundation of this material, they commenced diving for the weeds which grew at the bottom of the water, bringing up small bunches of it, and clambering up the sides of their nest (the bottom of which was in the water), they made a layer of this, hollowed out in the middle. They worked only in the morning and very late in the evening. Their eggs were six in number, and when first laid, quite white, and nearly oval.

During the time of sitting, whenever the old bird left her nest she covered her eggs most carefully. The singular part of this proceeding was, that she always dived for a quantity of green weed, which grew at the bottom of the pond, and used this, wet as it was, to cover her eggs. By the time that they had been laid for a few days they·became green and dirty-looking, having quite the appearance of being addled—and no wonder, as the nest was constantly wet from below, the water coming up through the rushes and weeds of which it was composed; and she gave them a fresh wet covering every time that she left them, arranging it around the eggs, so that the edges of the nest gradually became higher and higher. The bird appeared to be very frequently off during the daytime, remaining away for hours together, playing about on the water with her mate. After a fortnight of this kind of sitting, I one day saw her followed by six little dabchicks, scarcely bigger than large beetles, but as active and as much at home on the water as their parents. A very windy day came on, and the young birds collected in a group behind a floating rail, which being half grounded at an angle of the pool, made a kind of breakwater for them. The old birds swam out of this harbour when I came, but the little ones crept close up to the railing, uttering a feeble squeak like a young chicken. Huddled up in a group, they certainly were the smallest and quaintest-looking little divers that I ever saw.

I have heard it argued that it was impossible that eggs could be hatched in a situation constantly exposed to so much wet and damp, but those of this kind of grebe are certainly an exception. I do not know why the bird should always bring the covering from below the water, but she invariably did so, and the pool being in a convenient place for my watching them closely, I took some trouble to be sure that my

observations were correct. It is a pretty, amusing little bird, and quite
harmless: I have always much pleasure in watching their lively actions
in the water. Where undisturbed, they soon become bold and confident.
These little fellows used to swim close to me, and after looking up in my
face with an arch cock of their tiny head, turn up their round sterns and
dip under the water. They often remained so long under water, that the
circles made in the calm pool from their last dive were quite obliterated
from the surface before the saucy-looking little fellows would rise again,
often in exactly the same spot, when they would look at me again, as if to
be sure of who I was; then, turning half over in the water, they would
scratch their neck with their curiously-formed foot, shake their apology
of a wing, and dip under again.

One day my dog jumped into the water for a swim, and the motions of
the birds were then very different. They dived rapidly to the other end of
the pool, where they rose, showing only the very tip of their bill, which I
could distinguish by the small wave in the water made when it first came

up. After remaining in this position for a short time, they gradually lifted up more and more of their head, till, seeing that all danger was over and that the dog had left their pool, they rose entirely to the surface, and shaking their feathers resumed their usual attitudes, keeping, however, at a respectful distance and watching the dog. After the young ones were hatched and full grown they again disappeared, leaving us for the winter. *How* or *where* they went it is difficult to imagine.

About the middle of March the black-backed gulls are very noisy in the bay.

When the frogs begin to croak in the pools and ditches, the mallards are sure to be found in these places every evening and morning.

March 22nd, 1847. Fish have more sense or instinct than we give them credit for. I saw a trout to-day about six inches long that had been left in a small pool by a rise of the river, making its way over the *dry* stones across a ridge that separated the pool from the river, the distance being a full yard. When it saw us the trout immediately turned itself round, and mizzled back into the pool it had come from. This seems so very extraordinary a story that I should be almost afraid of telling it to any person.

March 23rd. The wood-pigeons are building in the shrubberies close to the window.

March 30th, 1847. Cold, sleet, and snow; the hills as much covered with snow as they have been all winter. Six swans came into the bay this evening, and near dusk flew westwards towards Lochlee.

It is amusing to see the arrival of the larger flocks about this time. A few small companies of pink-footed and white-fronted geese usually arrive early in the month, but about the 28th, and generally on some quiet evening, immense flights of the bean goose arrive in Findhorn Bay. They come in just about sunset, in four or five large flocks, and an

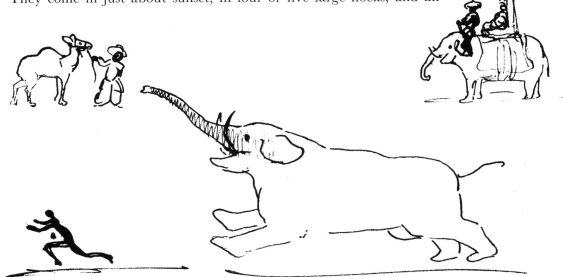

infinite quantity of gabbling and chattering takes place for several hours; but by daybreak they seem to have determined on their respective beats, and separating into smaller flocks disperse over the land, and do not collect again in very numerous flocks until they are about to leave that part of the country at the end of April or the beginning of May. The wild geese decrease in number every year: the gray lag goose is a very rare visitor to the oat-fields here, although so many breed in Sutherland.

The woodcocks are more numerous at this time of year in the larger woods than during any part of the winter: they pair early, and have probably before this time taken up their breeding quarters. Those which breed abroad do not leave this country till just before their time of laying. I am much inclined to think that most birds which migrate from us in the spring, pair some time before they take their departure.

It is a fallacy to suppose that pike are detrimental to the sport of the fly-fisher, that is, in the Highland lakes, where there is depth and space enough for both kinds of fish to live and flourish; of course pike kill thousands and tens of thousands of small trout, but the fault of most Highland lakes is that there are too many trout in them, and the fly-fisher works for a month without killing a trout above a pound weight; pike keep down the overstock, there are still plenty and more than plenty of trout remaining in the water, and of a better size and quality than where they are not thinned. I have invariably found this the case, and that I could catch a greater weight of trout in a loch where there are pike than where the trout had no natural enemies to keep down their daily increasing numbers, besides which, though the pike is piscivorous, he is also most decidedly as omnivorous as a pig or an alderman; a great part of the food of the pike consists of frogs, leeches, weeds, etc.; young wild ducks, water-hens, and even water-rats, do not come amiss to him.

March 31st, 1847. In the bay to-day mallard, sheldrake, widgeon, cormorant, curlew, oyster-catcher, whimbrel, red-shank, ring-dottrel, and large flights of different sandpipers. I observed a peculiarity in the flight of the oyster-catchers and whimbrels. Large flocks of these birds were constantly alighting on a small island near where I was concealed. The birds invariably flew down wind to 60 or 80 yards to the leeward of the spot on which they intended to pitch, and then turning round flew back against the wind, and alighted with their heads to windward. Of the hundreds that were on the island not one pitched in any other manner.

WILD DUCK

Scaup Ducks—Mallard—Strange Nesting Habits—Moulting—Taming Wild Ducks—
Widgeon—Long-tailed Ducks—Velvet Ducks and Scoters—Teal—Sheldrake—
Pochard—Eider-duck—Golden-eye

A few years ago I used to see a great many scaup ducks in the pools and burns near the coast, but now it is very seldom that I meet with a single bird of this kind. In general character and habits it resembles the pochard very much, as also in its manner of flight, of feeding, etc. It is oftener seen in pairs, and singly, perhaps, than the pochard, and is more frequently found on the sea. This is one of the few ducks frequenting the shore which has not a rank or fishy flavour: out of the numerous varieties of birds of the duck kind, I can only enumerate four that are really good eating, namely the common mallard, the widgeon, the teal, and the scaup duck.

The best of these is the mallard which breeds in all the bogs and marshes of this county, and also very frequently hatches its young in woods and quiet places at a considerable distance from the pool or lake to which it leads its young as soon as hatched. It is by no means an uncommon occurrence to find the eggs of this bird laid in an old crow's, or other bird's nest, at a considerable height from the ground. I never could exactly ascertain how the mother carries her young in safety to the ground. A curious instance of this bird building in a crow's nest was told me by a person whose veracity I am quite inclined to trust. My informant told me that he one day took six or seven wild duck's eggs out of an old crow's nest, in a fir-tree near Loch-na-bo. Ten days or a fortnight afterwards he saw an owl fly out of the same nest, and on climbing to it he found three eggs of the common horned owl, which bird also takes possession of a deserted crow's nest.

The wild duck frequently has her nest in places apparently the most unlikely; sometimes in the densest wood, at others close to a road or path, frequently in the long coarse grass or rushes at the edge of a lake. In fact, there seems no rule as to the situation or kind of ground, wet or dry, in which they breed. In a glen in Angus they nest freely in the holes left by fallen pebbles in the plum-pudding rock, at least 12, to 20 feet above the water. When strong enough, I suppose the young are thrust over the edge, and let fall in the stream. While laying and sitting, the old bird appears to be constantly adding down from her own body to the nest. On leaving her eggs for the purpose of feeding, etc., she covers them over most carefully, concealing even the path through the rank herbage to and from her nest. Their usual time of hatching with us is about the 25th to 28th of April; the number of eggs ten to thirteen. Many of the young, when first hatched, fall a prey to crows and other vermin, notwithstanding the great care which the mother takes of them.

As soon as hatched, the young ones take to the water, and it is very amusing to see the activity and quickness which the little fellows display in catching insects and flies as they skim along the surface of the water, led on by the parent bird, who takes the greatest care of them, bustling about with all the hurry and importance of a barn-yard hen. Presently she gives a low warning quack, as a hawk or carrion crow passes in a suspicious manner over them. One cry is enough, away all the little ones dart into the rushes, screaming and fluttering, while the old bird, with head flat on the water and upturned eye, slowly follows them, but not until she sees them all out of danger. After a short time, if the enemy has disappeared, the old bird peers cautiously from her covert, and if she makes up her mind that all is safe, she calls forth her offspring again, to feed and sport in the open water.

The young birds do not fly till they are quite full grown. I have observed that, as soon as ever the inner side of the wing is fully clothed, they take to flying; their bones, which before this time were more like gristle than anything else, quickly hardening, and giving the bird full power and use of its pinions. The old bird then leads them forth at night to the most distant feeding-places, either to the grass meadows where they search for snails or worms, or to the splashy swamps, where they dabble about all night, collecting the different insects and young frogs that abound in these places. As the corn ripens, they fly to the oat-fields in the dusk of the evening, preferring this grain and peas to any other.

During the month of July, however, many of the old ducks are quite unable to fly, having lost their quill-feathers, which appear to drop out all at once. The mallard loses his male plumage in May, assuming the appearance of the female, only rather darker. They have not re-acquired their full beauty till the end of October or first week in November. Though associating in large flocks during winter, they still keep in pairs; and when the flocks are on wing, they break off very soon into detached companies of two, four, six, etc., in which the pairs are

easily distinguished. This makes me inclined to think that the same drake and duck, whenever once paired, keep constantly together till divided by the gun or other accident. Some wild ducks which I had domesticated became gregarious, one drake serving many ducks, like tame poultry. But one season, having been neglected, and wandering out in the fields and ditches, they resumed their wild habits, paired, built, and lived in pairs quite conjugally. Foxes kill a considerable number of ducks, and the peregrine falcon frequently strikes down an old bird when found in a favourable situation, though so rapid is the flight of the mallard, that I have seen the falcon unable to gain a yard on him during a long chase. When the corn is exhausted in the fields, the wild ducks feed on the potatoes which are left on the ground, eating both sound and rotten roots indiscriminately.

I have frequently caught and brought home young wild ducks. If confined in a yard, or elsewhere, for a week or two with tame birds, they strike up a companionship which keeps them from wandering when set at liberty. Some few years back I brought home three young wild ducks: two of them turned out to be drakes. I sent away my tame drakes, and, in consequence, the next season had a large family of half-bred and whole wild ducks, as the tame and wild breed together quite freely. The wild ducks which have been caught are the tamest of all; throwing off all their natural shyness, they follow their feeder, and will eat corn out of the hand of any person with whom they are acquainted. The half-bred birds are sometimes pinioned, as they are inclined to fly away for the purpose of making their nests at a distance: at other times they never attempt to leave the field in front of the house. A pair or two always breed in the flower-garden. They appear to have a great *penchant* for forming their nests in certain flower-beds, and they are allowed to have their own way in this respect, as their elegant and high-bred appearance interests even the gardener, enemy as he is to all intruders on his favourite flowers.

These birds conceal their eggs with great care, and I have often been amused at the trouble the poor duck is put to in collecting dead leaves and straw to cover her eggs, when they are laid in a well-kept flower-bed. I often have a handful of straw laid on the grass at a convenient distance from the nest, which the old bird soon carries off, and makes use of. The drakes, though they take no portion of the nesting labours, appear to keep a careful watch near at hand during the time the duck is sitting. The half-bred birds have a peculiarity in common with the wild duck—which is, that they always pair, each drake taking charge of only one duck—not, as is the case with the tame ducks, taking to himself half a dozen wives. The young, too, when first hatched, have a great deal of the shyness of wild ducks, showing itself in a propensity to run off and hide in any hole or corner that is at hand. When in full plumage my drakes also have the beautifully-mottled feathers above the wing which are so much used in fly-dressing.

During the summer I have seen a very few widgeon about the Loch of

Spynie; but am more inclined to suppose that they were wounded birds, unable to follow the migrating flock, than birds remaining to breed. In Sutherland I have found the nest; and in Loch Naver and elsewhere the widgeon breeds regularly, though not in any great numbers.

The migrating widgeon begin to arrive early in October or at the end of September, and according to the weather they come in larger quantities. By the beginning of November there are immense numbers, and their shrill whistle enlivens all the larger lochs and swamps. Towards night every widgeon seems to be in motion, flying to their feeding-places, either in the shallow places or along the edges of the water, where they can get at the grass and water-plants which form their food. Their flight is very rapid, and, divided into small companies, they flit to and fro in every direction till they settle down to their food. During the day time they all collect and rest in the centre of the lochs. The widgeon, like the teal, is late in acquiring its full plumage, and in the flocks but a small proportion of drakes in full beauty are seen.

The widgeon is indeed the most perfectly proportioned of any waterfowl, and the plumage of the male is peculiarly bright and beautiful. Both on land and in the water it is a very active bird; when on shore it walks upright and rapidly, and on the water is unrivalled both in swimming and diving.

It is an interesting walk in the bright clear winter nights, to go round by the shore, listening to the various calls of the birds, the constant quack of the mallard, the shrill whistle of the widgeon, the low croaking note of the teal, and the fine bugle voice of the wild swan, varied every now and then by the loud whistling of a startled curlew, or oyster-catcher. The mallard and teal are the only exclusively night-feeding birds; the others feed at any time of the night or day, being dependent on the state of the tide to get at the banks of grass and weed, or the sands where they find shell-fish. All ducks are quite as wary in the bright moonlight as in the daytime, but at night are more likely to be found near the shore.

There is a very pretty and elegant little duck, which is common on our coast—the long-tailed duck. This beautiful bird is wholly a salt-water duck, and I never saw it higher than the mouth of a river. It does not arrive very early, but stays late; even in May it enlivens the sea-shore. Its movements and actions are peculiarly graceful and amusing, while its musical cry is quite unlike that of any other bird, unless a slight resemblance to the trumpeting of the wild swan may be traced in it. Lying concealed on the shore, I have often watched these birds, as they swim along in small companies within twenty yards of me; the drake, with his gay plumage, playing quaint antics round the more sad-coloured female—sometimes jerking himself half out of the water, at others diving under her, and coming up on the other side. Sometimes, by a common impulse, they all set off swimming in a circle after each other with great rapidity, and uttering their curious cry, which is peculiarly wild and pleasing. When feeding, these birds dive constantly, remaining under water for a considerable time. Turning up their tails, they dip under with a curious kind of motion, one after the other, till the whole flock is under water.

They swim in with the flowing tide, frequently following the course of the water to some little distance from the mouth of the river. When I see them in the heavy surf on the main shore, they seem quite at their ease, floating high in the water, and diving into the midst of the wildest waves. When put up, they seldom fly far, keeping low, and suddenly dropping into the water again, where they seem more at their ease than in the air.

On the open part of the coast they are often seen in company with the velvet duck. The latter very seldom comes into the bay, but keeps without the bar, quite regardless of storm or wind. Generally these heavy but handsome birds ride quietly on the sea in small companies, at the distance of about two hundred yards from the shore, apparently keeping over some ridge of sand or other feeding-ground, down to which they are continually diving. These birds drift along with the tide till it has carried them beyond the place where they feed; then they rise, and fly back for some distance, looking more like blackcocks than ducks, and dropping again into the water, they continue their diving till the tide has drifted them beyond the end of the feeding-ground; and then the same again and again.

Though in general appearance not unlike the velvet duck, the scoter is smaller and not so plump in appearance. This bird is not so common in the firth as the velvet scoter, and seems to leave us during the depth of winter, betaking itself southwards. I never heard of its being seen inland, and it appears to live wholly on small shellfish.

The teal can scarcely be called a winter bird with us, although occasionally a pair or two appear; but in the spring they come in numbers to breed and rear their tiny young in the swamps and lochs.

Nothing can exceed the beauty and neatness of this miniature duck. They fly with great swiftness, rising suddenly into the air when disturbed, and dropping as quickly after a short flight, much in the same manner as a snipe. In the spring the drake has a peculiar whistle, at other times their note is a low quack. A pair of teal, if undisturbed, will return year after year to the same pool for the purpose of breeding. Like the wild duck, they sometimes hatch their young a considerable distance from the water, and lead the young brood immediately to it.

I once, when riding in Ross-shire, saw an old teal with eight newly-hatched young ones cross the road. The youngsters could not climb up the opposite bank, and young and old all squatted flat down to allow me to pass. I got off my horse and lifted all the little birds up and carried them a little distance down the road to a ditch, for which I concluded they were making, the old bird all the time fluttering about me and frequently coming within reach of my riding-whip. The part of the road where I first found them passed through thick fir-wood with rank heather, and it was quite a puzzle to me how such small animals, scarcely bigger than a half-grown mouse could have got along through it. The next day I saw them all enjoying themselves in a small pond at some little distance off, where a brood of teal appeared every year. In some of the mountain lakes the teal breed in great numbers. When shooting in August I have seen a perfect cloud of these birds occasionally rise from some grassy loch.

As the winter draws to a close the teal alter their peculiar whistle, and are very restless in the marshes, constantly flying to and fro. The drakes do not acquire their plumage till later in the winter than most other water-fowl. Though so numerous in the spring and autumn, the greatest part of these birds go southwards during the winter. The nest and eggs are exactly similar to those of the mallard, but on a proportionately smaller scale. The number of eggs is about eight. I know no nest prettier than that of the teal when the eggs are near hatching and a full quantity of down surrounds them. Though so loose-looking a material, the whole may be lifted in a compact mass.

I should certainly call the sheldrake the most beautiful bird of the duck tribe that visits this country. Its clear black and white plumage, the beautiful bronze on the wing, and the bright red bill, give it a particularly gay and at the same time neat appearance. They arrive here in March or the end of February. They float in large flocks in the sheltered creeks and bays, swimming high in the water and making a great show. When the tide recedes, they take to the sands in search of their food, which consists of shell-fish, the sea-worms, etc. Their manner of catching the latter is curious. When the sheldrake perceives that he is above the hole of one of these insects, which he knows by the worm-casts similar to those of a common earth-worm, he begins patting the ground with his feet, dancing as it were over the hole. This motion on the sands generally brings the worm out of his abode. My tame sheldrakes, when they come to ask for food, pat the ground in an impatient and rapid manner, their natural instinct evidently suggesting this as the usual way of procuring food. Though among the most wary of birds when wild, their sharp eye detecting the least movement, yet they become extremely fearless and bold when once domesticated, and certainly no bird is more ornamental. They breed freely in a tame state, if allowed a certain degree of liberty.

In the wild they breed in rabbit holes several feet under ground. At day-dawn I have frequently seen the drakes waiting on the hillocks near which their females are sitting. Foxes often destroy the old birds by watching for them at the mouth of the hole where the nest is. As soon as hatched, the young take to the sea, and never come to land above high-water mark but in some sheltered places where the tide recedes to a distance. They appear to live wholly either on the sea or on the wet sands, where their food is plentiful. The young birds are so quick and active on the sands that it is almost impossible to catch them.

The pochard is not uncommon during the winter on Loch Spynie, Lochlee, and other large pieces of water. They arrive with the first cold or stormy weather, and remain till spring. On Lochlee I saw a pair of pochards late in the spring, after the rest of the wild-fowl had left this country. In due time the pair was increased to a small company, apparently a brood, and I have no doubt that they had been bred in the vicinity of the Loch. I had reason to believe that one of the original pair was a tame one which had escaped from my yard. I never on any other occasion saw the pochard during the breeding season in this country. It is a very active, quiet bird in the water, and dives rapidly. Indeed, the pochard feeds wholly under the water, and it is amusing to watch them when feeding, one after the other disappearing until perhaps not one bird is visible, then suddenly the whole surface is again alive with them. On the wing the pochard flies with great swiftness, making very rapid strokes with its short wings, which are small in proportion to the body. They keep in a compact flock during their flight, and before leaving a piece of water they fly several times to and fro, wheeling quickly, and increasing their height, when, if much frightened, they betake themselves to the sea.

The eider-duck is a rare visitant to this part of the coast. It is however sometimes seen in the Firth, but is too completely a marine bird ever to visit any fresh-water lakes. It breeds in some of the more northern rocky islands of Scotland, though even in these it is now rare. In Iceland, where the eider-duck breeds in considerable numbers, they are carefully protected for the sake of the down, with which they cover their eggs, and which the natives take in great quantities.

The eider-duck breeds regularly on the islets in the Forth between Aberlady and North Berwick. I have taken eggs from a nest in Ebrus. It is a beautiful sight to watch the mother and her newly hatched chicks swimming about in the smooth hollow of the wave. They are not frightened at the passing boat. I have seen a duck remain an oar's length off until she had gathered one by one her dusky little brood, not under but above her wings, where there seemed scarce standing-room for them all. When she had got every one "on board," but not till then, she sailed away for more undisturbed waters.

The golden-eye does not breed in this country. In Norway it breeds in a hollow tree, often entering at a hole made by the large woodpecker. The golden-eye arrives here early, and remains late in the spring. It frequents almost every loch and stream, though always in small numbers—generally in pairs or singly. The flight is rapid, and the sound of the wings is so peculiar, as to be distinguished amongst a large flock of other water-fowl. It is not a wild or shy bird, but very active in diving— as it feeds wholly under the water. The golden-eye duck differs so very much in size and plumage at different ages and according to sex, that it is sometimes difficult to decide whether a bird is a golden-eye or not. But from long observation I am inclined to suppose that many ducks, such as those called the morillon, etc., are but golden-eyes at different stages of maturity.

A curious anecdote of a brood of young wild ducks was told me by my keeper to-day. He found in some very rough, marshy ground, which was formerly a peat-moss, eight young ducks nearly full grown, prisoners, as it were, in one of the old peat-holes. They had evidently tumbled in some time before, and had managed to subsist on the insects, etc., that it contained or that fell into it. From the manner in which they had undermined the banks of their watery prison, the birds must have been in it for some weeks. The sides were perpendicular, but there were small resting-places under the bank which prevented their being drowned. The size of the place they were in was about eight feet square, and in this small space they had not only grown up, but thrived, being fully as large and heavy as any other young ducks of the same age.

Green finch.

Moorhen.
or Fin

APRIL

Arrival of the Wheatear—The Corn Bunting—White Hares—Aurora Borealis—A
Hurricane—Eels and Toads—Habits of the Water-ouzel—Jackdaws—Habits of Tame
Wild Duck—Lampreys—The White-fronted Goose—Arrival of Birds—The Thrush
and Blackbird—The Ring-ouzel—Siskin's Nests—A Little Gull

April 1st, 1847. Walked to Lochlee. The widgeon very much
decreased in numbers. Great flocks of fieldfares and redwings
singing on the trees.

April 2nd, 1853. Rennie brought me a roundish white egg with a
smooth shell which he found in a rabbit hole—length $1\frac{7}{8}$ inch; breadth
$1\frac{1}{2}$ inch—apparently the egg of the tawny owl.

April 3rd, 1847. At this season the salmon and trout appear to lie in the
dead water of a pool, or quite at the tail of the stream, so as to be out of
the strength of the river, not having the same power of resisting the water
as they have in the warmer weather.

4th. The water-ouzels have entirely disappeared from the burn near
the sea, having, I suppose, gone farther up the country to breed.

About the 4th or 6th of April the wheatear first makes its appearance
here; it is seen on the stone walls and along the sea-shore.

The corn bunting is one of the first birds which utters its spring note.
Before the winter is well over, sitting on the topmost twig of a bush, it
utters a loud shrill note. Frequently too it utters this cry while on the
wing, hovering over the hedge, with its feet hanging down at full stretch.
It is a very common bird, and to be seen near all farmyards, in every
hedge, and on every stone wall. It is larger than a sparrow or greenfinch,
and rather heavier than a lark, which bird it resembles much in general
colour, though of a different shape. In the winter the buntings collect in
large flocks. When they fly from tree to tree they keep in a close compact
body pitching again suddenly.

[65]

Corn Bunting

6th. Walked to the wood at Black Stab with the boys, who found some rooks' eggs and peewits' eggs.

Some gray geese were seen to-day. We caught a beautiful brent goose in a trap on a grassy island, which is generally covered by the sea at high water. Immense numbers of these geese float with every tide into the bays formed by the bar. As the tide recedes they land on the grass and feed in closely-packed flocks.

April 6th, 1851. We went to Dulsie for crossbills, but only saw one pair of old birds which crossed the river. We had a most beautiful day. There is evidently a scarcity of fir cones in that particular wood, which I have no doubt has made the birds move to some other district. The nests which we found were those of the crossbill without doubt, built exactly like those which we found last year. No other nest is like them.

I found the same day a tree-sparrow lying dead under the wall of the old Castle of Duffus—a place standing alone in that flat country, a mile from the Loch of Spynie. No doubt they breed plentifully here. Blackbirds and hedge-sparrows have eggs near hatching in the garden.

April 6th, 1853. Two white hares killed near Dr. Maclean's house [close to Elgin] yesterday; a very unusual occurrence to see these animals so far from their mountain home.

April 7th, 1847. I was out late with the keeper to-day, and we saw a very brilliant aurora borealis, or, as they term it here, "The Merry Dancers." He told me that often when the aurora was very bright, and the flashes rapidly waving through the sky, he had thought that he heard the merry dancers emit a faint rustling noise, like the "moving of dead leaves," but this was only when the night was quite calm, and there was no other sound to disturb the perfect stillness. The statement came from him quite uncalled for by any remark of mine, and was entirely the result of his own observation. I was pleased to hear him say this, as I had more than once imagined that the aurora, when peculiarly bright and rapid in its movements, DID actually make exactly the sound that he described; but never having heard it asserted by anyone else, I had always been rather shy of advancing such a statement.

The aurora is seldom seen, or at least seldom attentively watched in this country, in situations where there is not some sound or other, such as voices, running water, or the rustling and moaning of trees, to break the perfect stillness: but it has occasionally happened to me to be gazing at this beautiful illumination in places where no other sound could be heard, and then, and then only, have I fancied that the brightest flashes were accompanied by a light crackling or rustling noise, or, as my keeper expressed it very correctly, "the moving of dead leaves."

In the northern mountains of Sutherland, where the aurora is frequently very bright and beautiful, there is a fascinating, nay, an awful attraction in the sight, which has kept me for hours from my bed watching the waving and ever-changing flashes dancing to and fro. I have watched this strange sight where the dead silence of the mountains

Greenfinch

was only broken by the fancied rustling of the "*dresses*" of the "merry dancers," or by the sudden scream or howl of some wild inhabitant of the rocks, until an undefinable feeling of superstitious awe has crept over my mind, which was not without difficulty shaken off.

The aurora, bright as it sometimes is in this country, must be far more wildly and vividly splendid in the more northern and Polar regions. Here it is almost invariably the forerunner of change of weather, or of rough winds and storm.

April 8th, 1847. It blew a hurricane to-day from the west-north-west, with cold showers. We anticipated this kind of weather from the brightness of the aurora last night. Large flocks of brent geese driven into the bay; the birds scarcely able to move from the ground in exposed places. I saw a sea-gull caught by the wind in the air and turned entirely over five or six times before it could recover its balance and get its head to windward.

April 7th, 1852. I see eels beginning to show in the dead pools of the river. I see the remains of toads which have been killed, and partly devoured; in every instance only the hind legs have been eaten; I suppose by the hooded crow. The toad catches insects with extraordinary rapidity. Some who live in a cask of water in the yard catch the flies when they settle near them. The toad on seeing a fly creeps up with great caution till within an inch or two, and then with a motion so rapid that the eye cannot follow it, the fly is caught and swallowed. Apparently the toad darts out his tongue; but it is impossible to see exactly how the fly is caught. All one sees is a rapid opening and shutting of the toad's mouth, down which the fly (which was an inch or more from it) disappears as if by magic. The frogs also feed on the flies, but do not catch and swallow them with the same wonderful quickness.

April 10th, 1852. A water-ouzel in the burn has two eggs. The nest is built in a broken bank. The bats fly about now round the buildings and garden.

For several years a pair of water-ouzel built their nest and reared their young on a buttress of a bridge across what is called the Black burn, near Dalvey. This year I am sorry to see that, owing to some repairs in the bridge, the birds have not returned to their former abode. The nest, when looked at from above, had exactly the appearance of a confused heap of rubbish, drifted by some flood to the place where it was built, and attached to the bridge just where the buttress joins the perpendicular part of the masonry. The old birds evidently took some trouble to deceive the eye of those who passed along the bridge, by giving the nest the look of a chance collection of material.

I do not know, among our common birds, so amusing and interesting a little fellow as the water-ouzel, whether seen during the time of incubation, or during the winter months, when he generally betakes himself to some burn near the sea, less likely to be frozen over than those more inland. In the burn near this place there are certain stones, each of

which is always occupied by one particular water-ouzel: there he sits all day, with his snow-white breast turned towards you, jerking his apology for a tail, and occasionally darting off for a hundred yards or so, with a quick, rapid, but straight-forward flight; then down he plumps into the water, remains under for perhaps a minute or two; and then flies back to his usual station. At other times the water-ouzel walks deliberately off his stone down into the water, and walks and runs about on the gravel at the bottom of the water, scratching with his feet among the small stones, and picking away at all the small insects and animalcules which he can dislodge. On two or three occasions, I have witnessed this act of the water-ouzel, and have most distinctly seen the bird walking and feeding in this manner under the pellucid waters of a Highland burn.

It is in this way that the water-ouzel is supposed to commit great havoc in the spawning beds of salmon and trout, uncovering the ova.

The water-ouzel has another very peculiar habit, which I have never heard mentioned. In the coldest days of winter I have seen him alight on a quiet pool, and with outstretched wings recline for a few moments on the water, uttering a most sweet and merry song—then rising into the air, he wheels round and round for a minute or two, repeating his song as he flies back to some accustomed stone. His notes are so pleasing, that he fully deserves a place in the list of our song-birds; though I never found but one other person, besides myself, who would own to having heard the water-ouzel sing. In the early spring, too, he courts his mate with the same harmony, and pursues her from bank to bank singing as loudly as he can—often have I stopped to listen to him as he flew to and fro along the burn, apparently full of business and importance; then pitching on a stone, he would look at me with such confidence, that, notwithstanding the bad name he has acquired with the fishermen, I never could make up my mind to shoot him. He frequents the rocky burns far up the mountains, building in the crevices of the rocks, and rearing his young in peace and security, amidst the most wild and magnificent scenery.

[68]

April 14th, 1847. We find no end of plovers' eggs.

April 17th, 1847. The arrival of the geese to-day was worth seeing. An immense body of 300 or 400 birds arrived first in one flock. As soon as they were above the sands every bird appeared to commence calling, making together a noise that first attracted our attention, though we were nearly a mile from the place. After flying to and fro above the bay they broke off into different companies and dispersed through the country, looking for feeding-places. We could see the flocks as they wheeled round and round different new corn-fields looking for places to alight.

April 18th, 1851. The golden eagle probably has hatched ere now. The eggs are worth a guinea apiece.

April 18th, 1847. Riding by the heronry on the Findhorn I saw the Altyre keeper searching in all the jackdaws' nests that he could reach for the remains of the herons' eggs. These active little marauders live in great numbers in the rocks immediately opposite the herons, and keep up a constant warfare with them during the breeding season, stealing an immense number of their eggs. The keeper took handfuls of the shells of the herons' eggs out of some of the jackdaws' holes: the injury to the heronry from this cause must be very great, as the plundering seems to be incessantly going on.

The time at which roe lose the velvet from their horns seems to depend on the lateness or earliness of the season. This year (1848) is backward, and as late as the 15th of this month I see that the horns of the bucks are still covered with the velvet. In early seasons their horns are quite clean by the 4th or 5th of the month. When the larch and other trees become green, the roe wander very much, taking to the smaller woods and grassy plantations in search of some favourite foliage or herbage.

When a crow leaves her nest on being disturbed, her quiet, sneaking manner of threading her way through the trees tells that she has young or eggs in the thicket, as plainly as if she uttered cries of alarm. These birds are early breeders: I found a hooded crow's nest, with eggs nearly hatched, on the 16th April.

April 19th, 1848. My retriever put up a wild duck on the 16th in some very high and close heather at some distance from any water. I found that she had her nest in the very centre of the heather, and in the densest part of it. The nest was very beautifully formed; it was perfectly round, and looked like a mass of the finest down, with just sufficient coating of small sticks, etc., outside to keep the down together. These were thirteen eggs in it, which we took home and put under a bantam hen: they were hatched in a few days, and I allowed them to go at liberty with their foster-mother in the kitchen garden, where they soon became perfectly tame.

When the gardener digs any part of the ground, the little fellows immediately flock about his spade, so that it is difficult for him to avoid hurting them, as they tumble about on the newly turned-up earth,

[69]

darting at the worms which come into view; whenever they see him take his spade they run after him as if they thought that his only object in digging up the ground was to find them food. One tiny fellow, who is weaker than the rest, and who consequently gets pushed out of the way by his stronger brethren, waits quietly to be lifted up on the flat of the spade, where the gardener allows him to stop, out of the reach of the others, while the little glutton swallows a worm nearly as big as himself. The moment the spade is laid flat on the ground he knows that his turn has come, and running on it looks out for the expected worm, and is quite fearless although raised on the spade several feet from the ground.

Most wild-fowl require very little extent of water, so long as they have grass fields to walk about and to feed in. No more water is necessary than is sufficient for them to wash and take an occasional swim in.

Our brent goose seems to eat scarcely anything but grass, and any snails and worms it may find in the field. He is a far more graceful bird on land than the pochard, for quick and active as the latter is in the water, his great flat feet, placed far behind, are of little service to him in walking.

April 19th, 1852. I was amused by watching the singular proceedings of two lampreys in a small ditch of clear running water near my house. They were about six inches in length, and as large round as a pencil. The two little creatures were most busily and anxiously employed in making little triangular heaps of stones, using for the purpose irregularly-shaped bits of gravel about the size of a large pea. When they wished to move a larger stone, they helped each other in endeavouring to roll it into the desired situation: occasionally they both left off their labours and appeared to rest for a short time, and then to return to the work with fresh vigour. The object of their building I am not sufficiently learned in the natural history of the lamprey to divine; but I conclude that their work had something to do with the placing of their spawn. I had, however, a good opportunity of watching them, as the water was quite clear and shallow, and they were so intent upon what they were at, that they took no notice whatever of me. I had intended to examine the little heaps of stones which they had made, but going from home the next day put it out of my recollection, and I lost the opportunity. It seems, however, so singular a manœuvre on the part of fish to build up regular little pyramids of gravel, bringing some of the stones from the distance of two feet against the current and rolling them to the place with evident difficulty, that the lampreys must have some good reason which induces them to take this trouble. It is a great pity that the habits of fish and animals living in water are so difficult to observe with any degree of exactness.

April 19th, 1853. Every bird is late this year. This season I do not think the wild ducks have eggs yet, though I found them nearly hatching three days earlier in 1848. The kestrel hawks are very numerous. I saw one fly into a tree calling loudly and carrying something, a small bird or mouse.

Presently another hawk of the same kind came, and the first bird immediately gave its prey up to the last comer, who carried it off. The bird which brought the mouse carried it in its beak, but the one that received it carried it off in its claws.

April 20th, 1847. Fished at Darnaway, but only one salmon rose all day. During a severe frost last year, I watched for some time a common kingfisher, which, by some strange chance, and quite against its usual habits, had strayed into this northern latitude. He first caught my eye while darting like a living emerald along the course of a small unfrozen stream between my house and the river; he then suddenly alighted on a post, and remained a short time motionless in the peculiar strange attitude of his kind, as if intent on gazing at the sky. All at once a new idea comes into his head, and he follows the course of the ditch, hovering here and there like a hawk, at the height of a yard or so above the water: suddenly down he drops into it, disappears for a moment, and then rises into the air with a trout about two inches long in his bill; this he carries quickly to the post where he had been resting before, and having beat it in an angry and vehement manner against the wood for a minute, he swallows it whole.

I tried to get at him, coveting the bright blue feathers on his back, which are extremely useful in fly-dressing, but before I was within shot, he darted away, crossed the river, and sitting on a rail on the opposite side, seemed to wait as if expecting me to wade after him; this, however, I did not think it worth while doing, as the water was full of floating ice, so I left the kingfisher where he was, and never saw him again. Their visits to this country are very rare—I only have seen one other, and he was sitting on the bow of my boat watching the water below him for a passing trout small enough to be swallowed.

April 20th, 1849. The willow wren arrives generally about this time.

April 22nd, 1851. Wheatears, swallows, and martins are come. The woods are full of siskins—very few crossbills; all the small birds have eggs, and young ones in the garden.

The white-fronted goose arrives in this country from its breeding quarters in the arctic and northern regions about the middle of October, in small companies of from six to twelve generally, and if left tolerably undisturbed frequents regularly the same swamp or piece of marsh till the end of April, feeding on aquatic plants, and in the spring frequently grazing on the young clover or green wheat more in the manner of the graylag than the bean goose, the latter confining itself as much as possible to grain. Their cry is very loud and peculiar, sometimes resembling wonderfully the loud laugh of a human being. Hence its name of "laughing goose".

April 25th, 1847-1848. For the last two years I have first seen the martins on the 25th of April, and the common chimney swallow on the 27th. The terns also come at the same time. Indeed in both years I have seen them on the same day, *i.e.* the 27th.

Amongst the curious instincts which birds display in providing themselves with food, one most resembling reason is that which teaches the common crow, on finding on the shore a shell containing fish, to fly with it to a height in the air, and then to let it drop in order to break the shell sufficiently to get at the fish enclosed in it. When the shell does not break the first time that the crow drops it, she darts down, picks it up, and ascends still higher, till she perceives that the height is sufficient for her purpose. Sometimes another crow darts in to carry off the booty; upon which a battle ensues in the air. Cunning as the crow is, she seldom finds any prize without letting all the neighbourhood know of it by her cries and gestures. The crows collect great numbers of sea-shells on particular favourite hillocks, which are often at some distance from the

sea. I have frequently observed in this country great collections of this kind, and from the state of the shells it would appear that they bring them to the same place for many successive years.

The thrush has a similar habit. When it finds a snail which it cannot extract from the shell, it carries it to some favourite stone which happens to have a convenient chink in it, fixes the shell so that it cannot slip, and then soon breaks it up, using its strong bill like a pickaxe. The blows of the bird when opening a shell in this manner may be heard to some distance. In my garden there are certain stones round which there are always a number of snail shells left broken by the thrushes, and I have frequently seen stones used in the same manner in the woods. Though not migratory, in the common sense of the word, the thrushes change their quarters at the approach of winter, leaving the large fir woods and higher grounds for the gardens and cultivated fields.

The thrush begins to sing early in January in mild weather, but at that period of the year neither sings frequently nor regularly. As the spring advances, it sings most indefatigably, usually commencing at the same hour of the day; and, seated on the same branch day after day, it pours forth its rich and loud song. The notes of the thrush are very varied. If carefully listened to, the songs of no two thrushes are quite alike, and in some the difference is very striking indeed—in so much so, that the songs of different birds in the same garden can be as well known from each other as the voices of different people.

Every year the blackbird becomes more numerous in consequence of the destruction of hawks and other enemies. There seems to me no bird which so often falls a prey to the sparrowhawk. Gliding through the thicket or shrubberies, the hawk's eye is attracted by the conspicuous colour of the blackbird. It is a more familiar bird than the thrush, and does not build its nest so often in the larger woods, preferring the neighbourhood of houses, and even frequenting gardens in the midst of towns. The blackbird's song has not the same variety as that of the thrush, but has even greater clearness and "precision" in the notes it can execute.

The blackbird when building in the garden picks up all sorts of substances to form the outside of her nest with—large pieces of rag, string, even pieces of newspaper, are all interwoven. They build either in low bushes or in the wall fruit trees. One built and brought up her young under a net placed on a cherry tree trained on the wall of my garden, always scrambling up and down from the bottom of the net, so little protection was it from their inroads. The blackbird is not uncommonly seen variegated with white, and I have seen some entirely white, or rather cream-coloured.

The ring-ouzel so much resembles the blackbird in shape and figure that at a little distance they may be easily mistaken for each other. On closer observation, however, the ring-ouzel is at once distinguished, not only by the white crescent on the breast, but also by the whole plumage being much less black, almost all the feathers having a margin of a lighter colour. Its cry and song are both unlike those of any other of the thrush tribe, both having a kind of wildness in them in keeping with the scenery in which this bird is usually found.

The general locality of the ring-ouzel is amongst the scattered birch and juniper, which are thickly spread amongst the rocky parts of the hill-side, and it inhabits the wildest and most solitary glens, where its song, coming unexpectedly on the wanderer, sounds doubly sweet and striking. Indeed, the song is in itself, without the accompaniment of wild and rugged scenery, very sweet and melodious. Since the destruction of hawks and "vermin" the ring-ouzel has increased very greatly, and its devastations amongst the few cherries that grow in the garden of the Highland manse or farm-house are very severe.

April 26th. In the woods near Lochnabo we found two siskins' nests with young ones well fledged. No bird is more familiar and tame when in confinement. A person in Elgin showed me a nest with four young ones, which he had taken the day before from a Scotch fir tree. In the same cage he had the two old birds belonging to the nest; these he had taken with bird-lime. The female at once commenced feeding her young while in the cage, and the male in a day or two followed her example; so that between them they reared their family with as much care, and with apparently as much pleasure, as if they had still been in the woods. An old siskin, in a few days after being caught, will eat out of the hand of its master, and very soon seems to form a kind of acquaintance and attachment to those who feed it. In the winter the siskins come in large flocks, feeding on the seeds of the alder and birch, and also on the thistle seeds, and those of many other weeds. It is a cheerful, restless little bird. Its song, though not varied or rich, is pleasing. In the spring it frequently utters a long harsh cry like the noise of a file.

April 29th, 1847. In the fir wood beyond Kinloss we found the nest of the long-eared owl with one young bird above half grown, with the brightest yellow eyes. There was a rotten egg in the nest. The owl had apparently taken possession of an old crow's nest on the top of a tall Scotch fir tree in an open place of the wood.

During this month one of my sons killed, near the Loch of Spynie, a little gull. It is one of the rarest of our visitors; indeed this is the only instance of its having been seen in the district. Throughout the kingdom this is a bird very rarely seen. It is supposed to come from the east of Europe.

BIRDS THAT COME IN THE SPRING

Peewits—Pugnacity of—The Redshank—Oyster-catcher—Other Sea Birds—Red-starts and Flycatchers—The Whitethroat—The Wheatear—The Sand-martin—The House-martin—Swallows—Swifts—Tree-creepers—The Calls of Birds

The peewit is the first bird that visits us for the purpose of nidification. About the middle of February a solitary peewit appears, or perhaps a pair, and I hear them in the evening flying from the shore in order to search for worms in the field. Towards the end of the month, great flocks arrive and collect on the sands, always, however, feeding inland; it is altogether a nocturnal bird as far as regards feeding: at any hour of the night, and however dark it is, if I happen to pass through the grass-fields, I hear the peewits rising near me. Excepting to feed, they do not take much to the land till the end of March, when, if the weather is mild, I see them all day long flying about in their eccentric circles—generally in pairs; immediately after they appear in this manner, they commence laying their eggs, almost always on the barest fields, where they scratch a small hole just large enough to contain four eggs—the usual number laid by all waders. They seem to commence several nests before they determine on laying their eggs in any one, as I frequently see three or four nests begun all near each other, and the peewits are far too quarrelsome for these to be nests of different birds. By the time their four eggs are laid, they generally collect a considerable quantity of straws, roots, or sticks, in their nests, appearing to increase it with every egg they lay.

It is very difficult to distinguish these eggs from the ground, their colour being a brownish-green mottled with dark spots. I often see the hooded crows hunting the fields frequented by the peewits, as regularly as a pointer, flying a few yards above the ground, and searching for the eggs. The cunning crow always selects the time when the old birds are away on the shore; as soon as he is perceived, however, the peewits all combine in chasing him away: indeed, they attack fearlessly any bird of prey that ventures near their breeding-ground; and I have often detected the *locale* of a stoat or weasel by the swoops of these birds: also when they have laid their eggs they fight most fiercely with any other bird of their own species which happens to alight too near them. I saw a cock peewit one day attack a wounded male bird which came near his nest; the pugnacious little fellow ran up to the intruder, and taking advantage of his weakness, jumped on him, trampling upon him and pecking at his head, and then dragging him along the ground as fiercely as a game-cock.

The hen peewit has a peculiar instinct in misleading people as to the whereabouts of her nest; as soon as any one appears in the field where the nest is, the bird runs quietly and rapidly in a stooping posture to some distance from it, and then rises with loud cries and appearance of alarm, as if her nest was immediately below the spot she rose from. When the young ones are hatched too, the place to look for them is, *not* where the parent birds are screaming and fluttering about, but at some little distance from it; as soon as you actually come to the spot where their young are, the old birds alight on the ground a hundred yards or so from you, watching your movements. If, however, you pick up one of the young ones, both male and female immediately throw off all disguise, and come wheeling and screaming round your head, as if about to fly in your face. The young birds, when approached, squat flat and motionless on the ground, often amongst the weeds and grass in a shallow pool or ditch, where, owing to their colour, it is very difficult to distinguish them from the surrounding objects.

When first hatched the young ones leave the nest and betake themselves to the shallow parts of swamps, where the old ones attend them with great care. During autumn and winter, and when collected in flocks, the peewits are very shy and watchful. As the dusk approaches they leave the lochs and swamps and fly with great rapidity to their feeding-places, which are generally in the grass fields. They do not then fly in flocks, but singly, or in scattered companies. Before daybreak they are again collected together on some favourite ridge or mudbank.

Some few remain during the whole winter, but the greatest number leave us about the last week of November and on the 25th of that month I have seen immense flocks of peewits in the fields, where they appear to collect previous to departing.

Towards the end of March, the ring-dotterel, the redshank, the curlew, the oyster-catcher, and some other birds of the same kind begin to frequent their breeding-places. On those parts of the sandhills which are covered with small pebbles, the ring-dotterels take up their station, uttering their plaintive and not unmusical whistle for hours together, sometimes flitting about after each other with a flight resembling that of a swallow, and sometimes running rapidly along the ground, every now and then jerking up their wings till they meet above their back. Both the bird and its eggs are exactly similar in colour to the ground on which they breed.

The motions of the redshank are very curious at this time of year, as they run along with great swiftness, clapping their wings together audibly above their heads, and flying about round and round any intruder with rapid jerks, or hovering in the air like a hawk, all the time uttering a loud and peculiar whistle.

The oyster-catchers sit quietly in pairs the chief part of the day on the banks or islands of shingle about the river or on the shore, but resort in the evenings to the sands in large flocks. Both these birds and peewits soon become tame and familiar if kept in a garden or elsewhere, watching boldly for the worms turned up by the gardener when digging. The oyster-catcher's natural food appears to be shell-fish only; I see them digging up the cockles with their powerful bill, or detaching the small mussels from the scarps, and swallowing them whole, when not too large; if, however, one of these birds finds a cockle too large to swallow at once, he digs away at it with the hard point of his bill till he opens it, and then eats the fish, leaving the shell.

When in captivity the oyster-catcher eats almost anything that is offered to it. From its brilliant black and white plumage and red bill, as well as from its utility in destroying slugs and snails in the garden, where it searches for them with unceasing activity, it is both ornamental and useful, and worthy of being oftener kept for this purpose where a garden is surrounded by walls; it will, if taken young, remain with great contentment with poultry without being confined. I have found its nest in different localities, sometimes on the stones and sometimes on the sand close to high-water mark—very often on the small islands and points of land about the river, at a considerable distance from the sea; its favourite place here is on the carse land between the two branches of the Findhorn near the sea, where it selects some little elevation of the ground just above the reach of the tide, but where at spring-tides the nest must be very often entirely surrounded by the water—I never knew either this or any bird make the mistake of building within reach of the high tides, though, from the great difference there is in the height of the spring-tides, one might suppose that the birds would be often led into such a scrape.

Unlike most birds of similar kind, the sandpiper builds a substantial, comfortable nest, in some tuft of grass near the river-side, well concealed by the surrounding herbage, instead of leaving its eggs on the bare stones or sand. It is a lively little bird, and is always associated in my mind with summer and genial weather as it runs jerking along the water's edge, looking for insects or flies, and uttering its clear, pipe-like whistle.

Besides the sea-birds that come into this country to breed, such as sand-pipers, peewits, terns, etc., there are some few of our smaller birds that arrive in the spring to pass the summer here. Amongst these I may name the redstart, the spotted flycatcher, the whitethroat, the wheatear, etc.

The redstart is not very common: it breeds in several places, however,

up the Findhorn; at Logie, for instance, where year after year it builds in an old ivy-covered wall. As far as I can observe and ascertain, it arrives here during the first week in May. The young, when able to fly, appear often in my garden, for a few weeks, actively employed in doing good service, killing numbers of insects. Wholly insectivorous, the first frosts of autumn deprive the redstart of its food, and it therefore leaves us early.

Every spring a pair or two of flycatchers breed in one of the fruit-trees on the wall, building, as it were, only half a nest, the wall supplying the other half. They cover the nest most carefully with cobwebs, to make it appear like a lump of this kind of substance left on the wall; indeed, I do not know any nest more difficult to distinguish. It is amusing to see the birds as they dash off from the top of the wall in pursuit of some fly or insect, which they catch in the air and carry to their young. The number of insects which they take to their nest in the course of half an hour is perfectly astonishing.

Another bird that comes every spring early in May to the same bush to breed is the pretty little whitethroat. On the lawn close to my house a pair come to the same evergreen, at the foot of which, on the ground, they build their nest, carrying to it an immense quantity of feathers, wool, etc. The bird sits fearlessly, and with full confidence that she will not be disturbed, although the grass is mown close up to her abode; and she is visited at all hours by the children, who take a lively interest in her proceedings. She appears quite acquainted with them all, sitting snugly in her warmly-feathered nest, with nothing visible but her bright black eyes and sharp-pointed bill. As soon as her eggs are hatched, she and her mate are in a great bustle, bringing food to their very tiny offspring— flying backwards and forwards all day with caterpillars and grubs.

Both this and the larger kind of whitethroat which visits us have a

[79]

lively and pleasing song. They frequently make their nest on the ground in the orchard, amongst the long grass, arching it over in the most cunning manner, and completely concealing it. When they leave their eggs to feed, a leaf is laid over the entrance of the nest to hide it; in fact, nothing but the eyes of children could ever discover the abode of the little whitethroat. Before they leave this country, these birds collect together, and are seen searching the hedges for insects in considerable but scattered flocks. They frequently fly in at the open windows in pursuit of flies, and chase them round the room quite fearlessly. The gardener accuses them of destroying quantities of cherries, by piercing them with their bills: they certainly do so, but I am always inclined to suppose that it is only the diseased fruit that they attack in this way, or that which has already been taken possession of by small insects.

The wheatear does not arrive till the first week of April, when they appear in considerable numbers on the sand-hills, flying in and out of the rabbit-holes and broken banks, in concealed corners of which they hatch. But I see the greatest number go still farther northwards to breed. About the first week in September they quit this country, frequently leaving a few stragglers, if the season is warm, for a few days after the departure of the main body. The wheatear is easily known by its white rump, which is very conspicuous as it flits with a jerking flight from stone to stone, and jerks its tail while standing. It has the habit of often singing while on wing and hovering in the air.

The wheatear a few years ago, and even now, though not to so great a degree, was very eagerly sought for and trapped by the shepherds on the south downs of Sussex for the London market. They are caught by means of horsehair snares placed in holes made on the smooth grass of the downs, by removing a turf of 14 inches long and 6 broad. This turf is then placed crossways on the hole, and the snares placed so as to catch the birds as they run into these holes for shelter. A heavy shower of rain, or any sudden alarm, induces the wheatear to run into these holes for shelter. Simple as the contrivance seems, great numbers were annually caught on their passage from their breeding grounds in the north to the warmer south, where they can find a supply of insects, their only food, during the winter. Their eggs are peculiarly beautiful, being of a pale blue delicately shaded with a darker colour at one end.

Early in April the sand-martin, or bank-martin arrives the first of the

th fly. May/47

Small black b

Invererne

Swift

Cock Wheatear

Hen Wheatear Nairn. June 1847

Lark

Tit lark

May 1847.
Invererne

exact size
Curlew
Lochdu Sepy

5 9

swallow tribe, and large flocks come pouring in apparently from the south-east. I generally see them first near Spynie, or other pieces of water, flying at no great distance above the tops of the rushes. They breed, in sandy banks, old quarries, and such places; sometimes in large companies. They feed wholly on insects, principally on gnats and similar creatures. When they have young to bring up, they collect a mass or ball of insects in their throat or mouth sometimes as large as a marble before they return to the nest, and the same is true of swifts. The nest is formed of dried grass, and warmly lined with feathers about two feet or eighteen inches from the mouth of the hole. It is peculiarly infested with fleas. The eggs are white, with beautifully transparent shells.

The house-martin usually arrives about the third week in April. At first they are in large flocks, but soon disperse. The nest is placed under eaves of houses and similar places. This martin also builds frequently along the sea-shore. Taking advantage of some suitable depression or hollow in the rocks, it attaches its nest, formed of mud, in the shape of a segment of a globe. The nest in these situations is very difficult to see, as it is neatly fitted into the angles of the rock.

The house-martin can always be distinguished from the bank-martin by its superior clearness of colouring, and by being slightly larger. The upper parts of the house-martin are black or nearly so. Those of the bank-martin are a mouse brown. The toes of the latter are not covered with the same white down as those of the former. From the middle of September till the time of their departure, martins and swallows haunt the large rushy pieces of water, such as Spynie, not hovering much in one particular part, but seemingly hunting it from one end to the other in search of insects.

The chimney-swallow is perhaps the least numerous of the swallow tribe in this country, and at the same time the handsomest. I see them for the first time about the 20th of April. Warm springs bring them a few days earlier. Like the martins they appear first in the vicinity of lakes, where their food is more abundant than elsewhere. The name of "chimney-swallow" denotes its habit of building in chimneys.

When a hawk appears in their neighbourhood the swallow is always

the first bird to give the alarm, and with loud cries chases the bird of prey to some distance. Though so swift of wing, the swallow sometimes falls a prey to the merlin. A single hawk has little chance against the rapid wing of a swallow, but I have seen two merlins pursue a swallow till it was caught, the hawks helping each other, one keeping above and the other below their prey, till at last, after a long chase, by some unlucky turn, the swallow came in a favourable position for one of the merlins, and was immediately seized in the air and carried off. It must be, however, rare that the swallow can fall a victim to any bird or beast of prey.

The swift is always associated in our minds with summer and fine weather. Always seen near towns or villages, it fixes usually on the steeples or highest buildings for its resting-place, and round these it wheels during the whole long summer day. In June and July the swift seems to be constantly on wing from two or three in the morning till the night sets in, which in this country is not till eleven o'clock. Indeed, as long as there is any light or twilight the swift continues its rapid but easy flight, in fine calm weather wheeling at a great height in the air; but in heavy damp weather it flies much nearer to the earth. Sometimes great numbers of swifts hunt for hours along the line of some piece of road, dashing one after the other within a foot or two of the head of the passer by, or it sweeps and skims along close to the surface of some stream or pool by the hour. In fact, wherever and at whatever height the insects happen to be flying, there are the swifts clearing the air of thousands and millions of gnats and other flies. The swift appears never to alight for the purpose of resting. It builds under the eaves of houses and in crevices of the walls. The materials for the nest are collected while the bird is on the wing, picked up off the ground, or caught while drifting in the air. The swift is easily distinguished by its rapid peculiar flight, by its larger size, its loud screams, and by its uniform black colour, excepting a slight shade of white under the chin. They arrive later than other swallows, and depart sooner.

We are visited too by that very curious little bird the tree-creeper. This beautiful little bird may be constantly seen running up the stems of the trees in a circular or corkscrew kind of direction in search of insects, beginning near the ground, running up and round the tree, then flying off to another tree which it searches for food in the same manner. I have seen it sometimes detach, and drop to the ground, a piece of bark as large as a person's hand. In the winter the creepers accompany the large flocks of titmice and golden-crested wrens in their peregrinations through the woods, the latter searching the branches and twigs for insects, while the former search the stems of trees. It is a very small bird, not heavier than a wren. In the breeding season it frequently becomes very familiar, and builds in some convenient hole or crevice in an outhouse, sometimes in a hollow tree.

Though the voice of the landrail is *per se* so peculiarly harsh and grating, there are few birds whose note falls more pleasantly on my ear—

associated as it is with the glad season of spring and summer. The monotonous cry of the cuckoo has nothing delightful in it beyond recalling to the mind pleasing ideas of spring and woody glades; yet I believe every one listens to this bird with pleasure. From seeing and hearing so many of them about the wild rocks and glens of Scowrie and Assynt, the cuckoo now always brings that rugged district before my eyes, instead of the tranquil groves where I formerly had seen it. The nest, which of all others the knavish cuckoo prefers to lay her eggs in, is that of the titlark; and in Scowrie and Assynt those birds abound.

Another bird, whose cry is invariably associated by me with one kind of locality, is the swift. I never hear the loud scream of this bird without having some well-remembered steeple or other lofty building brought vividly before my mind's eye: thus, also, the martin and swallow recall the recollection of some favourite stream, whose waters abound in trout, and whose banks swarm with the May-fly and grey drake.

The crow of the grouse is as inseparable in my mind from the mountains of Scotland, as the song of the ring-ousel is from its birch-covered glens, or the spring call of the peewit from the marshy meadows.

There is, I think, great pleasure in thus recollecting by the sounds and notes of living animals scenes which the eye has dwelt upon with delight, and so constant is every bird to its own locality, that the associations thus called forth are invariably correct.

MAY

Landrails—Sparrowhawk in the Shrubbery—The Robin—The Chaffinch and Goldfinch—Departure of the Wild Geese—A Peregrine's Nest—Song of the Redstart— The Cuckoo—Habits of the Crossbill—A Blackcap—Young Duck—The Willow Wren—The Wren—Eels—A Northern Diver—The Gold-crested Wren—The House-sparrow—Birds in my Garden—Song of the Sedge Warbler

In this region May is invariably ushered in by the croak of the landrail. Generally this bird is heard on the 1st. If, however, the grass and wheat fields are backward, it is not heard till the 2nd or 3rd, but never later than the 3rd.

Hoarse and discordant as their voice is, I always hear it with pleasure, for it brings the idea of summer and fine weather with it. Oftentimes have I opened my window during the fine dewy nights of June to listen to these birds as they utter their harsh cry in every direction, some close to the very window, and answered by others at different distances. I like too to see this bird, as at the earliest dawn she crosses a road followed by her train of quaint-looking, long-legged young ones, all walking in the same stooping position; or to see them earlier in the year lift up their snake-like heads above the young corn, and croak in defiance of some other bird of the same kind, whose head appears now and then at a short distance. At other times, one hears the landrail's cry apparently almost under one's feet in the thick clover, and he seems to shake the very ground, making as much noise as a bull. How strange it is that a bird with apparently so soft and tender a throat can utter so hard and loud a cry, which sounds as if it was produced by some brazen instrument. I never could ascertain whether this cry is made by the male or female bird, or by both in common: I am inclined to suppose the latter is the case.

Their manner of leaving the country is a mystery. Having hatched their young, they take to the high corn-fields, and we never see them again, excepting by chance one comes across a brood at dawn of day, hunting along a path or ditch side for snails, worms, and flies, which are their only food, this bird being entirely insectivorous, never eating corn or seeds. By the time the corn is cut they are all gone; how they go, or whither, I know not, but with the exception of a stray one or two I never see them in the shooting-season, although the fields are literally alive with them in the breeding-time. You can seldom flush a landrail twice; having alighted he runs off at a quick pace, and turning and doubling round a dog, will not rise. I have caught them more than once when they have pitched by chance in an open wood, and run into a hole or elsewhere at the root of a tree; they sometimes hide their head, like the story of the ostrich, and allow themselves to be lifted up. Their nest is of a very artless description, a mere hollow scratched in the middle of a grass-field, in which they lay about eight eggs. The young ones at first are quite black, curious-looking little birds, with the same attitudes and manner of running as their parents, stooping their heads and looking more like mice or rats than a long-legged bird.

May 1st, 1852. A sparrowhawk is constantly hunting the birds, and destroying them, in the shrubbery.

Swallows, martins, swifts, and wheatears, become numerous. The owls hoot now very much, and though none breed very near the house, I hear them every night in the ash-trees.

The young thrushes, blackbirds, robins, and hedge-sparrows, will soon be hatched; but the greenfinches, chaffinches, etc., although their nests are nearly completed, have not yet laid any eggs; the insectivorous birds being the first to build.

The redbreast and its habits are known to all, and with all this bird has been a favourite. Its tameness and perfect confidence in man are its greatest protection. Many instances occur of the robin entering boldly the house of rich or poor alike, and claiming its share of the breakfast table or such crumbs as it can pick up. It frequently happens that the same robin returns for several winters in succession to a house, claiming shelter and food with the confidence and familiarity of a domestic bird; nor are these favours ever refused.

It is, however, a very quarrelsome and pugnacious bird to others of the same species, fighting desperately and savagely. In consequence of this quarrelsome dispotion, though very numerous and widely scattered over the face of the country, each pair of robins requires a certain domain of its own. It is a very striking thing in this country, and one which I have often remarked, I cannot recollect stopping five minutes in any part of any wood, however wild or distant, without seeing a robin, and even in the remote and solitary places the bird seems as tame, and possessed of as much confidence, as if bred and protected in a garden. Whenever I stop to eat my biscuit or luncheon, when shooting

or wandering in the woods, a robin invariably appears, and often picks up the crumbs which I fling to it, close to my feet, or at most, waits only till I have retired a few paces.

At the beginning of winter the chaffinches make a partial migration. They first collect in large flocks, which seem to consist wholly of females or birds in female plumage. It is certain that during winter they are comparatively scarce. Again, in spring they reappear everywhere, uttering their loud clear note. Gardeners have generally a great enmity to these birds, as they are very destructive to some seeds—those of the radish, cabbage, etc. At the same time, they fully compensate for all the mischief done in this way by destroying vast quantities of insects and caterpillars.

The goldfinch is now very rare in this district, indeed it has almost entirely disappeared. A few years ago it was not at all uncommon, building its beautiful little nest in many of the orchards and gardens. At present I occasionally see a pair or two, but have not lately heard of any breeding here. The bird-fanciers of the country attribute its disappearance to some bird-catchers "from the south," who seem to have caught nearly all the old birds in the district. No bird is more easily taken by means of a net and call-bird than the goldfinch. Although nearly extinct in Morayshire, it is not uncommon on the opposite coasts of Ross-shire and Sutherlandshire.

The geese generally leave us about the 3rd or 4th May, but from the quantity of snow on the hills this season (1847) they should naturally remain longer. The gray-lag goose though I hear that within the memory of many now alive it was a very common bird, is now seldom seen in this county.

In some parts of Sutherland—for instance on Loch Shin, and other lonely and unfrequented pieces of water—the wild goose breeds on the small islands that dot these waters. If their eggs are taken and hatched under tame geese, the young are easily domesticated; but, unless pinioned or confined, they always take to flight with the first flock of wild geese that pass over the place during the migrating season. Even when unable to fly, they evince a great desire to take wing at this season, and are very restless for a few weeks in spring and autumn. In a lonely and little-frequented spot on the banks of Loch Shin, where the remains of walls and short green herbage point out the site of some former shealing or residence of cattle-herds, long since gone to ruin, I have frequently found the wild goose with her brood feeding on the fine grass that grows on what was once the dwelling of man. The young birds do not fly till after they are full grown, but are very active in the water, swimming and diving with great quickness.

There seems no doubt of the gray-lag goose being the original of our tame bird. They are exactly similar, bearing the same proportion to the farm-yard goose as the mallard does to the tame duck, and breeding also with the tame goose; not rarely, but without the least shyness or

hesitation, and the young produced breed freely, and are scarcely distinguishable from their parents, perhaps rather larger than the wild, and rather smaller than the tame birds.

There is much snow on the Monaghleahd mountains this year (1847); and in consequence of this melting gradually, from the heat of the noonday sun, the water rises at a certain hour daily; here, at Dulsie, the rise takes place about three or four in the morning. Having risen for an hour or two, it again falls to its usual level.

May 5th, 1852. I looked for the nest of the peregrine to-day in the cliffs between Burghead and Lossiemouth, and found that it is placed not as usual on a ledge of rock, but quite within a small hole, in a place apparently more suited for a jackdaw to build in. Below the nest at the foot of the cliff we found a drake teal partly eaten, but quite fresh. The falcon must have carried it about three miles. These cliffs are fine bold rocks looking over the sea, with lovely green little nooks covered with primroses and blue hyacinths. When the birds were disturbed they flew straight out to sea till they looked like specks, and then suddenly reappearing they alighted on the rocks.

May 6th. The salmon-fry begin to appear.

May 7th. I observe a flock of bean geese in the bay, probably the last I shall see this year, as it is time for them to be nesting in the far north. On this day, also, the spotted fly-catcher appeared in the garden, where it builds every year in one of the apricot-trees (in 1847 I saw it for the first time on the 13th). This lively little bird is a very regular visitor to this part of the country, though not one of the earliest. Indeed, it does not arrive until the 8th or 10th of May. Certain portions of the garden-wall and certain trees are taken possession of year after year. In my garden at Elgin at least six pairs breed. The old birds are very tame and familiar, apparently quite aware of their safety. They sit on some flower-stalk or convenient branch, darting off every minute after the passing insects. I have observed one peculiarity in this fly-catcher. If disturbed off their eggs they return almost immediately, not appearing to be frightened away for a long time like most other birds.

May 8th. I have to-day seen the redstart in Dulsie Woods, near the Findhorn. It was sitting on the summit of a fir-tree pouring out a remarkably rich though short song. It was some time before I could discover what bird was singing, as whenever I approached it glided down and flew to a different tree, again singing its soft but loud song.

May 9th, 1852. At Spynie heard the cuckoo for the first time this year.

The cuckoo, like the landrail, is connected in all my ideas with spring and sunshine, though frequenting such a different description of country; the landrail always inhabiting the most open country, while the cuckoo frequents the wooded glades and banks of the rivers and burns; flitting from tree to tree, alighting generally on some small branch close to the trunk, or chasing each other, uttering their singular call. So much has been written respecting their habit of laying their egg

[87]

in the nest of some other bird, that I can add nothing to what is already known. In this country they seem to delight in the woods on the hill-sides by the edge of loch or river, where I constantly hear their note of good omen. When the young ones are fledged, they remain for a week or two about the gardens or houses, very tame and unconscious of danger perching on the railings, and darting off, like the flycatcher, in pursuit of passing insects.

On their first arrival in Scotland they appear to haunt the higher grounds. In the mountains of Sutherland I have frequently seen considerable numbers together, and while passing over several miles of muirland the cuckoos have been in sight for several hours at a time, in small companies of two or three. When they come down to the more wooded parts of the country they seem constantly in motion, either flying in pursuit of each other, or from tree to tree, but always uttering their pleasant but monotonous note. I first hear them in this immediate vicinity about the third week of April, or sooner sometimes. One haunts my garden for a considerable portion of the spring. It is difficult to know exactly when the cuckoo leaves this country. The old ones seem to disappear before their young. The latter remain till about the middle or end of August.

Whilst fishing in the upper part of the river on the 8th of May, I saw numbers of crossbills and siskins in the same beautiful woods, and found two nests of the former, from one of which the young birds could not have flown above a day. The crossbill has some peculiar habits not much known to the ordinary observer. I have never discovered either the eggs or the young birds in the nest, owing much to the early and also uncertain periods at which it breeds. Their nests, as well as those of the siskin, are scarcely ever found, though both birds breed plentifully in this country.

I have seen the old birds feeding newly-flown young ones at different times from April to August. In June I have seen the crossbills in large flocks, a great proportion of which were evidently young birds; they appear, though not exactly to migrate, to wander much, and to shift their quarters from one wood to another according as they find a supply of fir cones, the seeds of which appear to form their only food in this country. When the crop of cones is deficient in one place, they betake themselves to some other wood where they are plentiful. They extract the seeds from the cones with the greatest skill and rapidity, holding the cone in one foot, and cutting it up quickly and thoroughly with their powerful beak, which they use much after the manner of a pair of scissors. When the flock has stripped one tree of all the sound cones, they simultaneously take wing, uttering at the same time a sharp harsh chattering cry. Sometimes they fly off to a considerable height, and after wheeling about for a short time, suddenly alight again on some prolific-looking tree, over which they disperse immediately, hanging and swinging about the branches and twigs, cutting off the cones, a great

[88]

many of which they fling to the ground, often with a kind of impatient jerk. These cones, I conclude, are without any ripe seed.

The call of the crossbill is peculiar, and attracts the attention immediately, as being unlike that of any other of our small birds. While feeding and climbing about the branches of a larch or fir tree they utter a gentle chirp to each other; sometimes, when suddenly alarmed, every bird in the flock is suddenly perfectly still, clinging close to the branches or stem of the tree.

The crossbill itself is a busy, singular-looking little fellow, as he flits to and fro, or climbs, parrot-like, up and down the branches; and the cock, with his red plumage shining in the sun, has more the appearance of some Eastern or tropical bird than any other of our sober northern finches. When engaged in feeding, these birds are often so intent on their occupation that they will allow a horsehair snare, attached to the end of a long twig, to be slipped round their necks before they fly away. In captivity they are very tame, but restless, and are constantly tearing with their strong mandibles at the woodwork and wires of their cage.

May 10th. During this month the oyster-catchers remain in larger flocks than at any other time of the year, although many are breeding far inland on the stony banks of the Findhorn, Spey, and other rivers.

The partridge covers its nest and eggs with perhaps greater cunning than any other bird; not only entirely concealing the nest itself, but so disposing the surrounding grass that no vestiges of its track to and fro can be seen; they commence laying here about the 10th of May. The landrails are about a week later.

May 11th, 1852. We heard a bird singing in the garden, whose note was new to me; on watching, we found it was a blackcap a very rare bird so far to the north. I have only on one other occasion ascertained the presence of this bird. In the following June and part of July I heard every day and all day, from 3 A.M. till 10 P.M., a strange song in the shrubberies close to the house. Though I thought I recognised the full rich song of the blackcap, I could not at first make sure. The bird skipped about so quickly and quietly in the densest part of the foliage, that although I heard it at all hours close to me, it was several days before I could see it

Balnagowan

sufficiently clearly to be sure of its identity. I saw no female with it, but from its singing so constantly near the same part of the garden, I was inclined to think that it had a mate.

May 12th, 1852. The banks of the river are now very beautiful, the sloe, the hawthorn, the gean, the bird-cherry, and other shrubs, being in full bloom.

May 16th, 1852. I found a merlin's nest with three eggs. The old birds appear to watch near it by turns to keep off the hooded crows from their eggs, till they begin to sit.

May 17th, 1847. In fishing to-day I caught a martin, which dashed at the artificial fly.

Everywhere on the lakes are broods of young wild ducks either swimming in close order behind their mothers, or all huddled together in a heap on some little island or projecting point of land.

As we were out driving the other day, a teal came fluttering out of the dry ditch by the roadside, and for above a hundred yards continued flying and running almost under the horse's feet. I found that she had a number of young ones unable to get over the wall, so we helped them into the adjoining wood. They were a long distance from the water, and had very rough ground to pass over to reach it. I remember exactly a similar circumstance happening to me in Ross-shire, when also I saved the lives of a young brood of teal by lending them a helping hand. These instances prove that, notwithstanding the instinct of birds, which generally enables them to keep their young out of harm's way, they occasionally get them into a situation not only of difficulty, but where any dog or mischievous boy coming along might destroy the whole brood.

At every ebb tide now, the terns fish with great perseverance for the sand-eels, on which they almost entirely feed.

The month of May this year (1847) appears to have quite changed its character; instead of being warm and genial, we have nothing but cold and cutting east winds; and the mountains have lost but very little of their winter covering of snow; indeed, on the higher inland mountains their white dresses extend down very nearly as low as in the winter. But notwithstanding the bad weather there is much to amuse and interest one in the sheltered parts of the low country. Every plant and flower is bursting into beauty, in spite of the cold blasts; and the small birds are in full activity, and seem at the height of their happiness. It is also a constant source of amusement to us to watch the various ways of building, and the different nests of the small birds. Each nest has its own character, and each bird its own place of concealment. The little willow wren forms one of the most interesting nests, which it places either under a bush in the flower-garden, or in a rough grass-field, where it forms a kind of dome-shaped nest, made to assimilate completely with the surface of the surrounding ground.

This diminutive visitor is very abundant. It arrives here about the 20th of April, and soon afterwards is heard in every wood and garden uttering its loud song, in which, however, there is no variety, as it incessantly repeats the same strain during the whole day. It is, however, a lively, merry little bird, constantly in motion and constantly singing, and always associated in my mind with the first return of spring. Like many other migratory birds, it is very regular in its attachment to particular places, and I have known it build its nest for several years in succession under the same shrub.

The common wren too, is very choice and careful in the structure of her nest, and sometimes builds in the most singular situations. I saw one this year which was built in a cactus, that hung from the roof of a greenhouse. Every time the little bird wished to add a leaf, or a piece of moss, she had to squeeze and twist herself in through a small hole left for the entrance of a vine stem. Her perseverance and determination were extraordinary; for in spite of all difficulties she managed to form an immense nest in this singularly chosen and picturesque abode. It is difficult to imagine what could have put it into her head to come into the greenhouse at all, and through so awkward an entrance, surrounded, too, as she was by places far more suitable and easy of access.

I observed a very curious thing with regard to a wren in the spring of 1852. A wren had built and hatched her eggs in a nest placed in a narrow hole in a wall. It seemed to me that as her young ones became full grown the nest would be rather small for them. The old birds became aware of this, and built a large nest in a tree opposite the first nest, and as soon as the young ones were able to fly at all, they betook themselves to the newly-built abode, which was larger than usual, and not lined. For some little time afterwards whenever there was a heavy shower, and these happened to be rather frequent, the whole brood, eight in number, took refuge in the new nest. They also roosted in it every night for a short time.

I was much interested one day in May, in watching the thousands of small eels which were making their way up the river. It was some distance from the mouth, and where the stream, confined by a narrow rocky channel, ran with great strength. Nevertheless these little eels, which were about six inches long, and as large round as a quill, persevered in swimming against the stream. When they came to a fall, where they could not possibly ascend, they wriggled out of the water, and gliding along the rock close to the edge, where the stone was constantly wet from the splashing and spray of the fall, they made their way up till they got above the difficulty, and then again slipping into the water, they continued their course. For several hours there was a continued succession of these little fish going up in the same way; and, for more than a week, the same thing was to be seen every day. The perseverance they displayed was very great, for frequently, although washed back several times, and eel would always continue its efforts till it managed to ascend. Towards winter they are said to descend the river again, in equal numbers. Trout and many birds feed constantly on these small eels, catching them with great ease in the shallows.

May 19th. Rennie brought home another owl's egg from a rabbit hole in the woods behind Woodside. The last which he brought was on the 2nd April.

May 19th, 1851. This morning at 3 A.M. I was at Spynie for the eggs of two birds which are very rare, the shoveller duck and the little water rail, and was fortunate enough, with the help of my retriever, to find a nest of each. They breed very rarely in this country.

May 23rd, 1847. The landrails have already several eggs, as have the lesser willow wren, and other late-coming birds.

I have often observed that the black-headed gull eats a great deal of corn in the newly-sown fields; and I now find that the lesser black-backed gull does the same, as I shot one which had a handful of corn (oats and barley) in its crop, mixed up with worms, grubs, etc.

May 26th, 1847. The fishermen at Nairn found a very fine northern diver drowned in the stake nets set for salmon. They tell me that it is not a solitary instance, as every year they get one or two at this season. It is not at all uncommon along the sea-coast during the winter, and more especially towards the spring. I have seen it, indeed, during most months of the year. Its manner of fishing is peculiar. As the tide comes in, the northern diver comes with it, fishing close to the edge of the water along the rocks, or even close to the sandy beach. I know no other bird of the kind which hunts so near the land. The food of this and other birds of the same kind does not so much consist of fish as of other small aquatic animals; sea slugs, small crabs, etc. etc., form its principal prey. When alarmed, it seldom takes wing, but dives out to a considerable distance, and with erect neck inspects the threatened or suspected danger. When once at a good height, however, its flight is strong and rapid. Although I have seen the northern diver on the coast during the breeding season, and I have also seen it accompanied by a young one, evidently a very few days old, I never could find the egg or hear of it being found. I have, however, little doubt that it breeds on some of the most northerly and solitary parts of the island. This bird, owing to its habit of fishing along the shore, is not unfrequently entangled in the salmon nets, where it is generally drowned. It is a large heavy bird; the one I saw to-day weighed about 16 pounds, but it is sometimes a pound heavier. The young birds, as far as I can learn, take three years to come to maturity.

May 28th, 1847. Walked to-day to Lochlee; saw the large nests made by the coots and dabchicks. The coot forms a very large nest amongst the rushes, made of grasses and water plants. So strong are these nests that I have stood upon one without its giving way. I once saw one on the loch which the bird had fastened to a floating tree that had grounded in a shallow, but which, having again got adrift, owing to a rise in the loch, had been driven by the wind until it stuck fast close to the shore, where the old bird was still at work. One bird seems to remain in the nest while its mate brings it rushes, which the stationary bird disposes of by adding them to the already large structure, till it seems sufficiently high above the water, and solid enough to resist wind and weather. The young are hatched about the 10th of May, and immediately take to the water, swimming round the old birds, who attend them with great care, pulling up the small water plants, etc., on which the young ones seem to feed. The coot is a very tame bird, and from its constant activity and familiarity is a great ornament to a piece of water. The young are covered with black hairy down, excepting about the head, which is nearly naked and of a bright orange colour, giving the little bird a very singular appearance. I have found the old coots in the month of July quite unable to fly, having lost the whole of their quill feathers in moulting, like the mallard and teal.

The golden-crested wren is the most restless little bird that I know, constantly in motion, flitting from tree to tree and from branch to branch in search of the minute insects which form its food. During the winter the fir woods seem to swarm with these birds, in company with different kinds of titmice, etc., who all pass in a constant stream through the woods, searching every tree as they travel onwards.

Whenever I sit down or remain quiet in a wood these birds appear flying from branch to branch, frequently coming within a few feet or less of my head, so intent are they on their hunting, keeping up a constant twitter or call to each other, as if to avoid losing their company. In the garden, too, a stream of these small birds frequently seems to pass over, hunting from one end of the place to the other, and then going on in a straight line. Though so small and delicate a looking bird, I never observed them to look distressed in severe weather. It seems that they do occasionally migrate, as a captain of a ship has told me that great numbers of the golden-crested wren have pitched on his ship while at sea, so fatigued that they could be easily taken by the hand.

The golden-crested wren is easily known by its bright crest of yellow orange colour, and by its very diminutive size. I never distinctly ascertained the presence of the *Regulus ignicapillus*, or fire-crested wren, in this country. It appears to be very slightly larger than the *Regulus regulus*, and is known by the crest being a deep fire colour edged with black. Very probably, however, they accompany the large flocks of the golden-crested wren. There is also another variety, or distinct species, very much resembling the golden-crested wren, which it only differs from in having no yellow crest at all.

The common house-sparrow abounds as much here as in most parts of the kingdom, and seems possessed of the same pert impudence and familiarity as elsewhere. In towns the sparrow acquires a dirty, sooty, and often ragged appearance, but in the country it is a far more beautiful bird than is generally supposed; owing to its being so common it is not noticed, though a male sparrow is as richly coloured and finely marked a bird as we have.

May 29th, 1852. Birds in the garden very numerous for a spot of ground so near the town—1. Wood-pigeon; 2. Cuckoo; 3. Missel Thrush; 4. Thrush; 5. Blackbird; 6. Robin; 7. Wren; 8. Willow Wren; 9. Whitethroat; 10. Hedge-Sparrow; 11. Long-tailed Tomtit; 12. Little Blue Tomtit; 13. Sparrow; 14. Tree-Sparrow; 15. Greenfinch; 16. Chaffinch; 17. Yellow Hammer; 18. Spotted Flycatcher; besides constant visitors, such as 19. Hooded Crow; 20. Jackdaw; 21. Siskin; 22. Sparrow Hawk, and other Hawks; 23. Larger Titmouse; 24. Cole Titmouse, etc., etc. Sixteen varieties breed constantly, besides the swallows, martins, swifts, about the house. There is scarcely a day now on which we could not procure specimens of each of these birds within twenty yards of the house; and, as I said, the eggs of sixteen of them within the garden. I might also mention golden-crested wren, bullfinch, etc., which are frequently in the garden.

May 28th, 1850. The loch (Spynie) is full of sedge warblers now. I heard a most extraordinary singing in some alders to-day; at one time it was like a person whistling, at another like a very sweet and full-toned blackbird, but always ending in a song like a sedge warbler. The bird, turned out to be a whinchat. I cannot understand its note, quite unlike any bird that I ever heard.

The whinchat though scattered widely during the summer, is nowhere abundant. On most stony and rough places in the district a pair is to be seen. But their arrival and departure seem more irregular than those of most similar birds.

No bird is more interesting than the sedge warbler. I do not hear it singing till the 15th or 16th of May; but about that time it commences, and for six or seven weeks scarcely seems to leave off its song night or day. In almost every clump of alders or willows, or in the long reeds of the lochs, the little sedge warbler sings through the whole night. Its common note, though not loud, is rich and sweet, and it seems to have a peculiar faculty of imitating other birds; indeed it is commonly called the "mocking bird". For some minutes it repeats its own peculiar song, then suddenly breaks off into some strange flourish, apparently imitating some bird which it has heard.

I one evening heard a bird singing whose voice was quite new to me, and resembled more than any other the rich full note of the blackbird. Though I knew the spot it was in to be frequented by a sedge warbler, it was some time before I could convince myself that the tiny bird which I saw swelling out its throat and singing with all its might was the utterer of so loud and rich a song. After some watching, however, I found that this was the case. From its singing during the night, this bird supplies the place of the nightingale with us.

I have seen the wryneck in the woods of Dulsie. It, however, can scarcely be classed amongst the birds of this district. It may be distinguished by its peculiarly beautiful plumage of brownish colour above, striped and spotted all over with various shades of the same colour and white. The tongue is very long and hard at the point. It projects it beyond the mouth considerably in catching its prey, which consists of insects. The toes are long, and placed two before and two behind. Its actions are similar to those of woodpeckers, running up and down the stems of old trees in search of insects. I never heard of its being seen on any other occasion in this country.

The dunlin breeds both in rough pastures near the sea-coast, and also about most of the inland swamps, lakes, etc. During the breeding season it utters a peculiar purring noise, from which it derives the name of "purre"; and, indeed, some authors consider the dunlin and purre different birds, instead of being the same bird in different plumage. They breed later than the peewits, redshanks, etc. I do not find their eggs till the second week in May. Several pairs frequently breed in the same part of a swamp.

May 28th, 1852. To-day we found the shoveller's nest, eleven eggs, in a very wet grassy place; the bottom of the nest quite wet—not a great deal of down—what down there was, was very black. The eggs are long and oval, darker than the widgeon, but not unlike the colour, slightly tinged with green; we have put nine of the eggs under a hen.

My terrier got into a hole where there were some young badgers; but the old ones attacked him and licked him completely; he had a very fine curl on his tail, but now it hangs down in the most dejected manner, having been bitten nearly through.

GULLS

Return of the Black-headed Gull—Gull's Nesting Places—Gulls on the Shore—
Voracity of Gulls—The Boatswain Gull—Terns—Their Nesting Places—Feeding on
Sandeels

As great a variety of the gull tribe frequents the Findhorn Bay and the Moray Firth as perhaps is to be seen in any one locality in Great Britain. To the uninterested passer-by a gull is a gull, and nothing more, whether the race is represented at the moment by that splendid bird, the great black-backed gull, or by the small but elegant black-headed gull, *Larus ridibundus* of Linnæus, or as Buffon, alluding also to its laugh-like cry, calls it, *la Mouette rieuse*. Yet, if closely observed, every kind of gull has its own peculiar ways and habits, all of which are worthy of note, and adapted to its own manner of feeding and providing for its wants.

During March and April the black-headed gull, which has been absent during the winter, returns in innumerable flocks. After sunset they hold long consultations on the sands of the bay, and when the night is calm I can hear them from my windows at the distance of nearly two miles chattering and clamouring for hours together. In the daytime they frequent the fields, and wherever a plough is at work there are the black-headed gulls in thousands, hovering over the ploughman's head, and keeping up such a continual screaming, that I have seen both man and horses fairly bewildered by the noise. A man left his plough and came to me the other day, as I was passing in the next field, to beg me to fire a shot or two at these noisy and uninvited followers. As fast as a worm or grub is turned up by the plough, down drop two or three gulls to scramble for it. In this manner they soon get the necessary supply of

[96]

Invererne
May 1847

Findhorn April 1847

on Old Bar - near Naira. June 1847

Lesser Tern

Tern

Dunlin

food, and return to join the assembly on the sands, where, having drunk and bathed, they remain for the rest of the day. After passing a fortnight or more in this manner, they betake themselves to their breeding-place, which is generally either some rushy and quiet pool or island on some mountain lake, where they can breed and rear their young unmolested.

There are several lochs in this neighbourhood where they breed. One they chiefly resort to is a small piece of water in the forest of Darnaway, where they are not allowed to be annoyed or disturbed during the time of incubation. In these places their nests are placed as close as possible to each other, and from the constant noise and flying backwards and forwards of the birds, one would suppose that the greatest confusion must prevail amongst their crowded commonwealth, but every bird knows and attends to her own nest, and though their cries sound angry and harsh, the greatest amity and the strictest peace are preserved.

It is difficult to conceive how each gull can distinguish her own spotted eggs, placed in the midst of so many others, exactly similar in size, shape, and colour; and when at length the young are hatched, and are swimming about on the loch, or crowded together on some grassy point, the old birds, as they come home from a distance with food, fly rapidly amidst thousands of young ones, exactly similar to their own, without even looking at them, until they find their own offspring, who, recognising their parents amongst all the other birds, receive the morsel, without any of the hungry little creatures around attempting to dispute the prize, each waiting patiently for its own parent, in perfect confidence that its turn will come in due season.

Though crossing and jostling each other in all directions, they never appear to quarrel or fight. On the contrary, the birds all unite and make common cause against any enemy, man or beast that approaches them, or whose presence seems to threaten danger.

I once took a boat to a mountain lake in Inverness-shire, where thousands of these birds bred on some small islands which dot the surface of the water. The gulls, though not exactly attacking me, dashed unceasingly so close to my head that I felt the wind of their wings, and I sometimes really feared some one more venturous than the rest might drive his bill into my eyes. They had probably never had a visitor to their islands before. The shepherds, having a kind of superstitious dread of the place, from its being supposed to be haunted ground, never attempt to cross to the islands by swimming or wading. The greater part of the largest island was absolutely covered with eggs, laid in small hollows scraped by the birds, with little pretensions to any other kind of nest. I could scarcely walk without treading on them.

The old birds looked like a shower of drifting snow over our heads, and were as noisy as a dozen village schools broken loose. There were numbers of young gulls recently hatched—curiously marked little tortoiseshell-coloured things, who tottered about the rushes without the least fear of us. All other birds seemed to be kept away from the lake by

the gulls, excepting a few mallards, who were swimming about in a state of bachelorhood, their wives and families being probably in some more quiet and solitary pools in the neighbouring peat mosses. When the mallards rose they were so completely puzzled and "*bebothered*" by the thousands of gulls who were darting and screaming about them, that they gave up attempting to fly away, and came plump down again into the water.

Close to the edge of the water, indeed so near that the nest was always wet, was the domicile of a pair of black-throated divers, or loon, with a couple of long greenish-coloured eggs. The old birds swam out to a short distance, and watched me with great interest, uttering their strange hollow call. There were several smaller islands, or points of rock, appearing above the water, on each of which a pair of black-backed gulls had made their nest, constructed with more care and skill than those of their black-headed cousins. These large birds allowed none of the others to approach them, and each couple kept undisputed possession on their own particular kingdom, not joining in the same sociable kind of society as other gulls. When I approached the black-backed gulls' nest, they did not dash round me like the smaller kind, but flew in circles at some height, uttering a loud warlike kind of shout,

much like the voice of a human being. The eggs of the black-headed gulls
are exactly like those of the common lapwing, and are equally good
eating; so I took home a great number, selecting them from the nests that
had only one or two eggs, knowing the owners of these would not have
commenced sitting. I returned in a week, and found every nest with its
full number in it. I was walking along the shore of the lake some weeks
afterward, when the birds had hatched, and the whole fleets of young
gulls of a dark grey colour were swimming about.

When lounging, on the sea-shore here, or lying in wait for seals, I have
frequent opportunities of watching unobserved the proceedings of the
gulls of different kinds. The large black-backed gull soars slowly along
the edge of the receding tide, with his sharp eye fixed on the beach, and
turning his head and neck to observe every object that may be left by the
tide. If anything is seen which his omnivorous appetite covets, down he
pitches on it, and with his powerful bill soon tears up and swallows it.
The sand-eel or small fish is swallowed whole. If a floating prize presents
itself, such as the remains of a large fish or dead bird, it is soon discovered
by one of the large gulls, who is not allowed, however, to enjoy his prize
alone; for every one of his fellows within sight joins in tearing it to pieces.
If a dead fish is left on the shore they alight a few feet from it, and, having
reconnoitred carefully, fall to and devour it. It is interesting to see these
strong birds battling against a high wind, always working to windward,
and taking advantage of every headland and cliff for a moment's shelter.
When going to windward in their search for food (indeed, they never fly
down wind if they can help it), and perceiving something edible, they
keep on a short distance beyond it, and then drifting back with the wind,
drop down upon it. I saw a seal last week (April) which had caught a
salmon, and was eating it above the water. A number of large gulls had
collected round him, and seemed inclined to dispute his prize, darting
down at it with clamorous cries.

The large grey gull, or wagel, the young of the great black-backed gull
hunts the shore in much the same manner; but is still more voracious.
Nothing comes amiss to this greedy bird. I have seen a dozen of them
feeding on a dead and putrid horse, digging it out with their powerful
bills like so many ravens. I have no doubt a dead human being would be
considered a fair and lawful prize also. While I am lying ensconced on
the shore for seals, this bird frequently comes hovering over me, as if well

inclined to pounce down. The grey gull, though frequently feeding in the fields, seems very seldom to take to fresh-water lakes.

The next-sized gull which is common here is the blue-back, a beautiful clean-looking bird, though, as far as fish is concerned, as great a glutton as the two last-named kinds. This bird is particularly conspicuous in its attacks on the salmon-fry as they descend the river in May. Thousands of them fish in the shallow pools at low-water in the bay, and every bird seems to feed wholly on these silvery little creatures as long as they are to be had. The quantity that they disgorge when shot is perfectly astonishing, and they must be one of the most destructive enemies that the salmon has. Besides these larger kinds of gulls, there are several smaller species, who hover constantly about the shore and sand-banks, drifting to and fro, and beating against the wind in search of any prey, and darting fearlessly into the very foam of the breakers to obtain it, or floating as buoyantly as corks at a respectful distance from the larger gulls, who may be engaged in tearing to pieces any cast-up carcass, and being content to catch at the smaller morsels which are detached unperceived by the rightful owners of the prize.

I was much amused the other day by the proceedings of a pair of Arctic Skua the black-toed gull, or boatswain. These two birds were sitting quietly on an elevated ridge of sand, near which a number of other gulls of different kinds were fishing and hovering about in search of what the waves might cast up. Every bird, indeed, was busy and employed, excepting these two black robbers, who seemed to be quietly resting, quite unconcerned. When, however, a gull had picked up a prize, these birds seemed instinctively to know it, and darting off with the rapidity of a hawk (which bird they much resemble in their manner of flight), they attacked the unfortunate gull in the air, and, in spite of his screams and attempts to escape, they pursued and beat him till he disgorged the fish or whatever he had swallowed, when one of them darted down and caught the substance before it could reach the water. The two then returned quietly to their sand-bank, where they waited patiently to repeat the robbery, should an opportunity occur. As the flock of gulls moved on with the flow of the tide the boatswains moved on also, hovering on their flank like a pair of plundering freebooters. I observed that in chasing a gull they seemed perfectly to understand each other as to who should get the spoil; and in their attacks on the largest gulls (against whom they waged the most fearless warfare) they evidently acted so as to aid each other. If another pair of boatswains intruded on their hunting-ground, they immediately seemed to send them farther off, not so much by actual battle as by a noisy and screaming argument, which they continued most vigorously till the new-comers left the neighbourhood.

I never saw these birds hunt for their own living in any other way than by robbing the other gulls. Though not nearly so large as some of the birds which they attack, their hawk-like swoops and great courage seem

to enable them to fight their way most successfully. They are neatly and powerfully made; their colour, a kind of sooty dull black, with very little gloss or shining tints on their feathers. The boatswains seldom appear here excepting during April and May.

No more beautiful birds can be found than the terns; their easy and graceful flight, and their pure satin-like plumage, render them universal favourites. The common tern breeds on most of the retired parts of the coast. These birds arrive in the end of April or beginning of May, and commence breeding towards the end of the latter month. When the day is bright and the sun hot, the terns do not appear to sit on their eggs, but, hovering constantly over them, leave them to the heat of the sun reflected from and increased by the warm shingle. But in rainy or even cloudy weather they sit upon their eggs like other birds. When the young are hatched the old birds lead a busy life, fishing for sand-eels which frequent the coast at that season. They hover in the air in the same manner as the solan goose, and drop suddenly into the water with a great splash, appearing almost invariably to be successful, and rising to the surface with their quarry in their bill. The rapidity with which a bird must move, to catch a fish in this manner, is one of the most extraordinary things that I know. A tern, for instance, is flying at about twenty yards high—suddenly he sees some small fish (generally a sand-eel, one of the most active little animals in the world),—down drops the bird, and before the slippery little fish (that glances about in the water like a silver arrow) can get out of reach, it is caught in the bill of the tern, and in a moment afterwards is either swallowed whole, or journeying rapidly through quite a new element to feed the young of its captor. Often in the summer have I watched flocks of terns fishing in this manner at a short distance from the shore, and never did I see one emerge after his plunge into the water without a sand-eel.

The terns which breed in the islands on a loch in the woods of Altyre, fully five miles in a straight line from where they fish, fly up to their young with every sand-eel they catch. I have seen them fly backwards and forwards in this way for hours together, apparently bringing the whole of their food from the sea, notwithstanding the distance; their light body and long swallow-like wings make this long flight to and fro less fatiguing to the tern than it would be to almost any other bird.

Great numbers of terns breed every year on the sandhills. The nests being frequently at so considerable a distance from the water, it has often been a matter of surprise to me how the young birds can live till they have strength to journey to the sea-shore. I never yet could find any of the newly-hatched terns near the nests, and am of opinion that the old birds in some way or other carry off their young, as soon as they are out of the egg, to some place more congenial to so essentially a water-bird than the arid ground on which they are hatched.

If a crow in search of eggs happens to wander near the terns' building-places, she is immediately attacked by the whole community, every bird joining in the chase, and striking furiously at their common enemy, who is glad to make off as quickly as she can. The terns, having pursued her to some distance, return seemingly well satisfied with their feat of arms. I have also detected the fox by the rapid swoops of the terns as they dash at him if he happens to pass near their nests.

There is one kind of tern that breeds on the sandhills, which is peculiarly beautiful, the Lesser Tern. This little bird, scarcely bigger than a swift, and of a pale blue in the upper part of her plumage, is of the most satin-like and dazzling whiteness in all the lower portions. It is a most delicate-looking creature, but has a stronger and more rapid flight than the larger kinds, and, when he joins in their clamorous attacks on any enemy, utters a louder and shriller cry than one could expect to hear from so small a body.

Amongst the flocks of terns I have sometimes clearly seen the "roseate tern" distinguished by the rose-coloured tint of its breast as it hovered over my head at no great height from the ground. In all probability specimens of most British terns may be met with on this coast at different times, but I have only marked down and described those birds which I have actually seen myself, or ascertained to have been killed in this district.

A favourite position of the tern is on the stakes of the salmon-fishers' nets. Frequently every stake has a tern on it, where, if unmolested, they sit quietly watching the operations of the fishermen. Indeed, they are rather a tame and familiar bird, not much afraid of man, and seeming to trust (and, as far as I am concerned, *not* in vain) to their beauty and harmlessness as a safeguard against the wandering sportsman. Excepting when wanting a specimen for any particular purpose, I make a rule never to molest any bird that is of no use when dead, and which, like the tern, is both an interesting and beautiful object when living.

These birds make but a short sojourn with us, arriving in April in great numbers, and collecting in flocks on the sands of the bay for a few days. They then betake themselves to their breeding-places, and, having reared their young, leave us before the beginning of winter.

JUNE

Eels in Lochlee—Red-necked Phalaropes on Loch Naver—Adders—The Blind Worm
Fishermen on the Bar—The Hair-worm—A Rose-coloured Starling—The Rocks of
Cromarty—Rock-pigeons—Goats—Tame Pochard—Tame Peregrine—Cormorants
Fishing with Cormorants—Lizards and Toads—Salmon—Leaping the Falls—Mr
Young's experiments—Spawning—A Fishing Story

June 7th, 1847. Went to Lochlee to put in a few lines baited with small trout. The people here say there are no fish in the loch; but as otters are often seen there, I fancy there must be some kind of fish.

June 8th. I found on my lines some very large eels of 4 and $3\frac{1}{2}$ lbs. weight. Although I frequently afterwards put in the line, I never caught any fish excepting eels. This proves how favourite a food of the otter eels must be, as these animals appear to live constantly at the loch, where they could have found nothing else to prey upon. We found a teal's nest with eight eggs in a small tuft of heather standing up like an island just large enough to hold the nest, in the midst of a wet place; the heather was high, and the nest and eggs were entirely concealed. If a dog had not frightened the bird off, we should never have discovered it. Nothing could be more neat and warm than the nest, carefully lined as it was with beautiful down, and arched over with heather and long grass.

June 10th, 1848. To-day I was at the breeding-places of the waders in Loch Naver, near Aultnaharrow, Sutherland, and saw great numbers of greenshank, redshank, curlew, snipe, etc. etc., amongst them several widgeon. The drake widgeon is peculiarly handsome in his summer plumage; the black-throated diver (or rain goose as the Highlanders call it) was not on the lake; but the birds which were most interesting (and to me new) were two red-necked phalaropes, which I watched for half an

hour while they fed, sometimes within a yard of my feet where I was sitting, close to a corner of the swamp.

Nothing could be more graceful than the movements of these two little birds as they swam about in search of insects, etc. Sometimes they ran lightly on the broad leaves of the water-lily, which served them for a raft and entirely kept them out of the water. Though not exactly web-footed, the phalarope swims with the greatest ease. The attachment of these two birds to each other seemed very great: whenever in their search for food they wandered so far apart as to be hidden by the intervening weeds, the male bird stopped feeding suddenly, and, looking round, uttered a low and musical call of inquiry, which was immediately answered by the female in a different note, but perfectly expressive of her answer, which one might suppose to be to the purport that she was at hand and quite safe: on hearing her the male immediately recommenced feeding, but at the same making his way towards her; she also flew to meet him: they then joined company for a moment or two, and after a few little notes of endearment, turned off again in different directions. This scene was repeated a dozen times while I was watching them. They seemed to have not the slightest fear of me, for frequently they came within a yard of where I was sitting, and, after looking up, they continued catching the small water-insects, etc., on the weeds without minding my presence in the least.

After having apparently exhausted the food in one pool, on a signal from the male they suddenly both took wing, and flew away to a fresh feeding-place two or three hundred yards off.

On the stones near the lake I picked up a large adder. As I held her up by her throat it was curious to see the fierce expression of rage the creature put on, and also how its long teeth projected, as if eager to be fastened in my hand, while a drop of bright yellow liquid oozed out at the points of each of its venomous fangs. I knew that this was the poison, but had no idea that these reptiles could produce so large a quantity at once.

A retriever of mine, having been bitten by an adder, conceived the most deadly hatred against them ever after, and killed a great number of them without being again bitten; his method was to snap quickly at the adder, biting it in two almost instantaneously, and before the reptile could retaliate. A favourite amusement of this dog, when he was in Sussex with me some time afterwards, used to be hunting the hedgerows for snakes and adders. He made a most marked distinction between the two, killing the former quietly and without hurry, but whenever he found an adder, he darted on it with a perfect frenzy of rage, at the same time always managing to escape the fangs of the venomous reptile, quickly as it can use them. The poisonous teeth of the adder greatly resemble the talons of a cat in shape, and can be raised or laid flat on the jaw according to the wish of their owner; indeed, the fangs of the adder, which are hollow throughout, are only raised when he is angry, and in self-defence. The common snake, which is quite harmless, has no such teeth. There are stories among the peasants, of adders being seen in Darnaway Forest, of great size and length, measuring five or six feet, but I do not believe that there are any larger than the usual size.

I have never seen the *Anguis fragilis*, or blind-worm, as it is called, but once in this country, though I am told it is not uncommon; a man brought me one last year which he had found floating down the river after a flood, as if swept off some rock by the sudden rise of the water. I mentioned the circumstance to some of my acquaintance, but could find no one who had either seen or heard of such a creature in this country. This one was alive when brought to me, but had received a cut which nearly divided its body in two, so that it did not long survive.

I saw two golden eagles together to-day. There are two nests with young eagles within view of the inn (Tongue) here, but quite inaccessible. I was unable to get up to the ptarmigan ground, as there has been constant mist on the mountains, which makes it impossible to reach the place where the birds breed.

June 13th, 1853. The wood-pigeon in the garden has eggs in the same nest in which she brought up young ones a few days ago. A woman brought to me yesterday a live roe; she calls it three weeks old, but it does not appear quite so old as she says; it drinks milk very readily.

June 15th, 1853. I found a woodcock's nest with four eggs. The old bird flew off, and fluttered along the ground to take off our attention; the nest was made of moss, small sticks, etc., and placed under some cut branches.

On the Bar, which is a kind of island at the mouth of the Findhorn, there is a solitary hut, where two or three fishermen pass the spring and summer. In the latter end of winter, when I have been wild-fowl shooting in that direction, I have often gone in there to screen myself from the cold. During the absence of the fishermen the hut is tenanted by rabbits, who make themselves quite at home, digging holes in the turf walls, etc. The life of the fishermen in this place must be like that of a lighthouse-keeper. During high tides they are quite cut off from the mainland, and although at low water their place of abode is no longer an island, yet that part of the shore opposite the Bar is a kind of wilderness little frequented by any one, being at a long distance from any road or path, with extensive tract of rough and all but impassable country stretching in every direction. It is, however, a favourite resort of mine, being the undisturbed abode of many wild animals. The roebuck and blackcock live in tolerable security there, and would increase to a very great extent were their young ones not killed by foxes and other vermin, who prowl about without danger of trap or poison.

June 15th, 1847. In the stagnant pools near the river Nairn there are great numbers of that singular worm called by the country people the hair-worm, from its exact resemblance to a horsehair. In these pools there are thousands of them, twisting and turning about like living hairs. The most singular thing regarding them is, that if they are put for weeks in a drawer or elsewhere, till they become dry and brittle, and to all appearance perfectly dead and shrivelled up, yet on being put into water they gradually come to life again, and are as pliable and active as ever. The country people are firmly of opinion that they are nothing but actual horsehair turned into living things by being immersed for a long time in water of a certain quality. All water does not produce them alike. To the naked eye both extremities are quite the same in appearance.

While fishing in the river one day at the beginning of June, my attention was attracted by a terrier I had with me, who was busily employed in turning up the stones near the water's edge, evidently in search of some sort of food. On examining into his proceedings I found that under most of the stones were a number of very small eels: where the ground was quite dry the little fish were dead, and these the dog ate; where there was still any moisture left under the stone they were alive and wriggled away rapidly towards the stream, seeming to know

instinctively which way to go for safety. Trout have undoubtedly the same instinct; and when they drop off the hook on the bank by chance, they always wriggle *towards* the water and never *away* from it. It is difficult, indeed almost impossible, to become much acquainted with the habits of fish but could we pry into their domestic circles, I have no doubt that we should find them possessed of a far higher degree of instinct and much greater cleverness in providing for their food and safety than we give them credit for. The instinct of fish in foretelling, or rather in foreknowing, the changes of weather is very remarkable; and the observant angler may almost prophesy with regard to the approach of rain or storms by seeing in what mood for rising at his flies the trout may be. In certain states of the weather the angler may put away his tackle without trying to take a single trout; but this can only be learned by experience and close observation.

June 16th, 1847. Walked to Lochlee, found that the hooded crows had taken all the eggs from the teal's nest which I discovered here on the 8th. I had frequently seen her in her downy nest since that time, but to-day both bird and eggs were gone; and when I went to the grassy hillock, which the crows used for a dining-table, there were the remains of the whole eight eggs.

June 21st, 1851. While I was shooting rabbits near the loch of Spynie, I saw a small bird fly high over my head; I called out "A rose-coloured starling!" and shot at it, bringing it down beautifully clean and scarcely injured. It was flying in company with two other starlings apparently of the ordinary colour, which escaped, so that I could not ascertain whether they were young of the same species, or common starlings. The head and neck are glossy black. Its crown feathers are elongated into a pretty long crest. The back, the rump, and the lower parts, are of a faint rose-colour. Different specimens vary in the shade of the rose-coloured parts, and in length of the crest. It is but very rarely met with in any part of Britain.

June 25th, 1847. I rowed to-day to the Old Bar, about four or five miles from here, found some eggs of tern and the lesser tern. Numbers of these birds were flying about; but the eggs are so very similar in colour to the stones amongst which they are laid, that it is not easy to find them. Going there we put out a line for flounders, and took it up on returning, catching about 50 flounders, a gurnet, and a large cod. The latter is as long and lean as an eel, and had lost one eye. The men took it to bait their crab traps with.

Sometimes on a fine June evening the sea-fish, such as gurnets and coal-fish, take a large white fly readily enough, and fight most powerfully when of any size.

June 28th, 1847. I took a boat to-day to cross over to the rocks of Cromarty. The breeze was gentle, but sufficient to take us merrily over; and putting out a couple of lines with large white flies, we caught plenty of gurnet, etc.

As we floated along the coast, stopping at the mouths of several caves, and occasionally landing, we put up several large flocks of pigeons, and here and there cormorants and other sea-birds. On one shelf of the rocks, far up above the sea, was the nest of the raven. It was once inhabited by a pair of eagles, but is now quietly tenanted by the raven. These birds had flown; but both young and old were flying about the tops of the cliff, croaking and playing fantastic antics, as if in great astonishment at our appearance; for I fancy that they have very few visitants here.

Some of the caves were of great extent, and very full of rock-pigeons, old and young. The birds were nearly all blue; here and there a sandy-coloured one, but no other variety. Having made our way a considerable distance along the coast, and the tide being now quite out, we landed on a green spot of grass that stretched down between the rocks to the water's edge. Above our heads, and in every direction, were heron-nests; some built in the clusters of ivy, and others on the bare shelves of rocks. The young ones were full grown, but still in the nests, standing upright and looking gravely at us.

Looking with my glass to the opposite coast of the firth, I could distinctly see the long range of sandhills between Nairn and the Bay of Findhorn, and could distinguish many familiar points and nooks. While resting here, too, a large seal appeared not above a hundred and fifty yards out at sea, watching us with great attention. As we returned homewards, the pigeons were in great numbers flying into the caves to feed their young. A pair of peregrine falcons also passed along, on their way to a rock where they breed, farther eastwards than we had been.

We saw too a flock of goats winding along the most inaccessible-looking parts of the cliff; and now and then the old patriarchal-looking leader would stop to peer at us as we passed below him, and when he saw that we had no hostile intention towards his flock, he led them on again, stopping here and there to nibble at the scanty herbage that was to be found in the clefts of the rocks. In one place where we landed, my dog started an old goat and a pair of kids, who dashed immediately at what appeared to be a perpendicular face of rock, but on which they contrived to keep their footing in a way that quite puzzled me. The old goat at one time alighted on a point of the rock where she had to stand with her four feet on a spot not bigger than my hand, where she stood for a minute or two seemingly quite at a loss which way to go, till her eye caught some (to me invisible) projections of the stone, up which she bounded, looking anxiously at her young, who, however, seemed quite capable of following her footsteps wherever she chose to lead them. We caught sight also of a badger, as he scuffled along a shelf of rock and hurried into his hole.

The hardy little blue rock-pigeon abounds on all the sea-coast of Scotland where the rocks are steep and broken into fissures and caverns—one moment dashing into its breeding-place, and rapidly flying out the next; then, skimming the very surface of the breakers, this little bird gives animation and interest to many a desolate and rugged range of cliffs as far north as Cape Wrath and Whiten Head, and it still frequents the rocks on this coast, though in small numbers, and is so intermingled with the house-pigeon, which it so exactly resembles, that it would be difficult to decide now if any of the real wild birds still remain.

In the caves on the Ross-shire coast, and all along the north, great numbers still are seen. They feed on the small patches of oats grown in the Highlands, and when farther southwards, in the stubble and corn-fields; they also swallow numbers of small snail shells, which are generally numerous amongst the grassy patches on the cliffs.

About three weeks ago our tame pochard had been carried away in a hurricane of wind. To my surprise, one day this month I saw this same pochard swimming about the loch alone, and apparently very tame. One of the children who was with me, and whose own especial property the bird had been, whistled to it in the same way in which he had been accustomed to call it, upon which, to his unbounded joy, it immediately came towards us, and for some time continued swimming within a few yards of where we stood, evidently recognising us, and seeming glad to see us again.

A few days afterwards we again saw him; but he was now accompanied by a flock of fourteen or fifteen others. This was remarkable, both on account of the time of year, and because this kind of duck is very rare in this region, and has never been known to breed in the neighbourhood; but all birds seem to have some means of calling and attracting those of the same species, in a way that we cannot understand.

My peregrine falcon, who still lives in the garden, now utters a call which is different from her usual shrill complaining cry, and which occasionally attracts down to her some wandering hawk of her own kind. The peregrine falcon is well named, for it is found in all countries.

Our bird, from good food, and having always had the run of a large garden, instead of being confined in a room or cage, has grown to a great size, and is in peculiarly fine plumage; with the dark slate colour of her upper feathers forming a beautiful contrast to the rich cream-colour of her neck and breast.

[109]

There is scarcely any common animal too large for her to attack when she is hungry. She will fly at a dog or cat as readily as at a rabbit or a rat. The latter animal she kills with great dexterity and quickness; and I have also found the remains of half-grown rabbits, who, having feloniously made their way into the garden, have fallen a prey to her powerful talons.

Few birds of the same kind vary so much in size as peregrine falcons. Some killed in a wild state are almost as large as the noble ger-falcon. Altogether the peregrine is the finest of our British falcons, both in size, courage, and beauty. It possesses, too, in the highest degree, the free courage and confidence which facilitate so greatly the process of training hawks to assist us in our field sports.

The cliffs of Gordonstoun, near Covesea, are frequented by the cormorant and though the bird does not breed on our rocky coast, yet it frequents some parts of it in great numbers.

The cormorant is easily trained to fish; it is a bold, confident bird, and soon becomes familiar with its master. A small strap buckled round the neck loosely, but sufficiently tight to prevent the bird from swallowing its prey, is necessary, as it would otherwise fill itself with fish, and then hunt no more. Restrained from this by the strap, the cormorant catches as many trout or fish as it can hold in its neck and throat, and this is a far greater quantity than might be supposed; and then, if well trained, comes to land to be relieved. It immediately disgorges those already caught, and commences anew to fish. When it has caught a sufficient number, or gets tired, it ought to have its strap taken off, and to be then fed and taken home. The cormorant should not be put to fish where eels are numerous, as it manages to swallow these in spite of its strap.

It is very amusing and curious to watch a cormorant pursuing a trout in clear water. On being turned into a pool, the bird immediately dives, and it can be seen searching under the broken banks, loose stones, etc., till it drives out a fish, when a chase takes place, so rapid that it would be difficult to know whether the cormorant was a fish or a bird, so quickly and apparently without exertion does it shoot through the water, turning the trout as a greyhound does a hare, and seldom failing to catch it. If the trout takes refuge under a stone or bank, the cormorant sometimes is at fault for a moment, but soon finds it again, and, as I said, generally ends in catching it. Altogether, fishing with a cormorant is a very amusing, though seldom practised sport.

In a wild state, after having fed, the cormorants sit in rows on some favourite rock or other suitable place, with their wings spread wide open like the figure of a spread eagle. Its favourite element is, however, the water, and it swims and dives with great speed and facility.

In the breeding season the adult bird has a short crest. It has also a white mark under the chin, and a conspicuously white patch on each of its thighs. In winter it has not these distinctive marks. The "crested cormorant" of some authors is the common cormorant in its adult and

summer plumage. The feathers of the tail are peculiarly hard, stiff, and have a worn appearance, as if the bird leant on them.

June 29th, 1847. Went to-day to the Old Bar to fish for flounders; we caught a great number, and one small turbot. Found also some terns' and ring-dottrels' eggs. The flounders, when opened, are full of small shell-fish. The sand-eels are caught in great number in the sand-banks, which are left bare by the ebb of the spring tides. The people procure them by turning up the sand to the depth of about three inches.

One of my children brought home a large lizard one day, and put it into a box, intending to keep it as a pet; boys having strange tastes in the animals which they select as favourites. The next morning, to the children's great delight, the lizard had become much reduced in circumference, but had produced four young ones, who were apparently in full and vigorous enjoyment of life. They were voted, at a consultation of the children, to be entitled to, and worthy of liberty, and were all (mother and children) carefully put into the garden, in a sunny corner under the wall. For my own part, I can see nothing more disgusting in animals usually called reptiles, such as lizards and toads, than in any other living creatures. A toad is a most useful member of society, and deserves the freedom of all floricultural societies, as well as entire immunity from all the pains and penalties which he undergoes at the hands of the ignorant and vulgar. In hotbeds and hothouses he is extremely useful, and many gardeners take great care of toads in these places, where they do good service by destroying beetles and other insects. In the flower-beds too they are of similar use.

Of quiet and domestic habits, the toad seldom seems to wander far from his seat or form under a loose stone, or at the foot of a fruit-tree or box-edging. There are several *habitués* of this species in my garden, whom I always see in their respective places during the middle of the day. In the evening they issue out in search of their prey. I found a toad one day caught by the leg in a horse-hair snare which had been placed for birds. The animal, notwithstanding the usual placid and phlegmatic demeanour of its race, seemed to be in a perfect fury, struggling and scratching at everything within his reach, apparently much more in anger than fear. Like many other individuals of quiet exterior, toads are liable to great fits of passion and anger, as is seen in the pools during April, when five or six will contend for the good graces of their sultanas

[111]

with a fury and pertinacity that is quite wonderful, fighting and struggling for hours together. And where a road intervenes between two ditches, I have seen the battle carried on even in the dry dust, till the rival toads, in spite of their natural aquatic propensities, became perfectly dry and covered with sand, and in this powdered state will they continue fighting, regardless of the heat, which shrivels up their skin, or of passers-by, who may tread on them and maim them, but cannot stop their fighting. There is more character and energy in a toad than is supposed. After the young ones have acquired their perfect shape, they appear to leave the water, and frequently the roads and paths are so covered with minute but well-formed toadlings, that it is impossible to put your foot down without crushing some of them.

During the spring and summer it is an amusing sight to watch the salmon making their way up the river. Every high tide brings up a number of these fish, whose whole object seems to be to ascend the stream. At the shallow fords, where the river spreading over a wide surface has but a small depth of water, they are frequently obliged to swim, or rather wade (if such an expression can be used), for perhaps twenty yards in water of two inches in depth, which leaves more then half the fish exposed to view. On they go, however, scrambling up the fords, and making the water fly to the right and left, like ducks at play. When the fish are numerous, I sometimes see a dozen or more at once.

The fish which escape the nets, and those which go up during floods and on Sundays, on which day they are allowed to have a free passage, seldom stop until they get to the deep quiet pools amongst the rocks some four or five miles up the water, where they rest till fresh water and opportunity enable them to continue their upward progress. Neither sea-trout nor salmon ever seem happy excepting when making their way up a stream. It is wonderful, too, against what difficulties, in the shape of falls and rapids, they will ascend a river. The jumping of the salmon up a fall is a curious and beautiful sight, and the height they leap, and the perseverance which they show in returning again and again to the charge, after making vain efforts to surmount the fall, are quite wonderful.

Often on a summer evening, when the river is full of fish, all eager to make their way up, have I watched them for hours together, as they

Peregrine. Inverness April 1847

Sparrow Hawk.

sprang in rapid succession, looking like pieces of silver as they dashed up the falls with rapid leaps. The fish appear to bend their head to their tail, and then to fling themselves forward and upwards, much as a bit of whalebone whose two ends are pinched together springs forward on being released. I have often watched them leaping, and this has always seemed the way in which they accomplish their extraordinary task. Both salmon and sea-trout, soon after they enter the fresh water, from the sea, make wonderful leaps into the air, shooting perpendicularly upwards, to the height of some feet, with a quivering motion, which is often quite audible. This is most likely to get rid of a kind of parasitical insect which adheres to them when they first leave the sea. The fishermen call this creature the sea-louse: it appears to cause a great deal of irritation to the fish. It is a sure sign that the salmon is in good condition, and fresh from the sea, when these insects are found adhering to him.

The growth of salmon when in the sea is wonderful, it having been indisputably proved that a salmon has grown eleven pounds six ounces during the short period of five weeks and two days: the fish having been marked on its passage to the sea, was caught again in the same river when ascending, after an interval of that duration.

The destruction of salmon during their passage to, and residence in, the sea must be wonderful, and defies all calculation. Did all the fish, which descend as fry, return as salmon, the rivers would not hold them. Their enemies are countless; every fish and every sea-fowl preys and fattens on them. At the mouths of rivers, and indeed at every shallow on their passage, thousands of gulls and other birds prey upon the fry, while trout and eels are feeding on them under water. As soon as they reach the sea too, fish of all kinds are ready to devour them.

Mr. Young* told me also that his young family of salmon fry which he hatched and kept confined in ponds connected with the river always become perfectly tame, and the moment that he steps on the plank laid across the ponds for the purpose of feeding the fish from, they all flock round him ready to dart at the food he puts in. In some of the ponds he had put a number of small eels, which soon grew in size, and became as tame and familiar as the young salmon. As the cold weather came on, the eels all disappeared, and he supposed that they had managed to escape, led by their instinct to take refuge in some deeper pools. However, one fine spring day, when he had long ceased to think of his slimy pets, he happened to pass over one of the planks, when he was delighted to see them all issue out from under the stones asking for food, as if a day only, instead of many weeks, had passed since he last had fed them. Does not this most clearly prove that eels lie dormant during cold weather?

I asked Mr. Young if he could explain why at the mouths of rivers, when angling, one always catches such a variety of trout—a variety

*Mr. Young was manager of the Duke of Sutherland's fisheries.

which does not exist at some distance from the sea, each and every stream having its own peculiar species. His opinion, founded on practical experiment and long experience, coincided much with mine founded on mere casual and unscientific observation, namely, that the sea trout and river trout sometimes breed with each other, thus forming a great variety of shade and colour. He also states that the female salmon will breed with a male trout, which he says has been clearly proved by close observation, in the following manner:—A pair of salmon, male and female, being seen forming their spawning-bed together, the male salmon was killed with a spear and taken out of the water. The female immediately dropped down the stream to the next pool, and after a certain interval returned with another male. He having shared the same fate as his predecessor, the female again went down to the pool, and brought up another male. The same process was gone on with of spearing the male, till the widowed fish, finding no more of her own kind remaining in the pool, returned at last accompanied by a large river trout, who assisted her in forming the spawning-bed, etc. with the same assiduity that he would have used had she been a trout instead of a salmon; the female appearing to be determined that her ova should not be left in the gravel without being fertilized by the male, thus taking the trout as a *pis aller*, and carrying out the proverb—"si on n'a pas ce qu'on aime, il faut aimer ce qu'on a".

The process of preparing the spawning-beds is curious. The two fish come up together to a convenient place, shallow and gravelly. Here they commence digging a trench across the stream, sometimes making it several inches deep. In this the female deposits her eggs, or ova; and she having left the bed, the male takes her place, and deposits *his* spawn on the ova of the female. The difference may be perhaps easily exemplified by the *soft* and *hard* roe of a herring; the former being that of the male, and without this the hard roe or ova of the female fish would be barren. When the male has performed his share of the work, they both make a fresh trench immediately above the former one, thus covering up the spawn in the first trench with the gravel taken out of the second: the

[114]

same process is repeated till the whole of their spawn is deposited, when the fish gradually work their way down to the salt water to recruit their lost strength and energy.

The spawn is thus left to be hatched in due time, but is sometimes destroyed by floods, which bury it too deep, or sweep it entirely away; at other times it is destroyed by want of water, a dry season reducing the river to so small a size as to leave the beds exposed to the air. The time required to hatch the eggs depends much on the state of the weather; in warm seasons they are hatched much quicker than in cold. The details I have here given are very imperfect; but perhaps they may induce those interested in the subject to read a little work published by Mr. Young, the result of his observations and experience for many years.

It is a common opinion that no food is ever found in the stomach of a salmon; but this is quite erroneous. On first entering the rivers they are often perfectly gorged with small eels; fry, and even good-sized herring are constantly found in them; showing that the salmon is as voracious a fish as his cousin the trout. When in fresh water they do not seem to have the same voracity. That they do feed on small fish, etc. however, in lake and river cannot be doubted, as we know that trolling with parr is as efficient a way of killing salmon in several waters as fly-fishing, though not so generally practised: nay, many a salmon dies an ignoble death from taking a worm.

This year I was fishing on a river in the North of Scotland, near a town where there was plenty of anglers, young and old, good and bad. There was one old piscator, who was most assiduous in his attention to the river, and whom I have seen for hours together at one small pool; changing his bait from fly to worm and from worm to fly, as he fancied the inclinations of the fish might be turned at the moment. One day we saw him in his usual position at the head of a rocky pool, and found that he had risen a salmon. After tempting the fish with every fly contained in an old bible, which served as a fishing-book, without success, he told us, as we greeted him in passing, that he *would* have the fish before dark: and sure enough, late in the evening, while taking a stroll up the river, we met the old gentleman coming home, and after a little coquetry on the subject, he produced *the* salmon, wrapped up in a snuffy pocket handkerchief, and crammed into his trousers, where he carried it in order to avoid notoriety on the subject. Not having permission, I fancy, to kill salmon in the river, he had killed the fish with a worm late in the evening, after everything else had failed.

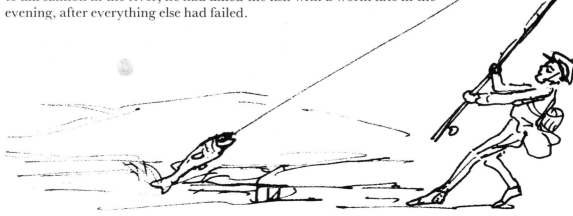

BIRDS OF PREY

Eagles—Peregrines—Ospreys—The Kite—Buzzards—The Hen-harrier—The
Sparrowhawk—The Kestrel—The Merlin—The Goshawk—The Hobby

I saw an eagle to-day passing southwards, apparently on his way from
the mountains of Sutherland or Caithness to the more southern
heights of the Grampians. The bird was flying very near the ground,
making his way against the wind, and pursued by a whole squadron of
grey crows, who had found out that he was a stranger, and taking
advantage of the unconcerned contempt with which he treated their
attacks, kept up a continual clamour and petty warfare against the royal
bird. The eagle, as he came over the more enclosed part of the country,
flew higher, as if suspicious of concealed foes amongst the hedges and
enclosures. I have almost every year during my stay in Morayshire seen
the eagles occasionally passing, at the beginning of winter invariably
going southwards, and again early in the spring on their return
northwards; in windy weather flying low, but when calm cleaving the
air at a great height. The eagle's flight, when passing from one point to
another, is peculiarly expressive of strength and vigour. He wends his
way with deliberate strong strokes of his powerful wing, every stroke
apparently driving him on a considerable distance, and in this manner
advancing through the air as rapidly as the pigeon or any other bird
which may appear to fly much more quickly.

I have seen him pounce (no, that is not the proper word, for he rather
rushes) down on a pack of grouse, and, with outspread wings, he so
puzzles and confuses the birds, that he seizes and carries off two or three
before they know what has happened. The mountain hare, too, is
carried off by the eagle with as much apparent ease as the mouse is borne
away by the kestrel.

[116]

The marten and the wild cat are favourite morsels. A tame eagle which I kept for some time killed all the cats about the place. Sitting motionless on his perch, he waited quietly and seemingly unheeding till the unfortunate animal came within reach of his chain. Then down he flew, and surrounding the cat with his wings, seized her in his powerful talons, with one foot planted firmly on her loins, and the other on her throat; and nothing more was seen of poor Grimalkin except her skin, which the eagle left empty and turned inside out, like a rabbitskin hung up by the cook, the whole of the carcass, bones and all, being stowed away in the bird's capacious maw.

Dead sheep, however, and other carrion form their principal food in those districts where the mountain hares are not very numerous; and on a large animal, such as a sheep, the eagle gorges herself so greedily that she is unable to rise from the ground quickly enough to escape an active man with a stick. Though certainly the eagles in some localities commit great havoc amongst the lambs, and also destroy the grouse when no larger game offers itself, it would be a great pity that this noble bird should become extinct in our Highland districts, who, notwithstanding his carnivorous propensities, should be rather preserved than exterminated. How picturesque he looks, and how perfectly he represents the *genius loci*, as, perched on some rocky point, or withered tree, he sits unconcerned in wind and storm, motionless and statue-like, with his keen, stern eye.

The eagle has not the same tractable and docile disposition as the falcons, and it is impossible to train an eagle to hunt with any certainty; she is as likely to attack the dogs of her master as the game which they have sprung, and would fly more readily to find a piece of carrion than to hunt a living animal. The temper, too, and disposition of this bird are changeable and treacherous.

We are occasionally visited, too, by the peregrine falcon, who makes sad havoc in the poultry-yard when he appears here. There is a nest of these birds always built in the inaccessible rocks of the Findhorn. Indeed, in the good old days of hawking, when a gentleman was known by his hawk and hound, and even a lady seldom went abroad without a hawk on her gloved hand, the Findhorn hawks were always in great request. The peregrine seems often to strike down birds for his amusement; and I have seen one knock down and kill two rooks, who were unlucky enough to cross his flight, without taking the trouble to look at them after they fell. In the plain country near the seashore the peregrine frequently pursues the peewits and other birds that frequent the coast. The golden-plover, too, is a favourite prey, and affords the hawk a severe chase before he is caught. I have seen a pursuit of this kind last for nearly ten minutes, the plover turning and doubling like a hare before greyhounds, at one moment darting like an arrow into the air, high above the falcon's head; at the next, sweeping round some bush or headland—but in vain. The hawk, with steady, relentless flight, without seeming to hurry herself, never gives up the chase, till the poor plover, seemingly quite exhausted, slackens his pace, and is caught by the hawk's talons in mid-air, and carried off to a convenient hillock or stone to be quietly devoured.

Two years ago I brought a young peregrine falcon down from near the source of the Findhorn, where I found her in the possession of a shepherd's boy, who fed her wholly on trout. For the first year the bird was of a dark brown colour above, with longitudinal spots on the feathers of her breast. On changing her plumage during the second autumn of her existence, she became of a most beautiful dark slate colour above, and the spots on her breast turned into crossbars, every feather being barred with black; her throat became of a beautiful cream colour. With great strength, she is possessed of the most determined courage, and will attack any person or dog whom she takes a dislike to. Her poultry-killing propensities oblige me to keep her chained in the kitchen-garden, where no other bird, except a tame owl, resides. The owl she appears to tolerate with great good-nature, and even allows him to carry off any remains of pigeon or crow that she leaves after she has satisfied her hunger. One day an unfortunate duck strayed within reach of her chain, and was immediately pounced on and devoured, leaving a numerous family of ducklings to mourn her loss.

The peregrine seldom strikes a bird on the ground, preferring to make its swoop at one on the wing, and either carries it off at once or strikes it with great force with the two hind talons, and then either letting it fall dead to the ground or catching it half-way in the act of falling. So strong on the wing is this bird that a full-grown partridge appears to be no incumbrance to its flight. The first thing that the hawk does on knocking down its prey, if it is not already dead, and often even if it is so, is to break the neck of the victim by bending the head back. It then begins with the brains, and after that eats all the most fleshy parts. The wild-fowl on seeing the peregrine approach betake themselves, if possible, to the water, knowing that as long as they keep to this element they are safe. I have often seen the falcon make several swoops close to the heads of ducks, etc., while swimming, as if endeavouring to make them rise, but always without success. She will not strike a bird too heavy to carry off at once while over the water, but waits till its prey is flying over the land. It must be a strong bird that can withstand the rapid powerful swoop and fierce blow of a peregrine. I have seen one strike the head off a grouse or pigeon with one blow, which divided the neck as completely as if it had been cut off with a sharp knife.

The osprey breeds in the forest of Glenmore. I have also frequently seen it flying over the lower part of the Findhorn and also hovering over the Loch of Spynie and in other places. Its flight and actions are peculiarly graceful and interesting. When unmolested, the osprey builds in the same place for many years adding only to the old nest. This is placed either on the highest part of some old ruin, on the peak of some rock which stands out from the water in a lonely highland loch, or, rarely, on the very summit of an old tree. The eggs are three in number; the ground of a cream colour thickly spotted and blotched with a beautiful mixture of chestnut and cinnamon colour. The young ones are covered with a coarse dark-coloured kind of hair at first, instead of the soft white down which protects from the cold the young of the peregrine falcon and other hawks.

I have seen the male sitting on the eggs, though usually he appears to assist the female more by bringing her fish than by taking his share of hatching. Their manner of fishing is very interesting. Hovering as a kestrel does over a mouse, the osprey seems to be motionless in the air till the prey is at exactly the right angle from her; then, dropping like a stone into the water, she seldom reappears without the fish in her powerful talons. Sometimes the osprey disappears completely under the water for a moment, at others she seems to catch the fish nearly on the surface. They appear to fish very often at a considerable distance from the nest, as I have seen the male bird coming at an immense height with a fish in his claws, and evidently from a distance of some miles, to feed his mate while sitting on her nest placed in the centre of some inland loch.

It is not many years since the kite was so common in this and in many other parts of the country as to be quite a scourge to the goodwife, being always a great destroyer of young chickens, young ducks, and such small and weak animals as are incapable of making much resistance. Although so large and powerful looking, the kite has none of the boldness and activity of any of the other hawk tribe in attacking its prey. The flight, however, of this bird is almost unequalled in beauty when it soars in wide circles high in the clear sky, as if sunning itself in the pure air of a higher region. Its wide and beautifully-marked wings and long forked tail give it a peculiarly picturesque appearance on these occasions.

Unless, however, driven by the necessity of providing for the hunger of its young, the kite preys only on small weak birds and reptiles, and, more frequently, on carrion of any description, fresh or stale. So little savage and courageous is its disposition, that I allow a tame kite to live amongst tame ducks and poultry, who seem to have no dread of it. When, however, there are young broods about, I do not trust her amongst them. A tame peregrine or even sparrowhawk would not live in the same kind of neutrality with them for two days without killing some of the poultry. The kite seems a very sociable bird when tame, and is very fond of being taken notice of, putting down its head like a parrot to be scratched, and altogether seeming to like being talked to and to have companions. It has the peculiarity of uttering its loud and not inharmonious whistle at all hours, even in the night, if it sees a light or hears a person passing. This bird is now very rare, and scarcely ever seen in this part of the country.

The buzzard is another of the hawk tribe which is gradually becoming rarer and rarer. Like the kite, too, the buzzard is a carrion-feeding bird, and seldom kills anything but small birds, mice, or frogs, excepting during the breeding-season, when it is very destructive to game; at other times the buzzard lives an indolent, lazy life. After having satisfied her hunger, this bird will sit for hours perfectly motionless on some withered branch, or on a projecting corner of rock, whence she commands a good view of the surrounding country, and can easily detect the approach of danger. A cowardly bird, except when excited by hunger, she submits patiently to the attacks of the smaller birds, and flies from the magpie or jackdaw. Like the kite, the raven, the eagle, and all birds who feed much on carrion, the buzzard has a lofty flight when in search of food. Soaring high up in the air, and wheeling in circles, she appears to examine the surface of the land for miles and miles, in hopes of detecting some dead sheep or other carcass.

Though she is one of the most ignoble of the hawk kind, I have a lingering affection for this bird, in consequence of her being connected in my remembrances with the rocky burns and hanging woods of the most romantic glens in the Highlands, where I have frequently fallen in with her nest and young. In this part of the country the buzzard has become very rare, and is only seen as an occasional visitor.

In the autumn my partridges suffer much from the hen-harrier. As soon as the corn is cut this bird appears, and hunts the whole of the low country in the most determined and systematic manner. The hen-harrier, either on the hill-side or in the turnip-field, is a most destructive hunter. Flying at the height of only a few feet from the ground, he quarters the ground as regularly as an old pointer, crossing the field in every direction; nor does he waste time in hunting useless ground, but tries turnip-field after turnip-field, and rushy field after rushy field, passing quickly over the more open ground, where he thinks his game is not so likely to be found. The moment he sees a bird, the hawk darts

rapidly to a height of about twenty feet, hovers for a moment, and then comes down with unerring aim on his victim, striking dead with a single blow partridge or pheasant, grouse or black-cock, and showing a strength not to be expected from his light figure and slender though sharp talons.

I saw on a hill-side in Ross-shire a hen-harrier strike a heath hen. I instantly drove him away, but too late, as the head of the bird was cut as clean off by the single stroke as if done with a knife. On another day, when passing over the hill in the spring, I was attended by a hen-harrier for some time, who struck down and killed two hen grouse that I had put up. Both these birds I contrived to take from him; but a third grouse rose, and was killed and carried off over the brow of a hill before I could get up to him.

There is a diversity of opinion whether the hawk commonly called the ringtail is the female of the hen-harrier. I have, however, no doubt at all on the subject. The ringtail is nothing more than the female or young bird. The male does not put on his blue and white plumage till he is a year old. I have frequently found the nest both on the mountain, where they build in a patch of rough heather, generally by the side of a burn, and also in a furze-bush. Though very destructive to grouse and other game, this bird has one redeeming quality, which is, that he is a most skilful rat-catcher. Skimming silently and rapidly through a rickyard, he seizes on any incautious rat who may be exposed to view; and from the habit this hawk has of hunting very late in the evening, many of these vermin fall to his share. Though of so small and light a frame, the hen-harrier strikes down a mallard without difficulty; and the marsh and swamp are his favourite hunting-grounds. Quick enough to catch a snipe, and strong enough to kill a mallard, nothing escapes him. Although so courageous in pursuit of game, he is a wild, untameable bird in captivity; and though I have sometimes endeavoured to tame one, I could never succeed in rendering him at all familiar.

There is another most destructive kind of hawk who frequently pays us a visit—the sparrowhawk. Not content with the partridges and other *feræ naturæ*, this bold little freebooter invades the poultry-yard rather too frequently. The hens scream, the ducks quack, and rush to the cover of the plantations; whilst the tame pigeons dart to and fro amongst the buildings, but in vain. The sparrowhawk darts like an arrow after one of the latter birds, and carries it off, though the pigeon is twice or three times his own weight. The woman who takes care of the poultry runs out, but is too late to see anything more than a cloud of white feathers, marking the place where the unfortunate pigeon was struck. Its remains are, however, generally found at some little distance.

Occasionally, when standing still amongst the trees, or even when passing the corner of the house, I have been startled by a sparrowhawk gliding rapidly past me. Once one came so close to me, that his wing actually brushed my arm; the hawk being in full pursuit of an unfortunate blackbird. On another occasion, a sparrowhawk pursued a pigeon through the drawing-room window, and out at the other end of the house through another window, and never slackened his pursuit, notwithstanding the clattering of the broken glass of the two windows they passed through. But the most extraordinary instance of impudence in this bird that I ever met with, was one day finding a sparrowhawk deliberately standing on a very large pouter-pigeon on the drawing-room floor, and plucking it, having entered in pursuit of the unfortunate bird through an open window, and killed him in the room.

The sparrowhawk sometimes builds on rocks, and sometimes in trees. Like all rapacious birds, he is most destructive during the breeding-season. I have found a great quantity of remains of partridges, wood-pigeons, and small birds about their nests; though it has puzzled me to understand how so small a bird can convey a wood-pigeon to its young ones. There is more difference in size between the male and female sparrowhawk than between the different sexes of any other birds of the hawk kind, the cock bird being not nearly so large or powerful a bird as the hen. Supposing either male or female sparrowhawk to be killed during the time of incubation, the survivor immediately finds a new mate, who goes on with the duties of the lost bird, whatever stage of the business is being carried on at the time, whether sitting on the eggs or rearing the young.

The kestrel breeds commonly with us about the banks of the river, or in an old crow's nest. This is a very beautifully marked hawk, and I believe does much more good than harm. Though occasionally depriving us of some of our lesser singing birds, this hawk feeds principally, and indeed almost wholly, on mice. On wing it may be very easily distinguished by its hovering motionless over the fields, a habit which gains it the name of "windhover" in many parts of England. It remains, as it were, suspended in the air with scarcely any perceptible motion of its wings, and this for a considerable time, watching the movements of some unfortunate mouse, and waiting for the right instant to make its stoop. The bird whose manner of hunting most resembles that of the kestrel is the osprey. The osprey hovers in precisely the same manner while watching for trout in the clear streams of the north. The kestrel breeds principally in rocks, but occasionally in trees.

Another beautiful little hawk is common here in the winter, the merlin. This bird visits us about October, and leaves us in the spring. In its adult state, it is very like a miniature peregrine, and has the same bold and tractable disposition. It is easy to train, though of a delicate constitution in confinement; and it seldom if ever survives its first moulting when deprived of liberty. Its flight is very rapid and beautiful, and its manner of striking its prey resembles wholly that of the peregrine. In a wild state it preys on small birds, snipes, and even partridges.

The merlin is easily known from the kestrel or sparrowhawk when on wing by its more rapid and direct flight, resembling that of the

peregrine, and by its long-pointed wings which reach to the extremity of the tail. In the days of falconry the merlin was in great request, and was the favourite hawk of ladies, because of its fine temper, and also its size not rendering it too great a weight for a lady's wrist. I have sometimes trained the merlin to fly at small birds, such as larks, etc., and I know nothing of the kind more beautiful than the flight of two merlins in pursuit of a lark when the latter mounts well into the air, as it does when pursued, in rapid circles, till nearly lost to sight, sometimes suddenly dropping to the ground and concealing itself so quickly and completely in the herbage as to escape the quick and keen eye of its pursuer, who, however, generally alights at the same spot, and searches for its prey with a keenness unequalled perhaps by that of any other hawk. So courageous is this beautiful little bird, that if trained to do so it will fly at and strike either grouse or black game, though without much effect. I have seen my tame merlins eat worms and insects, and this too when not pressed by hunger; so that I have no doubt that this sort of food is frequently resorted to by most of the small hawks when larger game is difficult to procure.

The goshawk is now nearly extinct in this country. A few years ago it bred regularly in the forest of Darnaway, and it may still do so. It also breeds in the forest of Glenmore, near Grantown, on the Spey. The female is a large and very powerful bird, with a peculiarly keen and cruel-looking eye. The length of a mature bird is about two feet; there is a great difference between the male and female as to size, the latter being much larger and heavier than the former.

[123]

The goshawk, like other short-winged hawks, seems to catch his flying prey more by surprise than by rapidity of flight; gliding quickly through the cover, it suddenly pounces on partridge, pheasant, or wood-pigeon, and seldom hunts in the open country excepting for young hares and rabbits. It is rather a favourite with some falconers, and is flown with great success at rabbits and even at hares. When flown at birds, if unsuccessful in its first dash, the goshawk is apt to perch on the nearest tree or hedge, and there to remain patiently as if expecting the reappearance of its prey. This habit, and its less interesting manner of flight, render it less a favourite with myself than the peregrine.

The temper of the trained goshawk, too, is said to be more capricious and changeable, and to require much humouring. Our ancestors, who understood hawking far better than we do, had the same opinion of the goshawk, and I find in an old book on the subject the remark that "she is very choice and dainty, and requires to have a nice hand kept over her." The same work remarks the habit of a goshawk of taking to a tree when disappointed in her first flight.

The hobby, a beautiful little hawk, like a miniature peregrine falcon, is not very common here. This kind of hawk leaves us before the winter. I have seen its nest in a fir or larch tree. A strong courageous bird, the hobby attacks and preys on pigeons and partridges, though so much larger than himself.

Since the introduction of English traps and keepers, all birds of prey are gradually decreasing in this country, whilst blackbirds, thrushes, and other singing birds increase most rapidly. In the highland districts of Moray, where a few years back a blackbird or thrush was rather a rare bird, owing to the skill and perseverance of gamekeepers and vermin-trappers in exterminating their enemies, they now abound, devastating our fruit-gardens, but amply repaying all the mischief they do by enlivening every glade and grove with their joyous songs. This year (1846) the thrushes and blackbirds were in full voice in January, owing to the mildness of the winter; and I knew of a thrush who was sitting on eggs during the most severe storm of snow that we have had the whole season.

Nairn. 1880

JULY

Roe—Torment of Midges—A Landrail's Nest—A Partridge's Nest—Hatching Eggs—
Waders—Herring   Fishing—Flounders—A   Hoopoe—A   Lesser   Red-pole—
Kittiwakes—Guillemots—Their Nesting Habits—Puffins—Solan Geese

July, is to me a most interesting season. Every day that I walk by the
lochs and swamps I see fresh arrivals in the shape of broods and flocks
of young teal and wild ducks, and this year there are numbers of
pochards swimming about in compact companies. Occasionally, too,
when I am walking near the covers, an old roe, accompanied by her two
large-eyed fawns, bounds out of some clump of juniper or brambles; and
after standing for a short time to take a good look at me, springs into the
wood and is soon lost to view: or an old solitary buck, driven by the
midges from the damp shades of the woods, startles me by his sudden
appearance near the loch side, springing over the furze and broom, on
his way back to the more extensive covers.

The roe have a singular habit of chasing each other in regular circles
round particular trees in the woods, cutting a deep circular path in the
ground. I never could make out the object of this manœuvre, but the
state of the ground proves that the animals must have run round and
round the tree for hours together.

Tormented by midges and ticks, the bucks often wander restlessly
through the woods at this season, uttering their bark-like cry; so like
indeed is this sound to the bark of a dog, that it often deceives an
unaccustomed ear. Of all torments produced by insects I can conceive
nothing much worse than the attack carried on by the myriads of midges
which swarm towards evening in the woods, particularly where the soil

[125]

is at all damp. For a time the smoke of a cigar or pipe protects one; but no human skin can long endure the inexpressible irritation produced by these insects.

July 1st. In walking over a field, the grass of which had been cut the day before, but was not yet carried, I disturbed a landrail, who was still sitting on her eggs, notwithstanding the great change that must have come over her abode, which, from being covered with a most luxuriant crop of rye-grass and clover, was now perfectly bare. How the eggs had escaped being broken, either by the scythe or by the tramping of the mowers' feet, it is difficult to understand; but there was the poor bird sitting closely on her eggs, as if nothing had happened, and on my near approach she moved quietly away, looking more like a weasel than a bird as she ran crouching with her head nearly touching the ground.

In another part of the same field I passed a nest of landrails in which the young ones were on the point of, or rather, in the very act of being hatched, some of the young having just quitted the shell, while others were only half out of their fragile prison. Both old birds were running around the nest while I stooped to look at their little black progeny, and were uttering a low kind of hissing noise, quite unlike their usual harsh croak. The mowers told me that they had seen several nests in the same field, but had avoided breaking the eggs whenever they perceived them in time.

The partridges here are chiefly hatched about the last week in June. Like the landrail, the hen bird sits very close, and during that time will almost allow herself to be taken up in the hand, especially when near her time of hatching. They seem to be quite confident in the forbearance of my boys, who have an intimate acquaintance with almost every nest in the neighbourhood of the house, the old bird allowing them to peer closely into her nest, and even to move aside the grass and herbage which conceal it, when they want to see if she is on her eggs. A retriever one day caught an old hen partridge on her nest, but let her go again on my rating him, without doing more damage to her than pulling out some feathers. Notwithstanding this she returned to the nest, and hatched the whole of the eggs the next day. Had she not been so near her time of hatching, I do not suppose that she would have returned again.

All birds have the same instinctive foreknowledge of the time of hatching being near at hand, and do not, when this is the case, leave their nest so easily as when disturbed at an earlier period of incubation. Some small birds are much tamer in this respect than others. A bullfinch will often allow herself to be taken off her nest, and replaced again, without showing the least symptom of fear. Indeed, this bird if put into a cage with her nest of young ones will continue to feed them as readily as if her habitation was still in its original situation. Blackbirds also are very unwilling to fly off from their eggs. The common wren, on the contrary, immediately forsakes her nest if it is at all handled and examined before she has laid her eggs. She will abandon it if she merely observes people

looking too closely at it; but when she has commenced to sit I have known her to be caught on her nest, and replaced, and still not forsake it. A small blue-headed tomtit formed her nest this year in a chink in my garden wall, and allowed the children to take out an egg to examine it from underneath her, without leaving the nest. In fact, instead of being frightened at the intrusion of their hands into her little warm, well-feathered domicile, she pecked courageously at their fingers, hissing and spluttering at them, and never seeming inclined to fly off.

When the young ones were hatched, the activity and perseverance of the old birds in providing them with caterpillars and blue-bottle flies were perfectly wonderful. They appeared to fly backwards and forwards to their young family every minute of the day, always bringing some insect in their bills. The good done by these little birds in destroying grubs and flies ought to earn them an immunity from all danger from trap or gun. Gardeners are always too much inclined to wage war against all small birds, forgetting that they invariably feed their young, not with seeds, but with different kinds of grubs and caterpillars, in this way amply repaying any little mischief they may do to the early-sown seeds. For my own part, I never trust a gun in my gardener's hands, but let the blackbirds and thrushes take as many cherries as they like, in return for which they destroy thousands of grey snails, etc., besides giving me many a moment of pleasure by their song.

About the second week in July the young wild ducks begin to fly. Those hatched high up in the country usually make their way down to the sea-side in that month. They follow the course of some stream or river till they arrive at their destination. Like the fable of the ostrich hiding her head when pursued, the young wild ducks when chased on the river will frequently dip their heads under the water, and keeping them there till they are nearly drowned, fancy themselves secure, although their whole body is exposed. If taken up, and put into some enclosed yard or garden, they will soon become tolerably tame, and get very fat if well fed. The whole of my poultry-yard (as far as ducks are concerned) is supplied by a breed of half-wild and half-tame ducks, originating in some young drakes caught, and turned out with the tame ducks—the tame drakes being all sent away, in order to ensure the proper cross in the breed. The birds are very much improved for the table by this cross, and are quite as tame as the common domestic duck, only showing their wild parentage in an inclination to hide their nests, and to build at a distance from home—always, however, if allowed so to do, bringing home their broods as soon as they are hatched. At other seasons they never seem inclined to wander, though they are always to be seen at the very earliest dawn of the morning, before it is quite light, spread out over the grass-field adjoining the house, hunting it in a regular line of advance for worms and snails. As the evening comes on, too, it is amusing to see them bent on the same pursuit, and displaying the greatest activity and skill in catching the large evening moths, as these insects rise from the grass or fly low over it.

About the second week of July the shore and sands are enlivened by vast flocks, or rather clouds, of dunlins, ring-dottrels, and other birds of the same kind, who now, coming down from their scattered breeding-places, collect in immense companies. When the tide ebbs, all these birds are employed in searching for the minute shell-fish and animalculæ, on which they feed; and vast indeed must be the supply required. About the lochs and swamps the young snipes and redshanks begin to fly.

The young sea-gulls, too, are numerous about the Bar and sandbanks, and are easily distinguished from the old ones by their fine mottled brown plumage.

Great numbers of all these birds must be killed by foxes, for every day I observe their fresh tracks along the shore and round the lochs. Near a fox's hole in one of the woods I saw an incredible collection of remains and *disjecta membra* of ducks, turkeys, fowls, game of every kind, and even of roe: apparently a litter of young foxes had been brought up in it.

July 10th, 1847. At Lochlee the young wild ducks are now just ready to fly.

On the 12th of July (1848) the Nairn herring-boats are all launched to reap their uncertain harvest. Of late years the supply does not seem to be nearly so regular or so much to be depended on as formerly; and frequently the men are but badly repaid for all their expense and risk. The cost of a herring-boat here, complete with its rigging, nets, etc., is not much less than ninety pounds; and the wear and tear of the nets is very great, owing to bad weather and other causes: the hull alone of the boat costs about twenty-seven pounds. There are five men to each boat; and Nairn alone sends out about sixty boats, so that from that small place not less than three hundred able-bodied men are for six or seven weeks employed in the pursuit of this valuable fish. The herrings are generally bought up beforehand by the fish-curers at Helmsdale, on the Sutherland coast, and at other parts, who contract to take the whole produce of the season's fishing at a fixed price; so that, notwithstanding the immense number caught, the supply of fresh herrings through the country is but scanty. The fish are, with as little delay as possible, packed in casks with brine, and in this state are exported to all parts of the world. The barrels are made principally of birch. Fir will not answer the

purpose, as it gives a taste of turpentine to the whole contents of the barrel. I have been out in a herring-boat during the fishing; and a very beautiful thing it is to see the nets hauled in with thousands of herrings, looking in the moonlight like so many pieces of the brightest silver flashing in the calm water. When not employed with the nets, the men generally fish with hooks for cod, halibut, etc.; all fish caught in this manner being the perquisite of the man who catches them; and frequently they make a good profit by this, as the cod collect in vast numbers about the herring-fishing grounds, and are caught as quickly as the hooks can be dropped into the water. Sometimes the cod, their great indistinctly-seen forms looking like the pale ghosts of fish, come close to the surface round the boats, and seize the bait as soon as it touches the water. Hauling these heavy gentry up from the depth of several fathoms is very severe work for the hands.

The herrings seem the most persecuted of all living creatures. From the moment when the great shoals of them appear in the north and north-west, they are pursued by thousands and tens of thousands of birds and countless numbers of fishes; and wherever the herring shoals are, *there* are these devourers. From the aristocratic salmon to the ignoble and ferocious dogfish, all follow up and prey upon the shoals; whilst their feathered foes mark out their track by the constant screaming and plunging into the water which they keep up during their pursuit. The solan geese from mid-air dash with unerring aim on the bright and silvery fish; whilst the cormorants and other diving sea-fowl pursue the dense crowd with indefatigable eagerness. In addition to all this, seagulls of every kind, like the skirmishers of an army, keep up a constant pursuit of all stragglers or wounded fish which come near enough to the surface to be caught by these birds, who have neither the power of the solan goose, to pounce hawk-like on their prey, even when at some depth in the water, or the diving power of the cormorant or guillemot, who can pursue them deep down into the sea. Altogether, a shoal of herring with its numerous accompaniments is a most amusing and interesting sight, independent of the consideration of the great importance of this fish to mankind, the number of people to whom it serves as food, and the number who are employed in its pursuit.

July 26th, 1853. In Pluscardin Wood I found a woodcock's nest with three eggs, at the foot of a tree. The forester told me he had flushed the old bird off it seven days back. She appeared not to have returned.

July 27th. My retriever brought to me, while looking for ducks in Spynie, a water-rail about two or three days old; the old one following the dog, and uttering cries of alarm and anger. He also caught and brought an old coot with its quill feathers all out, so that it could not fly. The dog always kills an old coot, though he does not hurt a wild duck in the least. I suppose that the reason is, that the coot scratches him severely with her sharp claws.

Among the available products of the sandy creeks and bays on this coast are immense quantities of excellent flounders. These fish come in with every tide, and though the great bulk of them return to the deep water, numbers remain in the pools which are formed at low water upon the sands. We occasionally drag some of these pools with a small trout-net, and are sure to catch a large quantity of these fish in one or two hauls. The flounders are of two kinds, the gray-backed flounder, and a larger sort which has red spots. The latter, however, is a far inferior fish, the flesh being soft and flabby. Notwithstanding the abundance and excellence of the flounders, left, as it were, for any person to pick up, with scarcely any exertion, the country people very seldom take the trouble to catch them, excepting now and then by the line, in a lazy, inefficient way.

July 27th. The Dunrobin keeper has just written to me that he has killed a very fine hoopoe in the middle of Golspie. I have never seen it in this country.

I also heard of the rose-coloured ousel being killed on the bent-hills near Dornoch. These birds must have been driven over by the east winds, as neither of them are inhabitants of Britain. Indeed, many a rare and foreign bird may visit the uninhabited and desert tracts of bent and sand along the east coast without being observed, excepting quite by chance; and the probability is, that nine persons out of ten who might see a strange bird would take no notice of it.

In the woods near Loch Rannoch I saw a great many red-starts, siskins, crossbills, and red-pole.

The lesser red-pole is a very small but interesting species of linnet. Some specimens seem scarcely larger than the golden-crested wren. The red-pole is easily caught with bird-lime, and very soon becomes tame and familiar, and apparently attached to its prison. I have more than once allowed them to fly out of the window, leaving it open for their return, and they have always come back to their cage, after taking a wander about the garden. In winter the red-poles collect in large flocks, either feeding on the weeds by the road or ditch side, or on the seeds of the birch or alder, hanging on the twigs like tomtits in all sorts of attitudes, and so occupied with extracting the seeds from their covering, that they may be caught by means of a horse-hair noose placed on the end of a stick. It is rather a matter of discussion whether this bird, and a variety called the mealy red-pole by bird-catchers, is the same species. I have, however, no doubt of their being quite distinct. The "mealy red-pole" is considerably larger, and has a peculiar "mealy" look about its plumage, which appears as if the bird had been sprinkled over with flour. I have seen it also only in small companies of from two to six. It feeds like the lesser red-pole on alder and other seeds, but as far as my observation goes, does not hang upon the branches, and put itself into the same tomtit-like attitudes as the latter bird. It is much more rarely seen, and I have not had many opportunities of closely comparing the two birds.

Let me wind up my notes of this bright summer month with a word or two of the gulls that now brighten air, earth, and water.

The kittiwake gull is about the size of the common gull. It breeds on the rocky cliffs of this sea-coast. I never, however, found it breeding in this immediate neighbourhood, though the birds are to be seen commonly during most of the year. The sea-gull described in Bewick as "the tarroch," is the young of the kittiwake.

The nesting-places of sea-gulls and some other kinds of water-fowl are curious things to see. The constant going to and fro, the screaming and wheeling about of the old birds, and the apparent confusion, are perfectly wonderful. The confusion is, however, only apparent. Each guillemot and each razor-bill amongst the countless thousands flies straight to her own single egg, regardless of the crowds of other birds, and undeceived by the myriads of eggs which surround her.

The common guillemot has no breeding-place on the Moray coast, but is common enough in the Firth. At the places where they breed the guillemots collect in immense numbers. Each pair has but one egg, which is of a very large size in proportion to their body. They build no nest, laying their single egg on the bare rock. A community of these birds in the breeding season is a most interesting sight. Thousands of them crowd on every ledge of rock which can afford the smallest standing room; and a constant flight seems to be kept up to and from the sea. As a new-comer arrives and wishes to settle on the rock, there is a general murmur and jostling together of those already provided with room, before he is admitted on to their ledge; and frequently an outsider is pushed or shouldered unceremoniously off the rock. Their food does not so much consist of fish as of small bivalves, marine insects, etc.

The puffin is a quaint and curious-looking little bird. It breeds in the same localities as the guillemot, razor-bill, etc., but places its egg in any convenient hole under ground, or under the rocks, at a distance of a yard or so from the surface. Woe to the fingers which pry incautiously into these dwellings, as the puffin's large and powerful bill closes on them with the sharpness and spring of a rat trap. This bird is but rarely seen far from its breeding place, and, though very numerous in those places, is but a rare visitor along our coast. The most striking peculiarity about the bird, and one that renders it unmistakable, is its bill; this is at least an inch and a half deep at the base, the part next to the head is a fine pale blue, the remaining half to the tip is red or orange colour.

During the herring season, or when any shoals of small fish frequent the coast, the solan goose is not at all uncommon along our coasts. From a very great distance the accustomed eye can distinguish the pure white plumage of the bird, with no other colour visible excepting the black tips to the wings, as with strong and rapid flight it sails to and fro at the height of forty or fifty feet above the water; sometimes suddenly checking itself in the air, hovering motionless for a few seconds, and then dropping like a stone into the water, rising quickly again to the surface with a remarkably buoyant motion, much as a bladder would, which had been forcibly drawn below the surface, and again suddenly allowed to rise. The bird immediately takes wing again and continues its hunting, till, apparently satisfied, it flies off and is lost to the eye. Seldom seeming to rest on the water, the air seems to be its native and proper element. The gannet breeds on the Bass Rock in the Firth of Forth, Ailsa Craig, and on other solitary and precipitous rocky islands.

During the winter season the solan geese disappear from the Bass Rock, going no one knows where. Their abiding places are probably regulated more by the supply of food than by the weather.

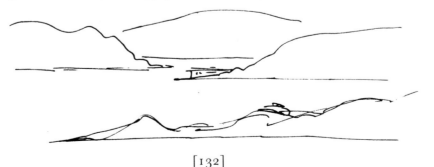

WEASELS AND STOATS

Escape of the Ferrets—Weasels—Stoats—Track of a Stoat—The Polecat—The Marten-cat

The bloodthirstiness and ferocity of all the weasel tribe is perfectly wonderful. The proverb *"L'appétit vient en mangeant"* is well applied to these little animals. The more blood they spill, the more they long for, and are not content till every animal that they can get at is slain. A she-ferret, with a litter of young ones, contrived to get loose a few nights back, and instinctively made her way to the henhouse, accompanied by her six kittens, who were not nearly half grown, indeed their eyes were not quite open. Seven hens and a number of tame rabbits were killed before they were discovered; and every animal that they killed, notwithstanding its weight and size, was dragged to the hutch in which the ferrets were kept, and as they could not get their victims through the hole by which they had escaped themselves, a perfect heap of dead bodies was collected round their hutch. When I looked out of my window in the morning, I had the satisfaction of seeing four of the young ferrets, covered with blood, dragging a hen (which I had flattered myself was about to hatch a brood of young pheasants) across the yard which was between the henhouse and where these ferrets were kept; the remainder of them were assisting the old one in slaughtering some white rabbits. Their eagerness to escape again, and renew their bloody attacks, showed the excited state the little wretches were in, from this their first essay in killing.

In the same way the wild animals of the tribe must be woefully destructive when opportunity is afforded them. Sitting opposite a rabbit-hole, I one day saw a tiny weasel bring out four young rabbits one after the other, and carry, or rather drag them away one by one towards her own abode in a cairn of loose stones; and, a few days ago, I saw one

[133]

bring three young landrails in as many minutes out of a field of high wheat. In fact, as long as she can find an animal to kill, so long will a weasel hunt, whether in want of food or not. I have frequently seen a weasel, small as he is, kill a full-grown rabbit. The latter is sometimes so frightened at the persevering ferocity of its little enemy, that it lies down and cries out before the weasel has come up. Occasionally these animals join in a company of six or eight, and hunt down rabbit or hare, giving tongue and tracking their unfortunate victim like a pack of beagles.

There is no doubt that in some degree they repay the damage done to game, by the number of rats and mice which they destroy (the latter being their favourite food). The weasel will take up its abode in a stack-yard, living on the mice and small birds that it catches for some time, and the farmer looks on it as a useful ally; till, some night, the mice begin to grow scarce, and then the chickens suffer. Eggs, fresh and rotten, are favourite dainties with the weasel.

I once witnessed a very curious feat of this active little animal. I saw a weasel hunting and prying about a stubble field in which were several corn-buntings flying about, and every now and then alighting to sing on the straggling thistles that rose above the stubble. Presently the little fellow disappeared at the foot of a thistle, and I imagined he had gone into a hole. I waited, however, to see what would happen, as, from the way he had been hunting about, he evidently had some mischief in his head. Soon a corn-bunting alighted on the very thistle near which the weasel had disappeared, and which was the highest in the field. The next moment I saw something spring up as quick as lightning, and disappear again along with the bird. I then thought it time to interfere, and found that the weasel had caught and killed the bunting, having, evidently guided by his instinct or observation, waited concealed at the foot of the plant where he had expected the bird to alight. A friend of mine, who was a great naturalist, assured me that, tracking a weasel in snow on the hill-side, he found where the animal had evidently sprung upon a grouse; and, on carrying on his observation, he had convinced himself that the bird had flown away with the quadruped, and had fallen to the ground about thirty yards off, where he found it with its throat cut; and the tracks of the weasel again appeared, as if he had come down with the bird, and having sucked its blood, had gone on his way, looking for a new victim.

The stoat is also very common here, and equally destructive and sanguinivorous—if I may use such a word. Being larger, too, he is more mischievous to game and poultry, and not so useful in killing mice. I often see the stoat hunting in the middle of an open field: its activity is so great that few dogs can catch it. When pursued, it dives into any rat's or mole's hole that lies in its way. I find that a sure mode of driving all animals of this kind out of a hole, is to smoke tobacco into it. They appear quite unable to stand the smell, and bolt out immediately in the face of dog or man, rather than put up with it. Tobacco-smoke will also

bring a ferret out of a rabbit-hole, when everything else fails to do so. In winter the stoat changes its colour to the purest white, with the exception of the tip of the tail, which always remains black. The animal is then very beautiful, with its shining black eyes and white body. The fur is very like that of the ermine, but is quite useless, owing to the peculiar odour of the animal, which can never be got rid of. It is worthy of note that the stoat does not emit this odour excepting when hunted or wounded.

The track of the stoat is very like that of a young rabbit, and may be easily mistaken for it. They travel over an amazing extent of ground in their nocturnal rambles, as their marks in the snow can testify. The edges of rivers and brooks seem their favourite hunting-places. By some means or other they manage to catch eels. I tracked a stoat from the edge of a ditch to its own hole, at the distance of several hundred yards. He had been carrying some heavy body, as I could plainly see by the marks in the snow; and this, on digging out the hole, I found to be an eel about nine inches long. No bait is better for all kinds of the weasel tribe than fish, which they seem to have a great liking for, and evidently feed upon whenever they inhabit a neighbourhood where they can procure them.

The polecat is now comparatively rare in this country, in consequence of the number of gamekeepers and vermin-trappers: they still, however, frequent the banks of the river, where they take shelter among the loose stones and rocks. There is no difference in appearance between the polecat and the brown ferret, which also partakes very frequently of the shyness of his wild relative, being much more apt to become cross-tempered and ready to return to a state of nature than the tamer white ferret. The polecat is extremely destructive—nothing comes amiss to it. I found in the hole of a she-polecat, besides her young ones, three kittens that had been drowned at the distance of at least a quarter of a mile. Besides these, her larder contained the remains of hares, rabbits, and of an infinity of birds and several eels.

There was a wood-pigeon that had young ones nearly fullgrown in an ivy-covered tree close to the window of my dressing-room. One morning I saw the old birds flying about in distress, but I could see no hawk or bird of prey about. Presently down fell one of the young birds, and in a moment afterwards the other young one also fell to the ground, both bleeding at the throat. I immediately loaded my gun, and had the satisfaction of shooting a large polecat, which came climbing down the tree and was just preparing to carry away one of the young pigeons.

Like the stoat, the polecat has a beautiful fur, rendered useless by the strong odour of the animal. Notwithstanding the quantity of game and other creatures killed by the polecat, he does not appear to be very quick on the ground, and must owe his success in hunting more to perseverance and cunning than to activity.

Formerly I frequently mistook the track of the marten-cat for that of a hare, when seen in the snow. Its way of placing its feet, and of moving by

[135]

a succession of leaps, is quite similar to that of the more harmless animal, which so often serves it for food. The general abode of the marten is in woods and rocky cairns. He is a very beautiful and graceful animal, with a fine fur quite devoid of all smell, but owing to its great agility it must be one of the most destructive of the tribe. When hunting, their movements are quick and full of elegance, the effect of which is much heightened by their brilliant black eyes and rich brown fur, contrasted with the orange-coloured mark on their throat and breast. The marten, when disturbed by dogs, climbs a tree with the agility of a squirrel, and leaps from branch to branch, and from tree to tree. In this part of the country they are now seldom seen. This animal is not wholly carnivorous, being very fond of some fruits—the strawberry and raspberry, for instance.

Though generally inhabiting cairns of stones, the marten sometimes takes possession of some large bird's nest, and relining it, there brings up her young, which are remarkably pretty little creatures. I endeavoured once to rear and tame a litter of young martens which I found in an old crow's nest, and I believe I should have succeeded had not a terrier got at them in my absence, and revenged himself on them for the numerous bites he had felt from martens and polecats in his different encounters with them. I have more frequently seen this animal abroad during the daytime than any of the other weasels.

The eagle is said to prey frequently on the marten-cat, but I never happened to witness an encounter between them; my tame eagle, however, always seemed to prefer them to any other food. I have no doubt that the eagle on its native mountain pounces on any living creature that it can conquer, and therefore must frequently kill both marten and wild cat, both which animals frequent the rocks and high ground where this bird hunts.

From the strength and suppleness of the marten, he cannot fall a very easy prey to any eagle of this country, and probably when pounced upon he does not die without a severe battle.

There are said to be two kinds of martens here, the pine-marten and the beech-marten; the former having a yellow mark on the breast, and the latter a white one. I do not, however, believe that they are of a distinct species, but consider the variety of shade in the colour of the breast to be occasioned by difference of age, or to be merely accidental.

The Findhorn near Forres. Sept 6th 1880.

AUGUST

Birds preparing to Migrate—The Dottrel—Regularity of the Coming and Going of
Birds—Crabs—The Sea-angler—The Deal Fish—Nightjars

During the first part of this month the mountain-bred birds, such as
golden plover, dottrel, curlew, etc., are daily seen to collect more
and more in flocks on the sea-shore or other places which suit their
habits. In the lower parts of the country the dottrel is now a very rare
bird, and it is seldom that many of them are killed, although they are so
tame and easy of approach as to have obtained for themselves the local
name of the "foolish dottrel." It is one of the peculiarities of this bird that
one pair only breeds on the same hill. Whilst you may see thousands of
golden plover on a hill-side during the breeding season, you will never
find above one pair of dottrel on each ridge. The ring-dottrel and other
shore birds become at this season more numerous day by day. Many
insectivorous birds, also, such as the whitethroat, redstart, etc., seem to
draw gradually towards the eastern coasts of the kingdom, as if in
readiness to depart. The wheatears almost entirely leave the wild rocky
mountains of the North, where they breed.

The regularity of the appearance and disappearance of birds in
different districts is one of the most striking and interesting parts of their
history, and is a subject worthy of more attention than it has hitherto
received. It is well known to many sportsmen that woodcocks appear in
certain woods, and even under certain holly bushes, or other favourite
spots, on the same day of the same month year after year; and in like
manner and with equal punctuality, do numberless smaller birds, of less
notoriety and less consequence to the sportsman, make their annual
flittings northwards or southwards. On referring to notes which I have
made during several years, I find that I have seen many migratory birds

[137]

for the first time in each year, on either the very same day of the month or within one day of it.

Even in the insect world the same punctuality in their change of abode is kept up, and an observant *out-of-door* entomologist will tell almost to a day when any particular moth or butterfly will first appear. The exclusiveness of some butterflies as to their locality is a very striking peculiarity of this insect. You may, year after year, find a certain kind in great numbers within a space of a hundred yards, but you may search in vain for a single specimen over the whole surrounding country; although both as to plants and soil it may seem as favourable for their production as the spot to which they confine themselves. I was told by a clever entomologist that I should find any number of specimens of a particular butterfly, which I wanted to procure, in a certain stone quarry, or rather where a quarry had once been, during the first and second week in August, but at no other time. My friend was perfectly right. Then and there, and then and there only, could I find this particular butterfly.

At the beginning of August I frequently find the crabs which frequent the rocks left exposed at low water either just about to change their shell or just after having changed it. Nothing can be more curious than the manner in which they contrive to draw their legs and claws out of their last year's covering, casting their entire shell perfectly whole and unbroken. I found the crabs about the rocks with their shells quite soft, having cast their covering of the last year. On some occasions the cast shell is found quite whole, even to the covering of the eyes and horns. On the 10th September 1848 [at Whitburn, Northumberland] I found one in this state, the crab having apparently only just finished the operation

[138]

of extracting itself, as it was lying in the crevice of the rocks close to the empty shell. What is remarkable, the animal, immediately on having cast its shell, increases considerably in size.

In fact, the only time that the crab has to grow in, is just after casting, as its skin commences immediately to harden into a new shell, and this done, all increase of size is impossible. Before casting, the flesh of the crab seems to be entirely turned into a watery substance enclosed in a tough skin, which enables it to draw itself whole out of the shell. Any one who has seen a crab must know how impossible it would be for the animal to drag its claws and legs through the small joints of these parts unless the flesh were totally changed in size and substance. Altogether, the power of a crab to cast its shell entire without breaking the covering of a single limb is one of the most extraordinary things in nature. Almost invariably a crab, while her shell is soft, is protected by a male crab, who remains with her, and, on the approach of danger, covers her with his body and claws, and dies rather than leave his helpless charge. Take him away, and put him at a distance of several yards, and he will return immediately to protect the helpless female. In a few days, however, the skin hardens into shell, and the crab no longer needs protection.

During the herring fishing it frequently happens that some strange and rarely seen monster of the sea gets either entangled in the nets or is cast upon the shore while pursuing the shoals of smaller fish. Among others, I have more than once seen a most hideous large-headed fish, which the country people call sometimes "the sea-devil," sometimes "the sea-angel," but whose more regular cognomen is, I believe, "the sea-angler." The first name he owes to his excessive and wicked-looking ugliness; the second must have been given him ironically; whilst the third is derived from his reputed habit of attracting fish to their destruction by a very wily ruse. He buries himself, it is said, in the sands by scraping a hole with his two most unseemly and deformed-looking "hands," which are placed below what may be called his chin. Being in this way quite concealed, he allows some long worm-like appendages which grow from the top of his head to wave and float above the surface of the sand; fish, taking these for some kind of food, are attracted to the spot, when the concealed monster by a sudden spring manages to engulph his victims in the fearfully wide cavity of his mouth, which is armed with hundreds of teeth sloping inwards, and as hard and sharp as needles, so that nothing which has once entered it can escape. So runs the tale, the exact truth of which I am not prepared to vouch for.

August 4th. We caught a young woodcock full grown in one of the woods near here. A dog disturbed it in the cover, and it flew fluttering into the road, where it allowed itself to be caught by the hand, although it was quite as large as an old bird, and its wings apparently fully feathered.

August 5th, 1847. A rare and singularly formed fish was brought to me to-day by the fishermen. It is called the "Deal fish," or, locally, the "Saw-fish." The latter name is very expressive of its shape and proportions, the fish being flat *vertically*, instead of, like a sole or flounder, *horizontally*. The following is the description of the fish, which I set down at the time:—

Length, 3 feet 6 inches. Depth, 7 inches. Greatest thickness, between half and three quarters of an inch. Colour, bright silver, with one very thin crimson fin running the whole length of its back. The tail very transparent, fan-shaped, and of a bright crimson. A large flat eye; and a small mouth, which the fish had a peculiar power of elongating to a considerable extent.

It had managed to get hooked through the back, by a common haddock-hook. I wished to have preserved the skin, as I believe that there are not above one or two perfect specimens extant; but, unluckily, through a mistake the fish was destroyed.

August 23rd, 1852. Immense numbers of wild ducks come now to feed on the standing barley.

August 24th, 1853. On Monaghty hill I put up three nightjars—an old one and two young ones. They were lying close together on the heather. The old one fluttered away, pretending to be lame; the young ones were as large as the old, but with short tails. The nightjar arrives late in the spring. I never recollect seeing one till after the middle of May. It is probable that it would not find a sufficient quantity of large moths and beetles, on which it feeds, before that time of year. During the whole day the nightjar remains perfectly quiet, either lying flat on the ground or on a dead or fallen branch of a tree. In the latter case the bird lies lengthways on the branch, and not across it like any other bird, and its mottled gray and brown colour makes it nearly invisible.

In this manner the bird will allow a person to approach nearly close to it before it moves, although watching intently with its dark eye to see if it is observed. If it fancies that you are looking at it, up it rises straight into the air, and drops again perpendicularly in some quiet spot, with a flight like that of an insect more than of a bird. With the shades of evening comes its time of activity. With rapid and noiseless flight the nightjar flits and wheels round and round as you take your evening walk, catching the large moths and beetles that you put into motion. Sometimes the bird alights in the path near you, crouching close to the ground, or sits on a railing or gate motionless, with its tail even with its head. Frequently, too, these birds pitch on a house-top, and utter their singular jarring noise, like the rapid revolving of a wheel or the rush of water, and the house itself appears to be trembling, so powerful is their note. It is a perfectly harmless, indeed a useful bird; and I would as soon wantonly shoot a swallow as a nightjar. I admire its curiously-mottled plumage, and manner of feeding and flying about in the summer and autumn evenings, which make it more interesting when alive than it can possibly be when dead. Often when I have been fishing late in the evening, has the nightjar flitted round, or pitched on a rock or bank close to me, as if inclined to take an interest in what I was at—confident, too, of not being molested. Its retreat in the daytime is usually in some lonely wild place. Though feeding wholly at night, I do not think that it is annoyed by sunshine, as it frequently basks in an open spot, appearing to derive enjoyment from the light and glare which are shining full upon it; unlike the owl, whose perch in the daytime is in some dark and shady corner, where the rays of the sun never penetrate.

There is scarcely any bird which is so careless about the spot where it places its eggs—indeed, it makes no nest at all, not even scraping a hollow place in the ground. The nightjar lays her two eggs on a bare but perfectly secure place. In this country they are placed near the edge of a wood or plantation, on a spot of ground free from heather.

The old blackcocks have not yet got their curved tail feathers.

I find that towards the end of August, when the hill lakes and swamps are much disturbed by grouse-shooters, the wild ducks bring down their young broods in great numbers, both to the bay and to the lochs.

The sheldrakes, who were so numerous a few weeks ago about the sandbanks and bar, have now nearly all disappeared; and their place is supplied by innumerable curlews and other waders, all of whom appear to find their food in the moist sands left by the ebb tide, which in this country contain an endless supply of shell-fish of different kinds, from the minutest species, fit only to feed the dunlin and sandpiper, to those which serve for food to the oyster-catcher, whose powerful bill is well adapted to breaking up the strongest cockles and mussels which are found in this district.

GAME BIRDS

A Grouse's Nest—Habits of Grouse—Blackgame—Ptarmigan—Partridges—Affection
for their Young—Pheasants—Woodcock—Carrying their Young—Migration of
Woodcock—Snipe

I found the nest of a grouse with eight eggs, or rather eggshells, within
two hundred yards of a small farm-house on a part of my shooting-
ground, where there is a mere strip of heather surrounded by cultivated
fields, and on a spot particularly infested by colley-dogs, as well as by
herd-boys, *et id genus omne*. But the poor bird, although so surrounded by
enemies, had managed to hatch and lead away her brood in safety. I saw
them frequently afterwards, and they all came to maturity. How many
survived the shooting-season I do not know, but the covey numbered
eight birds far on in October. If the parent bird had selected her nesting-
place for beauty of prospect, she could not have pitched upon a lovelier
spot. The nest was on a little mound where I always stop, when walking
in that direction, to admire the extensive and varied view—the Bay of
Findhorn and the sand-hills, the Moray Firth, with the entrance to the
Cromarty Bay, and the bold rocky headlands backed by the mountains
of Ross-shire. Sutherland, Caithness, Inverness, and Ross-shire are all
seen from this spot; whilst the rich plains of Moray, dotted with timber,
and intersected by the winding stream of the Findhorn, with the woods
of Altyre, Darnaway, and Brodie, form a nearer picture.

It is a curious fact, but one which I have often observed, that dogs
frequently pass close to the nest of grouse, partridge, or other game,
without scenting the hen bird as she sits on her eggs. I knew this year of a
partridge's nest which was placed close to a narrow footpath near my
house; and although not only my people, but all my dogs, were

constantly passing within a foot and a half of the bird, they never found her out, and she hatched her brood in safety.

Grouse generally make their nest in a high tuft of heather. The eggs are peculiarly beautiful and game-like, of a rich brown colour, spotted closely with black.

The old birds are very attentive to and careful of the young brood, and remain with them till the following spring. On the approach of and during wet and rough weather, grouse pack, as it is called, that is, assemble in large companies. Although in some peculiarly early seasons, the young birds are full grown by the 12th of August, in general five birds out of six which are killed on that day are only half come to their strength and beauty. In October there is not a more beautiful bird in our island; and in January a cock grouse is one of the most superb fellows in the world, as he struts about fearlessly with his mate, his bright red comb erected above his eyes, and his rich dark-brown plumage shining in the sun.

Notwithstanding the immense numbers killed by gun, net, and snare, not including those which fall a prey to crows, hawks, foxes, and other vermin, grouse are still numerous enough to be a source of great profit in the way of rent to the proprietors of the heath-clad mountains of this country. That they are not already extinct in most districts is owing, I truly believe, to the preservation carried on by those who rent the shootings.

Since my recollection of grouse they have very much changed their manner of feeding. The small crops of oats which year after year encroach on the moor lands have taught these birds to appreciate corn as their food instead of the tender heather shoots on which formerly they fed. Now, instead of finding the crop of the grouse full of this latter food, you find that they have been feeding on oats like a pheasant or barn-door fowl. As long as anything is to be found on the stubbles the grouse come from long distances every evening and morning to feed on them. Early in the season too they feed in great numbers in the standing corn. Great numbers are destroyed by means of snares in the corn-fields, more particularly while the sheaves of oats are left on the ground.

It is often asserted that the black game drive away the grouse, but I am not at all of that opinion; I do not consider that they at all interfere with each other. The same description of ground is not liked by both kinds of birds. The blackcock prefers rocky hill-sides, with plantations and boggy pieces of ground, clothed with coarse grass and different kinds of plants; while the grouse delights in wide open tracts where the heather is not too rank, and where there is plenty of young heath, on the shoots of which they can feed. Burning the heather judiciously and at proper seasons is of great service to grouse, as it gives them heather of different ages—the young to feed on, and the older parts for shelter.

Black game for the most part breed in plantations. The nest is placed in a tuft of rank heather, or under a small tree or bush. She takes great

care of her young, attending them anxiously till they are full grown. It is not easy to ascertain, but I doubt whether they breed the first year—at least there are always more hens of black game without broods than I can account for in any other manner.

When able to run, the old hen leads the young ones to the vicinity of some wet and mossy place in or near the woodlands, where the seeds of the coarse grass and of other plants, and the insects that abound near the water, afford the young birds plenty of food. The hen takes great care of her young, fluttering near any intruder as if lame, and having led him to some distance from the brood takes flight, and making a circuit returns to them. The cock bird sometimes keeps with the brood, but takes good care of himself, and running off leaves them to their fate. Wild and wary as the blackcock usually is, he sometimes waits till you almost tread on

[144]

Black Cock
Grey Hen
A.S... Aug 1907

Different woodcocks

him, and then flutters away. At other times, being fond of basking in the sun, he lies all day enjoying its rays in some open place where it is difficult to approach him without being seen.

In snowy weather the black game perch very much on the fir-trees, as if to avoid chilling their feet on the colder ground: in wet weather they do the same.

During the spring, and also in the autumn, about the time the first hoar-frosts are felt, I have often watched the blackcocks in the early morning, when they collect on some rock or height, and strut and crow with their curious note not unlike that of a wood-pigeon. On these occasions they often have most desperate battles. I have seen five or six blackcocks all fighting at once, and so intent and eager were they, that I approached within a few yards before they rose. Usually there seems to be a master-bird in these assemblages, who takes up his position on the most elevated spot, crowing and strutting round and round with spread-out tail like a turkey-cock, and his wings trailing on the ground. The hens remain quietly near him, whilst the smaller or younger male birds keep at a respectful distance, neither daring to crow, except in a subdued kind of voice, nor to approach the hens. If they attempt the latter, the master-bird dashes at the intruder, and often a short melee ensues, several others joining in it, but they soon return to their former respectful distance. I have also seen an old blackcock crowing on a birch-tree with a dozen hens below it, and the younger cocks looking on in fear and admiration.

Strong as the blackcock is, he is often killed by the peregrine falcon and the hen-harrier. When pursued by these birds, I have known the blackcock so frightened as to allow himself to be taken by the hand. I once caught one myself who had been driven by a falcon into the garden, where he took refuge under a gooseberry bush and remained quiet till I picked him up. I kept him for a day or two, and then, as he did not get reconciled to his prison, I turned him loose to try his fortune again in the woods. Like some other wary birds, the blackcock, when flushed at a distance, if you happen to be in his line of flight, will pass over your head without turning off, as long as you remain motionless.

A bold bird by nature, the blackcock, when in confinement, is easily tamed, and soon becomes familiar and attached to his master. In the woods instances are known of the blackcock breeding with the pheasant. I saw a hybrid of this kind at a bird-stuffer's in Newcastle: it had been killed near Alnwick Castle. The bird was of a beautiful bronzed-brown colour, and partaking in a remarkable degree of the characteristics of both pheasant and black game. I have heard also of a bird being killed which was supposed to be bred between grouse and black game, but I was by no means satisfied that it was anything but a peculiarly dark-coloured grouse.

Our other species of grouse, the ptarmigan, is found only on the highest ranges of the Highlands. Living above all vegetation, this bird finds its scanty food amongst the loose stones and rocks that cover the summits of Ben Nevis and some other mountains. It is difficult to ascertain indeed what food the ptarmigan can find in sufficient quantities on the barren heights where they are found. Being visited but rarely, these birds are seldom at all shy or wild, but, if the day is fine, will come out from among the scattered stones, uttering their peculiar croaking cry, and run in flocks near the intruder on their lonely domain.

When the weather is windy and rainy, the ptarmigan are frequently shy and wild; and when disturbed, instead of running about like tame chickens, they fly rapidly off to some distance, either round some shoulder of the mountain, or by crossing some precipitous and rocky ravine get quite out of reach.

In severe weather they often burrow under the snow to get shelter, and also to find their scanty food. The greatest destruction made amongst ptarmigan is when the shepherds first put their flocks to the tops of the hills, which is generally done about the time when the young birds most easily fall a prey to the dogs.

Wherever there is cultivation in this country there are partridges. Towards winter, however, there seems to be a partial movement of these birds from the small patches of cultivated ground on the higher districts to the richer and warmer districts. The soil is particularly well adapted for the breeding of partridges, being dry, full of grain, and with a tolerable mixture of furze and broom, in which they can hatch in security. The wide drains in some parts of the country are dangerous traps for the very young birds, as they frequently cannot climb up their steep sides. Partridges, however, when very young do not wander much from the high corn or bank of broom near which they are hatched. Weasels, stoats, and, worse than all, tame cats, destroy a great many young partridges; while hawks, such as the peregrine falcon and the sparrowhawk, and the hen-harrier, are very destructive to the old birds.

The nest of the partridge is often placed in a very frequented neighbourhood, or close to a road or footpath. The old bird, however, conceals not only her eggs but also the track which she makes through the herbage in going to and from her nest, with the greatest care and cunning. They lay from twelve to eighteen eggs. The male bird accompanies the brood throughout the season, taking as much care of them as the female does. Both in pheasants and partridges the number of cock birds reared far exceeds the hens. I have been told by men who have reared several hundreds of both pheasants and partridges that there are two cocks for every hen in both kinds of birds.

The farmer cannot complain of the mischief done by partridges. The crop seldom contains anything but small seeds and a few blades of grass or clover. Sometimes they take to eating turnips even in fine open weather, but cannot commence a hole in a sound root, only picking small pieces off one already broken by rabbits or rooks. The hen partridge is a most careful and affectionate mother, showing the

strongest signs of distress on any danger approaching them, and even giving battle to crows and other enemies in their defence. In more than one instance I have seen an old partridge fly at a dog which had come near her brood.

In this country the pheasant is rare excepting in places where they are preserved from poachers, and fed during the winter. If the latter is not attended to, in consequence of their wandering habits they are apt to stray far from home, and to fall a prey to poachers, etc. The pheasant eats all sorts of food, grain, insects, roots, and even carrion. Though destructive to crops, where too numerous, the pheasant is of some service in scratching up and eating great numbers of grubs and caterpillars, amongst which it is said to be particularly fond of the wireworm, one of the greatest plagues that the farmer is subject to, unless kept down by rooks, pheasants, etc. Acorns, beech-mast, etc., are also much sought after by the pheasant. The pheasant will breed without much hesitation with the common fowl, more particularly if brought up with pullets without seeing any of their own species. The mule bird, however, is inferior in beauty and proportions to both its parents. I have also seen mules between the pheasant and black game. The rich brilliancy of the pheasant's plumage renders him certainly the handsomest of all our birds. When quiet and undisturbed he will soon become familiar, feeding boldly about the house door, and forming a great ornament and addition to the beauty of the garden, more particularly during the spring, when, with erect crest and comb, he struts and crows at all hours of the day, spreading his tail and quivering his wings in the most fantastic manner.

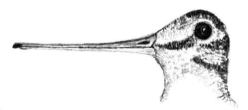

I have again, this year (1848), seen the old woodcocks carrying their young down to the soft, marshy places to feed. Unfitted as their feet appear to be for grasping anything, the old birds must have no slight labour in carrying their whole family (generally consisting of four) every evening to the marches, and back again in the morning. They always return before sunrise.

Occasionally I have come upon a brood of young woodcocks in a dark, quiet, swampy part of the woods, near which they had probably been bred. In a case of this kind we may suppose that the old birds are saved the trouble of conveying their young to a distant feeding-place; but as the young birds are frequently hatched in long heather in dry situations, and far from any marshes, they would inevitably perish in the nest were they not daily carried backwards and forwards by their parents. The quantity of worms required to sustain one of these birds would astonish those town-bred naturalists who gravely assert that the woodcock "lives on suction."

The nest is placed at the foot of a tree in a patch of long heather, or indeed in any sheltered place; most frequently in the driest and densest parts of the woods. It is formed of dry grass, leaves, etc., and is shallow, and made without much apparent care. The eggs are four in number, of a pale yellowish brown, blotched and spotted with reddish brown. As soon as the young are hatched, the old birds are obliged to carry them to the feeding-ground, which is often at some distance. The young, though able to run immediately, are tender helpless little things, and could by no means scramble through the tangled heather and herbage which often surround their nest, perhaps for many hundred yards.

It long puzzled me *how* this portage was effected. That the old birds carried their young I had long since ascertained, having often seen them in the months of April and May in the act of doing so, as they flew towards nightfall from the woods down to the swamps in the low grounds. From close observation, however, I found out that the old woodcock carries her young, even when larger than a snipe, not in her claws, which seem quite incapable of holding up any weight, but by clasping the little bird tightly between her thighs, and so holding it tight towards her own body. In the summer and spring evenings the woodcocks may be seen so employed passing to and fro, and uttering a gentle cry, on their way from the woods to the marshes. They not only carry their young to feed, but also if the brood is suddenly come upon in the day-time, the old bird lifts up one of her young, flies with it fifty or sixty yards, drops it quietly, and flies silently on. The little bird immediately runs a few yards, and then squats flat on the ground amongst the dead leaves, or whatever the ground is covered with. The parent soon returns to the rest of her brood, and if the danger still threatens her, she lifts up and carries away another young bird in the same manner.

I saw this take place on the 18th May; the young were then larger than, or fully as large as, a snipe. I have, however, seen young woodcocks nearly full grown at the end of April, and I have again seen the young ones about half grown at 26th of July, and at different intervals between. I have also seen eggs of this bird at different times between March and the end of July. The inference, therefore, is, that the woodcock either breeds twice in the season, or is very irregular as to her period of so doing. The young birds are of a light reddish brown colour, mottled and striped with darker brown.

In the evening the woodcock's flight is rapid and steady, instead of being uncertain and owl-like, as it often is in the bright sunshine. I consider their vision to be peculiarly adapted to the twilight, and even to the darker hours of night—this being the bird's feeding-time. In very severe and protracted snowstorms and frosts I have seen them feeding at the springs during the daytime; but in moderate weather they pass all the light hours in the solitary recesses of the quietest parts of the woods, although occasionally one will remain all day in the swamp, or near the springs on the hill-side, where he had been feeding during the night. When they first arrive, about the month of November, I have sometimes fallen in with two or three brace far up on the mountain, while grouse-shooting. The first frost, however, sends them all to the shelter of the woods. No bird seems less adapted for a long flight across the sea than the woodcock; and it is only by taking advantage of a favourable wind that they can accomplish their passage. An intelligent master of a ship once told me, that in his voyages to and from Norway and Sweden, he has frequently seen them, tired and exhausted, pitch for a moment or two with outspread wings in the smooth water in the ship's wake; and having rested themselves for a few moments, continue their weary journey.

Although those that remain here breed so early in the year, the woodcocks that migrate do not leave England till the end of March or beginning of April. In the wild extensive woods of Sussex, I have often seen them in the evenings, about the beginning of April, flying to and fro in chase of each other, uttering a hoarse croaking, and sometimes engaging each other at a kind of tilting-match with their long bills in the air. I remember an old poaching keeper, whose society I used greatly to covet when a boy, shooting three at a shot, while they were engaged in an aerial tournament of this kind.

The snipe also begins to breed in March, though it is not quite so early a bird as the woodcock. Snipes hatch their young in this country, breeding and rearing them in the swamps, or near the springs on the mountains. During the pairing time the snipes fly about all day, hovering and wheeling in the air above the rushes where the female bird lies concealed, and uttering their peculiar cry, which resembles exactly the bleating of a goat, and from which they have one of their Gaelic names, which signifies the air-goat.

About the end of July and first week in August the snipes descend from the higher grounds, and collect in great numbers about certain favourite places. They remain in these spots for a week or ten days, and then disperse. The rest of the season we have but few in this part of the country.

SEPTEMBER

Wild Weather—The Climate of Morayshire—Widgeon—Arrival of the Jack-snipe—The Turnstone—A Sea-eagle—The Age of Birds and Animals—Departure of the Swallows—Finnock

In this part of Scotland we have much wild and stormy weather in September; and many English sportsman, towards the end of the month, when located in some small shooting-lodge in the wild and distant glens of the inland mountains, begins to think of taking his way southwards. The incessant rain driving pitilessly down the glen where his confined and badly built cottage is placed, rivers turned into torrents, burns changed into rivers, and the grouse unapproachably wild, all combine to drive away many a southern sportsman before the end of this month; and yet October and November often are better months than the latter part of September.

Here, in Moray, we have a more favourable climate, and it is very rarely that there is any long continuance of bad weather in the lower parts of the county. Many a storm passes harmlessly over our heads to fall on the high grounds a few miles from the coast. These storms of rain or snow, although they pass over us, have always the effect of lowering the quicksilver in the weatherglass as certainly as if they fell here, instead of only threatening to do so.

Very few birds and, comparatively speaking, few even of land animals, fall victims to floods. The rabbits manage to climb up into the highest furze bushes, or even into the branches of trees, and it is very seldom that any birds make their nests within reach of this danger. In the same manner that terns and other birds who lay their eggs on the sea-shore seem to have an instinct which teaches them the exact line to which the highest spring-tides ever reach, so do the land birds avoid building their nests in places to which the land floods ever ascend.

There is one very numerous class of birds, the sandpipers and others of the same kind, which are very little known. Even the best and most quoted authors of works on natural history are constantly in error with regard to the names and classification of these birds, and although I do not pretend to be acquainted with all, or nearly all, the varieties, I know enough of them to perceive that the numerous changes of plumage which each species goes through, according to their age, sex, and the season of the year, have completely misled most naturalists. Indeed to know these birds perfectly requires much greater attention and more minute examination than has yet been expended upon them. Such also is the case as regards sea-gulls and some kinds of hawks, though with these the difficulty is not so great.

September 8th. The earliest day on which I ever saw widgeon in Moray was the 8th of September, on which day they flew over my head on their way from the bay to some inland lake. The flock altogether consisted of eight or nine. In the same year I killed a jack-snipe on the 16th, which is far earlier than these birds are usually seen (I have never yet ascertained that they breed in Britain), and during the next ten days I killed four others in nearly the same place, some of which were undoubtedly young birds. It may therefore be supposed that a chance pair occasionally breed in the north, as it does not seem likely that those which I killed had been bred out of the island. In no other year have I ever seen a jack-snipe before the 8th of October; even that is very early. I have made much inquiry on this subject in Sutherland and in other likely localities; but have invariably found that where the jack-snipe has been supposed to have been seen during the breeding season, it has turned out to be the dunlin, or the common snipe. Neither their eggs nor young have ever been found, nor has the old bird been seen, for a certainty, in Britain during the summer season, excepting in the case of a single disabled bird.

Their general time of arriving is October and November. They do not leave till the middle of April. This bird is not so wild as the common snipe. I have sometimes found them in the most unexpected places—in dry wood, amongst tall trees, in sandy places quite away from water, and in other as unlikely looking spots. It is a very fat little bird. When it rises it utters no cry like the common snipe, and usually pitches again very soon.

September 10th, 1847. Went up to Glenalladale. Saw several eagles among the high mountains in that country; ptarmigan also, and some deer. The stags' horns this year are by no means remarkable for size; the spring was backward, and they had not good feeding at the season when they were getting their new horns.

September 17th, 1849. I see at the swamps some sandpipers which I cannot make out. There are vast numbers of every kind of wild-fowl arriving daily, and always some peregrines hunting.

The turnstone, a bird that breeds in Norway, arrives in this country at the first commencement of the month, but appears only to make it a temporary resting-place on its way to the south. They come, however, in small numbers, and remain but a short time, appearing on most parts of the coast. They are not at all a shy bird seeming too busy in searching under the gravel and stones for the insects on which they feed to think of any danger. Their name of turnstone is well applied, as they turn over the small stones with great perseverance and rapidity. It is a compactly made bird, and of a stouter form than most of our sea-shore birds.

Like many other birds, the eagle occasionally, though rarely, exhibits great varieties in the colour of his plumage. This year (1848), during the month of September, I saw a freshly-killed sea-eagle, or white-tailed eagle, whose colour was a fine silvery white, without the slightest mixture of brown. The bird was killed in Sutherland; and I was informed that another eagle had been seen in its company with the same unusual plumage. Our specimen had quite arrived at maturity, but did not appear to be very old. Partridges, pheasants, grouse, and many small birds, occasionally appear in a snow-white dress; but the birds of prey seldom change their colour. A black swan we read of as an example of a "*rara avis;*" what must then a white crow have been thought of by the augurs and omen-seekers! Yet rooks and Jackdaws, both parti-coloured and white, are by no means so uncommon with us as to be looked on as wonders.

This white eagle had been probably bred on some of the wild rocky headlands of the north coast of Sutherland, where not even the value of the eggs can at all times induce the shepherds to attempt their capture. The sea-eagle is, in its habits, a sluggish, vulture-like bird, feeding chiefly on the dead fish and other animal substances which are cast up by the sea on these lonely and rugged shores, and seldom attacking the lambs of the farmer to the same extent as the golden eagle does. Although it is frequently seen, and its sharp bark is heard, far inland, the usual hunting-ground of the sea-eagle is along the shore, where it can feed on its foul prey, undisturbed and unseen by human eye for months together. Like the golden eagle, this bird sometimes so gorges itself with

food as to become helpless, and if then met with may be knocked down by a stick, or captured alive before it can rise from the ground—a sad and ignoble fate for the king of birds! After all, the eagle is but a sorry representative of royalty and kingly grandeur; for although his flight is noble and magnificent, and his strength and power astonishing, there is a cruelty and treachery about the disposition of the bird which render it unfit to be educated and trained like the peregrine and other falcons; nor does it ever become attached to its keeper.

It is not easy to determine the length of years bestowed on any of the wild animals. There are no specific and well-ascertained facts on which to form a valid opinion. On all such subjects the most positive *assertions* are often so ill supported by *facts* that the naturalist should be most careful and guarded as to the evidence on which he founds his opinion. It seems, however, reasonable to suppose that the age attained by all animals bears a certain proportion to the time which they take in coming to their maturity in size and strength.

Judging by this criterion, the eagle may be set down as one of the longest lived of our British birds; as he certainly does not arrive at the full maturity of his plumage for some years. On the other hand, the swan puts on her white feathers at her first moulting, yet is said to live to a very great age; and there are well-authenticated instances establishing that this is the fact. Geese, too, live to a most patriarchal age. The period of life of tame falcons does not exceed eight to ten years—at least so I am assured by some of my acquaintances who have kept these birds. A wild hawk, barring accidents from shot or trap, has probably a better chance of longevity than a domesticated bird, however carefully the latter may be tended, as it is almost impossible to hit upon the exact quantity, quality, and variety of food which best conduces to their health, or to give tame birds as large a share of exercise and bodily exertion as in their wild state they would be constrained to take in pursuit of their daily prey. Common fowls live to the age of ten or twelve years, but become useless and rheumatic after six or eight. Such, also, is the case with

pigeons. I knew of a pair who lived for fifteen years, but they were barren for some years before their death.

The length of life of small birds is probably less; but it is difficult to form an accurate opinion on this point; for any deductions founded on canaries or goldfinches in a state of confinement must be fallacious, as caged birds are subject to numerous diseases from over-eating, from improper and too little varied food, and a thousand other causes which do not affect those who live in a state of natural and healthful liberty.

It is a curious fact that one scarcely ever finds the dead body of a wild bird or animal whose death appears to have been caused by old age or any other natural cause. Nor can this result from the fact of their being consumed immediately by animals of prey, as we constantly meet with the bodies of birds who have been killed by wounds from shot, etc. Either the wild animals on the approach of death creep into hidden corners of the earth (as donkeys and postboys are said to do), or nearly all of them, before they reach extreme old age, are cut off by their common enemy, mankind, or serve as food to birds and beasts of prey.

I have, however, killed both eagles and foxes who bore unmistakable marks of extreme old age; the plumage of the former being light-coloured, thin, and worn—so worn, indeed, as to lead one to suppose that the bird could not have moulted for several seasons;—and the foxes' faces being gray and their jaws nearly toothless; yet they were still in good, and even fat condition. In animals, age and cunning supply the place of strength and activity; so that the eagle and fox are still able to live well, even when they have arrived at the most advanced age assigned to them.

Very old deer become light-coloured and grayish, especially about the head and neck, and have a bleached and worn appearance over their whole body. Their horns, also, lose much of their rich appearance both as to colour and size, becoming not only smaller, but also decreasing in the number of their points. The Highlanders assign a great age to the red deer; indeed, they seem to suppose that it has no limit, save a rifle ball; and they tell wonderful stories of famous stags, who have been seen and

(The Sunday Hack)

Going out.

known for a long series of years in certain districts. Though these accounts are doubtless much exaggerated, it is tolerably certain that their life extends to from twenty to thirty years.

I have occasionally shot roebucks, and still oftener does, showing by their size, colour, length of hoofs, etc., that they had reached a tolerable old age; but, like all persecuted animals, the chance of their attaining their full extent of days is so slight, as scarcely to give us the means of ascertaining how long they would live if secure from danger.

Sheep of seven or eight years lose their teeth, more or less, and show symptoms of their best days being past. But these, like all other domesticated animals, do not afford a good criterion to judge by, as they are all under an artificial system as to food and manner of living, which makes them, like man, subject to many diseases and causes of decay, which would not affect them in a state of nature.

September 27th, 1847. Saw peewits and swallows still in the country.

On the 28th of September (1846?) the last house-swallow took his departure from this neighbourhood, although the season was so fine that there were several nests of young greenfinches about the garden even so late as the 30th of the month, and a wood-pigeon was sitting on its eggs in an ash-tree close to the house.

During the latter weeks of the fishing season (which legally ends on the 15th of September in all the northern rivers), the lower pools of the Findhorn are full of an excellent small sea-trout, locally called the finnock. My opinion is that the "finnock" is the grilse or young of the common sea-trout, bearing exactly the same relation and affinity to that fish as the grilse does to the salmon; but the natural history of the inhabitants of another element is too uncertain and difficult a subject for a mere casual observer to enter upon. At any rate, the finnock is not only an excellent fish for the table, but affords capital sport, rising freely, and playing boldly when hooked; and has altogether strong attractions for those anglers who somewhat love their ease.

September 30th, 1846. Peewits collect in great numbers near the shore; also golden plovers. Great flocks of young gulls are seen.

RED DEER

The Red Deer of Sutherland—Stag's Horns—Calving—Poaching Deer—Roe—
Damage done to Plantations—A Dangerous Pet—Mating

The tract of country preserved as a deer forest comprises a most extensive range of mountains, the best in all Scotland for the purpose.* Reaching away to the north-west and west, the forest takes in corrie after corrie, and mountain after mountain, of the most wild and romantic character. Fitted, too, for scarcely any other purpose than as a refuge for wild animals, the most determined utilitarian could not say that the ground was wasted, nor suggest a better use to which to apply it. It is far too barren to make sheep farming remunerative, and any other way of attempting to make the mountains in that district useful to mankind would be labour thrown away.

In this fine range the red-deer daily increase in number; so much so, that I have no doubt that, unless they are systematically shot down, they will, in the course of some few years, degenerate in size and beauty from the ground being overstocked; for, although there is plenty of room in the surrounding wild mountains for the deer to distribute and disperse themselves, still so much do they dislike being disturbed, and so determinedly do they adhere to the forests where neither sheep nor shepherds annoy them, that while these quiet places are overstocked, the deer are almost wholly drained out of all the surrounding mountains. I speak here only comparatively, for of course red-deer are to be found almost everywhere throughout the county; still all the sheep-farms have far fewer deer on them than they had before the forest was made,

*That part of Sutherland that lies to the north and west of Altnaharra.

notwithstanding that the number of these animals is probably greater on the whole than it was then. Certain slopes and hill-sides even close to the main road are never without deer, and the passer by seldom travels many miles without seeing some of these noble animals. They seem used to the sight of people on the road (although so few *do* travel by it); and on a carriage coming into sight the stag scarcely stops his feeding for a longer time than is sufficient for him to take a good gaze at his natural enemy, when he again continues his rapid grazing, although perhaps not much more than a rifle-shot from the roadside. In the middle of the day the deer are seldom to be seen except by a practised eye, as they are then at rest and lying quietly, with little more than their head and neck above the rough heath. In the early morning or towards evening they feed downwards towards the grassy sides of the rivers and burns. In very hot weather the stags, tormented by midges and flies on the lower grounds, keep on the high mountains and ridges, where they have the advantage of every cool breeze that blows. Hardy as he naturally must be, the stag does not seem to like exposing himself more than is necessary to extremes of heat and cold. In this respect the hinds seem more hardy than their antlered lords. For some time after they lose their horns in the beginning of May the stags seem to feel helpless and unarmed, retiring to out-of-the-way places, where they remain as quiet and stationary as they can, not wandering far from their hiding-place, till their horns having in some measure grown, they feel more able to keep their place amongst their fellows. I have often heard people affirm that they hide their horns invariably on casting them, but this is by no means the case; the horns are constantly found; I have frequently picked them up myself, and have seen great numbers that have been found on the hills. A man walking across a rugged and extensive range of mountain cannot expect to find very often an object so little conspicuous as a stag's horn, unless he is a forester or keeper, and as such living amongst the deer at all times. There is no doubt, too, that deer have the habit of chewing and breaking up horns or bones, or any substance of the kind, that they find in their wanderings; in the same manner that cattle in a field will chew for hours together a bone, old bit of leather, or any other hard substance, to the neglect of the clover or grass, or whatever food they may be surrounded by. It is probable also that the deer trample under the heather, in the course of their working at it, any horn that comes in their way.

When about to calve, the hinds retire to the most lonely and undisturbed places, where there is little risk of their young meeting with enemies while unable to escape. For a few days they appear to keep them in these safe solitudes, visiting them little during the daytime; but as soon as the calves have acquired a certain degree of strength, they become the inseparable companions of their mothers. Where the hind is, there is the calf following its dam over hill and dale. At first they are covered with white marks, but, losing these, they are of a darkish brown, and are well clothed with long hair by the approach of the winter. Although not

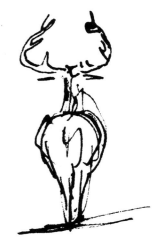

coming to full maturity for several years, the growth of young deer is very rapid for the first six or eight months. Did they not acquire strength rather quickly in proportion to their after growth, it would be impossible for them to keep company with the hinds in their numerous flights over mountainous and dangerous passes, impelled onwards by the sight or scent of some enemy real or imaginary. Eagles and foxes both make prey of the newly-born calves; though I am told that the parent will defend her young courageously and effectively against either of these enemies if she happens to be at hand when they are attacked: her manner of defence is by striking with her forefeet—a species of warfare in which the red-deer hind is a most active enemy, and difficult to cope with.

Deer, from their size and strength, are secure from the attacks of every other wild animal of the country.

Notwithstanding the vigilance and care of the foresters, who in this county are, I believe, all men of honesty and experience, the shepherds manage to kill many a deer at all seasons; nor is it possible for any number of keepers to prevent this entirely: though they may be as watchful as possible, the shepherd, from being constantly on the hill amongst the deer, and knowing by experience all their haunts at every time of day and at every season, has advantages over the keeper that no vigilance of the latter can counterbalance. A shepherd has for some days perhaps observed that a particular fine stag, with noble head and in good condition, frequents some certain grassy burn to feed in. There he grazes daily, going thither about four o'clock every evening; and having done so undisturbed several times in succession, he becomes careless, and on leaving the braeside on which he rests throughout the day, he feeds rapidly down the burnside till he arrives at the favourite spot of grass. The shepherd, knowing well that the deer will continue on this feeding spot until disturbed, watches his opportunity when the forester has taken some other direction, or has not left his home, or in fact when the coast is clear: he then takes his gun out of the stock, and easily concealing the two parts till he is safe in the solitudes of the mountain, he betakes himself to some hiding-place within an easy shot and to leeward of the place which he well knows the stag will visit at the feeding time. Having looked well to his copper cap or priming, he waits patiently till the animal is within twenty or thirty yards of him, when a handful of slugs or a bullet settles the business. The four quarters are then conveyed home as convenience and opportunity suit. If the antlers are good, they are another source of profit, there being a ready sale for them to some gun maker or bird stuffer, many of whom have constant correspondence with the shepherds, keepers, etc., for the purpose of buying deers' heads, birds' eggs, skins, etc., which they resell to visitors at Inverness, or even to sportsmen who, taking the stag's head to England with them, pass it off as a trophy of their own skill and prowess. I have known instances of this kind, although it is difficult to understand how a man can exhibit as his own shooting, and nail up over his hall-door, a stag's head, which he has bought for three or four pounds instead of shooting it, without being ashamed to behold such a memento of his own weakness and want of good faith.

In my opinion, the general run of the old stags' heads in Sutherlandshire are the handsomest of any in Scotland, in the way the horns are set on the head and in the shape of the horns themselves. The largest and oldest heads that I have seen in that county form a fine, widely-stretched circle, the tops of the antlers arching inwards towards each other. I never myself saw horns with so fine a spread and arch in any other county, though I do not pretend to say that such may not be seen elsewhere. A nobler sight than a herd of well-antlered stags standing clearly defined on the horizon, and combined with the surrounding scenery and all the *et cæteras* of the country which they inhabit, can scarcely be imagined.

As the spring advances, and the larch and other deciduous trees again put out their foliage, I see the tracks of roe* and the animals themselves in new and unaccustomed places. They now betake themselves very much to the smaller and younger plantations, where they can find plenty of one of their most favourite articles of food—the shoots of the young trees. Much as I like to see these animals (and certainly the roebuck is the most perfectly formed of all deer), I must confess that they commit great havoc in plantations of hard wood. As fast as the young oak trees put out new shoots the roe nibble them off, keeping the trees from growing above three or four feet in height by constantly biting off the leading shoot. Besides this, they peel the young larch with both their teeth and horns, stripping them of their bark in the neatest manner imaginable. One can scarcely wonder at the anathemas uttered against them by proprietors of young plantations. Always graceful, a roebuck is peculiarly so when stripping some young tree of its leaves, nibbling them off one by one in the most delicate and dainty manner. I have watched a roe strip the leaves off a long bramble shoot, beginning at one end and nibbling off every leaf. My rifle was aimed at his heart and my finger was on the trigger, but I made some excuse or other to myself for not killing him, and left him undisturbed—his beauty saved him. The leaves and flowers of the wild rose-bush are another favourite food of the roe.

Just before they produce their calves the does wander about a great deal, and seem to avoid the society of the buck, though they remain together during the whole autumn and winter. The young roe is soon able to escape from most of its enemies. For a day or two it is quite helpless, and frequently falls a prey to the fox, who at that time of the year is more ravenous than at any other, as it then has to find food to satisfy the carnivorous appetites of its own cubs.

A young roe, when caught unhurt, is not difficult to rear, though their great tenderness and delicacy of limb makes it not easy to handle them without injuring them. They soon become perfectly tame and attach themselves to their master. When in captivity they will eat almost anything that is offered to them, and from this cause are frequently destroyed, picking up and swallowing some indigestible substance about the house. A tame buck, however, becomes a dangerous pet; for after attaining to his full strength he is very apt to make use of it in attacking people whose appearance he does not like. They particularly single out women and children as their victims, and inflict severe and dangerous wounds with their sharp-pointed horns, and notwithstanding their small size, their strength and activity make them a very unpleasant adversary.

Though they generally prefer the warmest and driest part of the

*Roe have the first year one antler, second year two antlers, third year three antlers. This is always the case unless some accident happens to them. Sometimes they have four antlers, but seldom. The growth of the horns of all deer is irregular, depending much on the feeding which they get.—C. St. J.

August —   Teal   Missel Thrush

Ring Dotterel. Nairn. May 1847

Nov. 16/47

Black headed bunting
w. Findhorn /47

woods to lie in, I have sometimes started roe in the marshy grounds, where they lie close in the tufts of long heather and rushes.

Being much tormented with ticks and wood-flies, they frequently in the hot weather betake themselves not only to these marshy places, but even to the fields of high corn, where they sit in a form like a hare. Being good swimmers, they cross rivers without hesitation in their way to and from their favourite feeding-places; indeed, I have often known roe pass across the river daily, living on one side, and going to feed every evening on the other. Though very much attached to each other, and living mostly in pairs, I have known a doe take up her abode for several years in a solitary strip of wood. Every season she crossed a large extent of hill to find a mate, and returned after two or three weeks' absence. When her young ones, which she produced every year, were come to their full size, they always went away, leaving their mother in solitary possession of her wood.

Where numerous, roe are very mischievous to both corn and turnips, eating and destroying great quantities, and as they feed generally in the dark, lying still all day, their devastations are difficult to guard against. Their acute sense of smelling enables them to detect the approach of any danger, when they bound off to their coverts, ready to return as soon as it is past. In April they go great distances to feed on the clover-fields, where the young plants are then just springing up. In autumn, the ripening oats are their favourite food, and in winter, the turnips, wherever these crops are at hand, or within reach from the woods.

The difference in the colour and kind of hair that a roe's skin is covered with, at different seasons of the year, is astonishingly great. From May to October they are covered with bright red-brown hair, and but little of it. In winter their coat is a fine dark mouse-colour, very long and close, but the hair is brittle, and breaks easily in the hand like dried grass.

OCTOBER

Fine Weather in October—A Pigeon's Nest—Quail—Geese going South—Spawning Trout—Starlings—Hawks—Peregrine and Mallard—Ospreys—The Bohemian Waxwing

October is, in this country, one of the finest months of the whole year. The cold cutting winds of November are frequently preceded by bright, clear, sunshiny weather most enjoyable and invigorating to all whose avocations and amusements keep them much in the open air. The birds, both migratory and stationary, begin now to establish themselves in their winter quarters; and scarcely a day passes which is not marked by the arrival or departure, or the winter preparations of some of the feathered races in this country.

October 4th. During the mild season of 1847, I found a pair of young wood-pigeons in a nest near the house. A few days afterwards they were both dead, either from the old birds having been killed, or from the coldness of one or two of the succeeding days.

The rats return to the houses from the fields and the ditches.

Three or four quails were killed at the beginning of October, in the eastern part of the county. During the month of May I constantly heard the call of the old birds close to my house; and we saw them several times basking in the sun on one of the gravel walks.

Though I have never found their nest in this country, every spring, during the months of May and June, I hear and sometimes see the quails in the young corn and grass fields. Scarcely a shooting-season passes, too, without two or three or more being killed, more particularly in the flat country near Duffus. I also heard of one instance of a quail being killed in the neighbourhood of Cawdor in December. The spring call of the quail, though low and musical, is to be heard at a considerable distance. I have often had to follow the sound over several fields before I have reached the actual spot where it came from. This call consists of two soft notes like a whistle. Quails have always been remarkable for two peculiarities. One is the immense flights which migrate to the coast of Africa, the Grecian Islands, Turkey, etc. etc. These migratory flocks still afford food and an object of pursuit to thousands during their continuance; and countless must the numbers be of these birds, though not quite making credible the account of Pliny, that "the quails alight in such numbers on the rigging of ships as to sink them by their weight." The ancient Romans and Greeks seem to have been as fond of fighting quails as the Chinese, the Afghans, and other eastern nations still are— the bird still keeping up its character for pugnacity.

October 11th and 12th. Large flocks of wild geese passed to the south. There was at the time a considerable sprinkling of snow on the Ross and Sutherland mountains. None of the gray or bean geese seemed to alight anywhere in this neighbourhood during the autumn; but a flock of that very beautiful species the white-fronted goose took up their quarters about the fresh-water lakes.

18th. Spawning trout get into all the small ditches, and wherever they find running water. Hen-harriers and other hawks come down and hunt the low grounds. Redwings arrive in middle, fieldfares about the last week of the month.

A single very large wild swan appeared on the lakes on the 18th of October, and on the 20th he was joined by two more. The wild swans, on their first arrival, almost always fly into the bay from the south, coming in flocks of one hundred to two hundred together. The only way I can account for this, knowing that they must of necessity have taken their flight from the north, is, by supposing that they first alight on some of the mountain lakes between Findhorn and Strathspey. A large flight of these noble birds, as they circle round the fresh-water lakes on their first arrival, is one of the most beautiful sights imaginable. There is, too, a wild harmony in their bugle-like cry, as they wheel round and round, now separating into small companies, as each family of five or six seems inclined to alight, and now all joining again in a long undulating line, waiting for the word of command from some old leader, whose long acquaintance with the country and its dangers constitutes him a swan of note among the common herd. At last this leader makes up his mind to alight, and in a few moments the whole flock are gradually sinking down on the calm loch. After a brief moment or two spent in looking round them, with straight and erect necks, they commence sipping the water, and turning their flexible necks into a thousand graceful curves and attitudes.

In October and November clouds of starlings frequently roost in the reeds of Loch Spynie; as the dusk of evening comes on they wheel to and fro, sometimes settling on, and again rising from the reeds, till at last having arranged themselves to their satisfaction they remain quiet for the night. I was amused one evening by watching the attempts of a merlin to catch one out of an immense flock of starlings. The hawk appeared to have fixed his eye on one particular bird, and endeavoured to single it out from the rest. The pursued starling, however, whenever his pursuer was near overtaking it, dashed into the middle of the flock, when all its companions, to the number of many hundreds, closed round it in the air, forming a perfectly compact body like a solid mass, every bird uttering a loud scream simultaneously. In this manner they completely puzzled and beat off the hawk.

October 13th, 1849. I see in the loch scaup, pochard, and pintail, widgeon, teal, mallard, and golden eye, etc.

October is the month when the greatest number of widgeon arrive in the bay; and the mallards, also, keep up a constant quacking and calling on the sands. Every evening at sunset, or soon afterwards, the mallards fly to the stubble fields, preferring those where there is the least quantity of grass to cover the scattered grains. The water ouzels now come down to the burns near the sea; and these merry little birds resort to the very same stones year after year. They appear to be regular attendants on the small streams and burns where the trout spawn.

Grouse in October and September feed very much in the stubble fields, and are snared and trapped in great numbers by the shepherds and others, who have small oat fields far up in the hills; they frequently leave some of the sheaves on the ground for the express purpose of catching the grouse. The usual manner is with horse-hair nooses; they put a great number of these snares on each sheaf of corn, and catch dozens of grouse in a morning.

Immediately on the retiring of a flood in the river, great numbers of snipes are seen on the mud and refuse left by the water, feeding busily. Where they come from is difficult to say, as at this season, except on these occasions, we have no great abundance of these birds. Redshanks, in considerable flocks, follow their example. On the 16th I see redwings in the hedges; fieldfares do not appear until ten days afterwards. The wood-pigeons now fly considerable distances to feed on acorns.

Late in the afternoon I constantly see the roe feeding on those clover fields where there is sufficient second growth to attract them. They have now lost their red summer coat, and have put on their beautiful mouse-coloured winter covering, though the hair has not yet acquired its full length. As the leaves fall from the birch and oak woods the roe quit them, and take to the fir plantations, where they have more quiet and shelter. The foresters accuse these animals of being very destructive to their young oak-trees; and fond as I am of them, I am afraid I must admit the accusation is just, as they undoubtedly prefer the topmost shoot of a young oak-tree to almost any other food. Nevertheless, the mischief done to the woods by roe is trifling when compared to that of rabbits. Many an acre is obliged to be replanted owing to their destructive nibbling; and in some of the beautiful woods of Brodie, I saw the fine holly-trees of many years' growth, with stems of six inches in diameter, killed dead by being barked by rabbits.

October, 1849. The sea-gulls of every variety are very numerous, also sandpipers. Peregrine, merlin, sparrowhawk, kestrel, and hen-harrier daily. I hear of other hawks, but see these.

October 19th, 1847. Swans (*i.e.* one swan) and numbers of geese appear.

Most of the hill-bred hawks come down to hunt the fields, which are clear of corn, and also to feed on the plovers, etc., which frequent the shore. I sometimes see the peregrine in pursuit of wild ducks; and to-day I observed one give chase to an old mallard. The pursuit was rather curious, reversing the usual order of things, as the falcon's great object was to keep below the mallard instead of above him; the duck endeavouring all he could to get to the water, in which case he knew, as the hawk did also, that his chance of escape would be the greatest. Once in the water, his own element, by diving and swimming he would soon have baffled his pursuer. I don't know what was the end of the chase; the last I saw of them they were winging their way at a tremendous rate straight across the sea for the opposite coast of Ross. Either the hawk was not willing to strike his prey while over the water, or the mallard had a vigour of wing which enabled him to keep ahead of his murderous enemy.

[165]

My tame peregrine, after some years of perfect friendship and alliance with our pet owl, ended in killing and eating her! a piece of ungenerous barbarism which I should not have suspected so fine a bird would have committed. They seemed to have quarrelled over the remains of some bird that was given them for food. At any rate all that remained of the poor owl was a leg and some of the longer feathers.

At this season the osprey is sometimes seen soaring, with its kestrel-like flight, along the course of the river. I occasionally see one hovering over the lower pools; but, in general, this bird is seen here only *in transitu* from one side of the country to the other. The golden eagle, too, passes on his way at this season from north to south, frequently attended by a rabble rout of gray crows, who, when they have pursued the kingly bird for a certain distance, give up the chase, which is immediately taken up by a fresh band, who in their turn pass him over to new assailants. It would appear that each set follows him as long as he is within their own especial district, like country constables passing on a sturdy vagrant from one parish to another.

October 27th, 1847. The golden plovers collect in great flocks on the banks of the river to enjoy the morning sun.

The Bohemian waxwing or chatterer visits us at irregular and at long intervals. When it does appear, it is usually in considerable numbers, not in large flocks, but widely scattered. They feed on the berries of the hawthorn, mountain ash, and similar fruits. While flying from tree to tree, or perched on a topmost bough, they frequently utter a peculiar though not loud note, which at once strikes on the ear of the ornithologist as the cry of a strange bird. They are not at all shy. The name of waxwing indicates this beautiful little bird more decisively than that of chatterer, the most striking peculiarity in the bird being the small bright red appendages to their secondaries, giving the points of these feathers the appearance of having been dipped in sealing-wax.

OCTOBER WALK

Birds on the Sea-shore—Goosanders—The Peewits Leave—Gulls on the Shore—View of Cromarty Firth—The Sandhills of Moray—Seals—Their Scarcity—Habits—Arrival of the Swans—A Fox—Mallard Flighting

One of my most favourite walks is along the shore, beginning at the mouth of the river and following the edge of the bay till I reach the open firth; then, after continuing along the beach for three or four miles, I return through the wild uncultivated ground which divides the sea-shore from the arable lands. At this season the variety of birds which are to be seen in the course of this walk is astonishing. Bright and bracing is the autumn morning; the robin sings joyously and fearlessly from the topmost twig of some rosebush, as I pass through the garden, while the thrushes and blackbirds are busily employed in turning up the leaves which already begin to strew the walks as they search in conscious security for the gray snails, repaying us for the strawberries and cherries they have robbed us of; and welcome are they to their share of fruit in the season of plenty.

The partridges as I pass through the field seem aware that I am bent on a quiet walk of observation; and instead of rising and flying off as I pass them, simply lower their heads till I am beyond them, and then begin feeding again on the stubbles.

Looking quietly over the bank of the river, I see a couple of goosanders fishing busily at the tail of a pool. After watching them for a short time, as they fish for small trout, I walk on. If, however, I show any portion of my figure above the bank, their quick eye detects me, and after gazing for half a minute with erect neck, they fly off; at first flapping the surface of the water, or almost running along it; and then gradually rising, wend their way to a few pools higher up the river, where, alighting, they recommence their fishing.

The golden-eye duck and the morillon also are frequently seen diving for shell-fish and weed in the deep quiet pools, but never fishing in the shallow parts of the river like the goosander.

The peewits do not leave us till quite the end of October, and during most of the month are in immense numbers on the sands near the mouth of the river. In the dusk of the evening they, as well as the golden plover, leave the sands, and take to the fields in search of worms and snails, generally frequenting the ploughed land or the grass-fields. As I pass along the shore of the bay, large flocks of widgeon fly to and fro as the ebb-tide leaves uncovered the small grassy island and banks. Unlike the mallard and teal, both which are night-feeding birds, the widgeon feeds at any hour of the day or night indiscriminately, not waiting for the dusk to commence his search for food, but grazing like geese on the grass whenever he can get at it. Although towards the end of winter the shyest of all water-fowl, the widgeon, at this season, may be easily approached, and with a little care may be closely watched as they swim to and fro from bank to bank; sometimes landing, and at other times cropping the grass as they swim along the edge. If a pair of mallards is amongst the flock, the drake's green head is soon seen to rise up above the rest, as his watchfulness is seldom long deceived; with low quacking he warns his mate, and the two then rise, giving an alarm to the widgeon. The latter, after one or two rapid wheels in the air, return to their feeding-ground, but the mallards fly off to a considerable distance before they stop.

In crossing the sands of the bay to the neck of sandy ground that divides it from the main sea, there are many runs of water to be waded, some caused by the river itself, which branches out into numerous small streams which intersect the sands, and some made by two good-sized brooks which empty themselves into the bay. In all these streams there are innumerable flounders, large and small, which dart as quick as lightning from under your feet. Their chief motive power seems to lie in their broad tails, with which they propel themselves along at a wonderful rate; then suddenly stopping, they in an instant bury themselves in the sand; and it is only a very sharp eye that can detect the exact spot where they are by observing their outline faintly marked on the sand in which they are ensconced: sometimes also their two prominent eyes may be discovered in addition to their outline.

It is a favourite amusement with my boys in the summer to hunt and spear the flounders which remain at low water in the pools and runs of water in the bay. On a calm day, by wading to where the water is a foot or two in depth, they kill, with the assistance of a long light spear, a basketful of good-sized fish.

The large gulls keep up a system of surveillance over all the calm pools at low water, hovering over them, and pouncing down like hawks on any fish which may be left in them. As the tide ebbs, numbers of herons, also, come down to the water's edge, and keeping up step by step with the receding tide, watch for any fish or marine animal that may suit their appetite. It is amusing to observe these birds as they stride slowly and deliberately in knee-deep water, with necks outstretched, intent on their prey, their gray shadowy figures looking more like withered sticks than living creatures.

As for curlews, peewits, sandpipers, *et id genus omne*, their numbers in the bay are countless. Regularly as the tide begins to ebb do thousands of these birds leave the higher banks of sand and shingle on which they have been resting and betake themselves to the wet sands in search of their food; and immense must be the supply which every tide throws up, or leaves exposed, to afford provision to them all. Small shell-fish, shrimps, sea-worms, and other insects, form this wondrous abundance. Every bird, too, out of those countless flocks is not only in good order, but is covered with fat, showing how well the supply is proportioned to the demand; indeed, in the case of all wild birds it is observable that they are invariably plump and well-conditioned, unless prevented by some wound or injury from foraging for themselves.

On the mussel scalps are immense flocks of oyster-catchers, brilliant with their black and white plumage, and bright red bill, and a truly formidable weapon must that bill be to mussel or cockle; it is long and powerful, with a sharp point as hard as ivory, which driven in by the full strength of the bird's head and neck, must penetrate like a wedge into the shell of the strongest shell-fish found on these shores.

Beautiful, surpassingly beautiful, is the view before me, as I rest myself on a height of the sand-hills facing towards the north. The bright and calm sea close at hand, and the variously-shaped and variously-coloured cliffs and rocks of Cromarty and Ross, at a distance in reality of twelve or fifteen miles, but which, as the sun shines full upon them, appear to be very much nearer, and all these are backed by mountains of every form and outline, but of a uniform deep blue tipped with white peaks. The sea as smooth as a mirror, except where some sea-fowl suddenly splashes down into the water, making a few silvery circles, which soon disappear. Every here and there is a small flock of the long-tailed duck, diving and sporting in the sea, and uttering their strange but musical cry as they chase each other, swimming rapidly in small circles or taking short flights close above the surface; the whole flock dropping all at once into the water as if shot, not alighting gradually like the mallard and other ducks.

The rabbits which inhabit these sand-hills are certainly larger and heavier than those living in the more cultivated country, though their food must consist almost entirely of dry bent, with the variety of a little seaweed and the furze bushes, which they eat into numerous shapes, like footstools, ottomans, etc.

Foxes, almost as tall and powerful as greyhounds, frequent this desert region; and their fresh tracks are seen after every tide close to the sea-

shore, whither they have been in search of cast-up fish, wounded wild-fowl, and suchlike.

I never pass over these sand-hills without endeavouring to raise some new theory respecting their origin, and what was the state of the country which they now cover. That beneath the accumulation of sand there has once been a range of fertile fields, cannot be doubted, as in different places are seen furrows and other well-defined traces of cultivated land; yet no account exists of the destruction of these fields by the inroad of the sand; evidently the change was accomplished suddenly. In many parts of this sandy region there are distinct marks of rushing waters; ridges of both sand and shingle are cast up in a manner which could only have been effected by some tremendous rush of water; and strange pyramids of stones also are heaped up in several places, to all appearance by the same agency.

So fine and dry is the sand which composes the hillocks and plains of this curious district, that every beetle and fly that walks or crawls over its surface in calm and dry weather leaves its track as distinctly marked on the finely-pulverised particles, as the rabbit or hare does on snow. The footprints of the lizards, which abound, are very neatly and distinctly marked, till the first breath of wind drifting the sand erases the impressions.

Few remains of antiquity have ever been found here; indeed, these sands are rarely trodden by any foot save that of some poacher in search of rabbits. I have, however, seen a most curious bracelet-like ornament which was found here. It is made of fine bronze, in the shape of a snake, which, it has been supposed, had a head at each extremity, formed of some precious stone; these, however, are lost, the fastenings having corroded. In shape this relic appeared to me to resemble one of the bands which bound together the fasces carried by a Roman lictor. On further examination it has, I believe, been ascertained that the bronze must have encircled some ornament or weapon of wood, which has rotted away, leaving nothing but the more durable metal.

It has twice happened to me to find human skeletons, or rather the remains of skeletons, lying on the sand, laid bare by some drifting wind, or half disinterred by the subterraneous proceedings of the rabbits. In both cases the remains were evidently of great antiquity, but had been preserved by the dry sand.

Those curiously carved pieces of flint called elf-arrows are not uncommon in some parts of the sand-hills.

On one part of the sands, which forms a peninsula at low water, but an island when it is high, I perhaps discover two or three seals lying. Clumsy-looking as they are, at the slightest alarm they scuffle off with great rapidity into the water. Once there they feel secure, and rising at a short distance from the shore, they take a good look at the intruder on their domain. Ugly and misshapen as a seal appears on land, he is when in the water by no means an unsightly animal; and he floats and dives with a quiet rapidity which appears marvellous to the looker-on. You see a seal's head appear above the water; in a minute or two you are startled by its rising quietly in quite a different direction; and after gazing intently at you for a few moments with its dark, mild eyes, the sleek shining head disappears again below the surface without making a ripple on the water, leaving you almost in doubt as to whether it is a seal or a mermaid. The Highlanders, however, are by no means prepossessed in favour of the good looks of a seal, or "sealgh," as they pronounce the word. "You are nothing but a sealgh," is a term of reproach which, when given by one fishwoman to another, is considered the direst insult, and a climax to every known term of abuse.

It is curious to observe the seals resting on some shallow, with only their heads above the water, and their noses elongated into a proboscis-like shape. They will frequently lie in this manner for hours together, until the return of the tide either floats them off their resting-place, or some other cause induces them to shift their quarters.

Within the memory of some of the people here, seals were very numerous about this part of the coast, and were constantly killed by the farmers for the sake of their oil, and with no weapons except their hoes or spades, with which they attacked them when lying on the sand-banks. It is but seldom that I see them resting on the shore, but occasionally watch them in that situation, as they either lie sleeping on the banks or play about, which, notwithstanding their unwieldy appearance, they sometimes do. At other times they engage in the most determined battles with each other, fighting like bulldogs, and uttering loud mournful cries.

The young appear about July. When first born they are nearly white, and the hair is rough and long: they gradually become spotted and of a darker colour, like the old ones. The very young ones that I have seen here were probably born about the rocks and caves of the Ross-shire coast. Some rocks off the coast near Gordonston were till very lately the constant resort of seals, but owing to workmen having been employed there of late years in building a lighthouse and other works, they very seldom rest on them at present.

I have frequently been told that the seal cannot remain under water for more than a quarter of an hour without coming to the surface to breathe. I am, however, confident that this is not the case, and that he can continue for hours under the water when lying undisturbed and at rest. If caught and entangled in a net, he is soon exhausted and drowned.

I was assured by a man who was constantly in pursuit of seals, that one day, having found a very young one left by its mother on the rocks, near Lossiemouth, he put it into a deep round hole full of water left by the receding tide. For two hours, during which he waited, expecting to see the old female come in with the flow of the tide, the little animal remained, as he expressed it, "like a stone" at the bottom of the water, without moving or coming to the surface to breathe. He then took it out, and found it as well and lively as ever; and on turning it loose into the sea it at once began swimming about with some other young ones.

A seal has a very acute scent, and can never be approached from the windward. I conceive that their eyesight is less perfect; at any rate they are endowed with a certain dangerous curiosity which makes them approach and reconnoitre any object which they may have seen at a little distance and do not quite understand. I have seen a seal swim up to within twenty yards of a dog on the shore, for the purpose apparently of examining him, as an unknown animal. Music, too, or any uncommon or loud noise attracts them, and they will follow for a considerable distance the course of a boat in which any loud musical instrument is played, putting up their heads and listening with great eagerness to the unknown strains. I have even seen them approach boldly to the shore where a bagpiper was playing, and continue to swim off and on at a hundred yards' distance.

Notwithstanding their wariness and the difficulty of capturing them, seals are gradually diminishing in number, and will soon disappear from our coasts. This is owing chiefly to the constant warfare carried on against them by the salmon-fishers, who either destroy them or frighten them away from their fishing stations.

On the neck of land at which we have now arrived there is a hut inhabited during the season by a couple of salmon-fishers, whose business it is to attend to the stake-net, which stretches out from near their hut into the sea. A lonely life these men must lead from March to September, varied only by visits from or to their comrades, who are stationed at the depôt of ice at Findhorn, where the fish caught are deposited till a sufficient quantity is ready to load one of their quick-sailing vessels for London. But if their life is lonely it is not idle, as the exposed situation of their nets renders them liable to constant injury from wind and sea. At every low tide the men scramble and wade to the end or trap part of the net to take out the fish which have been caught, and to scrape of the net the quantity of seaweed that has adhered to it during the last tide. Although they do not always find salmon, they are seldom so unlucky as not to catch a number of goodly-sized flounders,

which fall to the share of the fishermen themselves; and perhaps once or twice in the season a young seal gets entangled and puzzled in the windings of the net, and is drowned in it. More frequently, however, the twine is damaged and torn by the larger seals, who are too strong and cunning to be so easily caught.

Frequently on this barren peninsula I have fallen in with a small colony of field-mice. They are in shape like the common large-headed and short-tailed mouse, which is so destructive in gardens, but of a brighter and lighter colour. These little animals must live on the seeds of the bent and on such dead fish as they may fall in with.

The sea in this bay, as well as in other similar ones on the coast, runs in so rapidly that unless one keeps a good look-out, there is a chance of being surrounded by the water, and detained till an hour or two after the tide begins to ebb again.

The first flock of swans which I have seen this season are just arriving in a long, undulating line. As they come over the sands where they will probably rest for the night the whole company sets up a simultaneous concert of trumpet-like cries; and after one or two wheels round the place, light down on the sand, and immediately commence pluming themselves and putting their feathers in order after their long and weary flight from the wild morasses of the north. After a short dressing of feathers and resting a few minutes, the whole beautiful flock stretch their wings again and rise gradually into the air, but to no great height, their pinions sounding loud as they flap along the shallow water before getting well on wing. They then fly off, led by instinct or the experience of former years, to where a small stream runs into the bay, and where its waters have not yet mingled with the salt sea. There they alight, and drink and splash about to their hearts' content. This done, they waddle out of the stream, and after a little stretching of wings and arranging of plumage, standing in a long row, dispose themselves to rest, every bird with head and long neck laid on its back, with the exception of one unfortunate individual, who, by a well-understood arrangement, stands with erect neck and watchful eye to guard his sleeping companions. They have, however, a proper sense of justice, and relieve guard regularly, like a well-disciplined garrison.

A desert of moss, heather, and stunted fir-trees, which takes an hour to walk through, affords little worthy of note, with the exception of that fine fellow of a fox who, as we pass on, surveys us from a hillock well out of reach. The gray crows flying and croaking over his head first called my attention to him. Nothing is to be seen now but the top of his head and the tips of his ears, as he lowers himself down gradually and quietly the moment he sees me look in his direction. But my dog has got the scent; and off he goes in a vain pursuit. Tractable and well broken as he is with regard to game, no sooner does he perceive the inciting odour of a fox or otter, than, heedless of call or threat, he is off in pursuit. Look now! away goes the fox at a quick but easy gallop, through the swamp, with his tail (*Anglicè* brush) well up in the air. A fox is always a great dandy about his brush; and keeps it free from wet and dirt as long as he possibly can: a sure sign of poor Reynard beginning to feel distressed is his brush appearing soiled and blackened. Ah! the dog has got on his scent again, and begins to press hard on his chase; but as I well know he has not the slightest chance against the light-heeled fox, who is always in racing condition, whereas the retriever, with his curly coat and good living, will be blown before he has run a mile, I continue my walk. Presently the dog returns panting like a porpoise; and, conscious of his irregular conduct, before he takes his usual place at my side, stops behind a little while, wagging his tail, and grinning in the most coaxing manner imaginable, till he has examined my face with that skill in physiognomy which all dogs possess; then seeing that I cannot help smiling at him, he jumps boldly up to me, knowing that he is forgiven.

As I approach home, and the evening comes on, several small flocks of wild ducks pass with whistling pinion over my head, on their way to some well-known stubble. The barley fields appear to be their favourite feeding ground at this season, probably because there is always more barley left on the ground than any other kind of grain.

The ferryman at the river where I pass tells me that he "is thinking that I have had a long travel, but that I have not got much *ven-ni-son*." In both surmises he is not far wrong, but I have enjoyed my long and rough walk as much—ay, and much more—than I should have done the best battue in Norfolk, or the best day's grouse-shooting in Perthshire.

NOVEMBER

Arrival of the Snow Bunting—A Tomtit—The Butcher Bird—Otter's Tracks—Stormy Weather—The Black-throated Diver—Habits of Hares—Golden Plover

November, month though it be of cold winds and sleet, is generally ushered in by flocks of that beautiful little bird the snow bunting. For three successive years I have first seen this winter visitor on the 1st of November, which is another instance of the regularity of birds in their migrations.

I do not know whether they arrive during the night, but I have constantly heard their note after it has been quite dark, the birds being at the time on wing; and this sometimes occurs several hours after nightfall.

When the snow-buntings first arrive, they are of a much darker colour than they are afterwards as the winter advances. If there is much snow, they put on a white plumage immediately. I do not know how this change of colour is effected, but it is very visible, and appears to depend entirely on the severity of the season. They feed a great deal on the shore. When flying they keep in close rank, but as soon as they alight the whole company instantly disperse, and run (not jump, like many small birds) quickly about in search of their food, which consists principally of small insects and minute seeds. They often pitch to look for these on the barest parts of the sand-hills, the dry sands always producing a number of small flies and beetles. They leave us late, some remaining till the first week of May.

November 5th, 1846. A beautiful little blue tomtit has taken up his abode voluntarily in the drawing-room. It would seem that at first he was attracted by the few house flies which at this season crawl slowly about the windows. These he was most active in searching for and catching, inserting his little bill into every corner and crevice, and detecting every fly which had escaped the brush of the housemaid. He soon, however, with increased boldness, came down to pick up crumbs, which the children placed for him close to me upon the table where I am writing, looking up into my face without the least apparent fear. From his activity and perseverance in exterminating flies, this bird appears well worthy of protection.

November 4th, 1846. Several peewits still remaining.

The thrushes, and blackbirds too, earn the favour of the gardener by their constant destruction of snails, in search of which, at this season, they are all day busily employed in turning over the dead leaves under the garden walls, and at the bottom of the hedges.

Last winter I saw a great ash-coloured shrike or butcher-bird in my orchard. The gardener told me that he had seen it for some hours in pursuit of the small birds, and I found lying about the walls two or three chaffinches, which had been killed and partly eaten, in a style unlike the performance of any bird of prey that I am acquainted with; so much so, indeed, that before I saw the butcher-bird, my attention was called to their dead bodies by the curious manner in which they seemed to have been pulled to pieces.

This is the season at which partridges migrate from the high grounds to the cultivated fields. Fresh unbroken coveys frequently appear near the mouth of the river: sometimes they come in flocks of twenty or thirty. In damp weather these birds seek the dry and warm ground on the sandy places about the lower islands, and appear entirely to desert the fields except at feeding time.

November 8th, 1846. By the edge of the river are tracks of four otters, two old and two young. They are evidently newly arrived, and will probably remain feeding about the mouth of the river till a flood drives them away. There are two or three small hillocks the size of molehills near the river, to which the otters invariably resort, and it seems that whenever an otter arrives in that part of the river, however great a stranger he may be, or however long an interval may have elapsed since an otter has visited the hillock, the new-comer goes out of the water to examine the place, as if the animal wished to judge by the freshness or staleness of the marks on it what likelihood there may be of any other otters being in the neighbourhood.

November 17th. Young otters are caught now apparently not three weeks old. I have before this fancied that the otter breeds at various seasons, not regularly, like most wild animals.

The trout now betake themselves to every running stream, working their way up the narrowest rills, in order to place their spawn.

In a creek of the sea where I sometimes watch for seals, I have seen two or three come in with the flow of the tide. After playing about for a short

Guillemot
near Nairn June 1847
H. C. St. John

Female Goosander Loch
Dun Droes
March
Nairn

71

time, they have disappeared under the water, and have not shown themselves again till the receding tide has warned them that it was time to leave the place. From the situation they were in, and the calmness of the water, the seals could scarcely have put up their noses to breathe without my having seen them. Apparently they sank to the bottom in a certain part of the bay, in order to be at rest, and remained there till the ebb was pretty far advanced, when they reappeared in the same place where I had lost sight of them, perhaps some hours before. It was a curious and amusing sight to see these great creatures swim up within a few yards of the ambuscade which I had erected close to the narrow entrance where the tide came in to fill the bay.

A flock of seals playing and fighting on a sandbank is one of the drollest sights which I know in this country. Their uncouth cries and movements are unlike anything else. In the Dornoch Firth and near Tain there are still great numbers of them, and every fine day they are in large flocks on the sandbanks; but on this coast they have been very much thinned off. My keeper tells me, that when he was a boy their number was very great, and that the inhabitants of the place could always kill as many as they wanted for oil, and for their skins, picking out the largest, and sparing the smaller ones; but, alas! cheap guns and salmon-fisheries have combined to make them scarce. Formerly, also, in the pools left by the sea within the old bar of Findhorn, numbers of seals were left at every ebb of the tide, and the farmers occasionally went down and killed a few to supply themselves with oil for the winter.

November 27th. Any unusual number of wild-fowl in the bay at this season generally prognosticates stormy weather or snow. I saw nearly fifty wild swans swimming and flying between this place and the town of Findhorn; and some large flocks of geese were passing over to the south.

[177]

The next day the ground was covered with snow, an unusual occurrence at this season. Of these swans one flock of six established themselves in the fresh-water lakes between this and Nairn, and the rest held on their way to the south. The Icelanders hail the appearance of the wild swan in the same manner as we do that of the cuckoo or swallow; it being with them the foreteller of spring and genial weather; whilst here they are connected in our minds with storms and snow-clad fields.

November 28th. The ground, as I anticipated from seeing the swans, is covered with snow.

The frost and snow send all the mallards down from the hill lakes to the bay.

The black-throated diver, though a smaller bird than the great northern diver, is equally beautiful in its plumage. It breeds on Lochindorb, but on no other loch in this district. On the northern lochs they breed very commonly, though generally only one pair frequents the same loch.

During the month of May, on a fine calm evening, I have seen great numbers of these birds in the Bay of Tongue, in Sutherland. The rocks and hillsides resound with their singular and wild cry, as they seem to be holding a noisy consultation as to their future movements. The cry is most peculiar and startling. I could scarcely persuade my companion, who was not used to these birds, that the sounds did not arise from a number of people shouting and laughing—till I pointed out to him the birds splashing and playing on the calm surface of the beautiful bay. As the evening advanced the divers gradually dispersed, going in pairs, after a few circles in the air over the bay, in a direct and rapid course, and at a great height over the surrounding mountains, each pair evidently wending their way to some well-known mountain loch, where their breeding quarters were decided upon. As each pair left the bay, the remaining birds seemed with one accord to salute their retiring companions with a universal shout of mingled laughter, howling, and every other earthly and unearthly cry. During their flight they frequently uttered a short shrill bark-like cry. On a quiet day this bird seems to rise with some difficulty from a small lake. But when the wind is high and the water rough they take flight with great readiness. Once on wing they fly very rapidly.

Owing to the value placed on both the skin and eggs of this bird by collectors, it becomes scarcer every year.

Hares have some peculiar habits which, from the animal itself being so common, are not often remarked, as few look on a hare as anything more than an article of food, whereas it is as interesting and beautiful a creature as exists. One peculiarity is that they have a particular fancy for sitting near houses, undeterred by the noise of the men and dogs who may inhabit them. When found sitting a hare sometimes seems fascinated in an extraordinary manner by the eye of a person looking at her. As long as you keep your eye fixed on that of the hare, and approach her from the front, she appears afraid to move, and, indeed, will sometimes allow herself to be taken up by the hand. A hare, when dogs are near her, is particularly unwilling to start from her form.

November 28th. Late in the evening the golden plovers come in considerable numbers to the bare grass fields to feed during the night; but when the ground is hardened by frost, they resort to the sands at the ebb-tide, both by night and day. Whilst the tide is high, these birds fly up to the hills, resting on those places where the heather is short; and they leave the hills for the sands as soon as the sea has receded sufficiently; and yet their principal resting-place is fully five miles inland.

I have observed the same instinct in the female sheldrakes when sitting on their eggs. Although several feet underground, they know to a moment when the tide has sufficiently ebbed, and then, and only then, do they leave their nest to snatch a hasty meal on the cockles, etc., which they find on the sands.

Though breeding in the wildest and most lofty districts, the golden plover comes down to the sea-shore and the low country as soon as the young are strong. Very early in the spring the plover utters its wild but soft note which distinguishes it from all other birds, resembling the whistle of a song bird. In the spring time, when they live wholly on the mountains, it is very interesting to see the golden plovers leave slope after slope as the evening shades steal over them, flying to the ridges still exposed to the warmth of the sun, collecting finally on the points which catch the last rays, and when everything is in shadow the birds fly down to feed on the swampy flats.

November 30th, 1852. I find the crops of the wood-pigeon full of the seed of the dock, although there is a great extent of newly-sown wheat in every direction.

INSTINCTS OF BIRDS AND ANIMALS

How Birds Conceal their Nests—The Camouflage of Eggs—Foxes' Cubs—Birds and Animals Protecting their Young—The Bills of Birds—The Feet and Claws of Hawks—Birds and Animals Performing Unsuitable Actions—Instincts of Birds about Food and Weather

The observation of the different plans that birds adopt to avoid the discovery and destruction of their eggs, is by no means an uninteresting study to the naturalist. There is far more of art and cunning design in their manner of building, than the casual observer would suppose, and this, even amongst the commonest of our native birds. The wren, for instance, always adapts her nest to the colour and appearance of the surrounding foliage, or whatever else may be near the large and comfortable abode which she forms for her tiny family. In a beech-hedge near the house, in which the leaves of the last year still remain at the time when the birds commence building, the wrens form the outside of their nests entirely of the withered leaves of the beech, so that, large as it is, the passer-by would never take it for anything more than a chance collection of leaves heaped together, and though the nest is as firm and strong as possible, they manage to give it the look of a confused mass of leaves, instead of a round and compact ball, which it really is. The wren also builds near the ground, about the lower branches of shrubs which are overgrown and surrounded with long grass: in these situations she forms her nest of the long withered grass itself, and twines and arches it over her roof, in a manner which would deceive the eyes of any animal, excepting those of boys. When her nest is built, as it often is, in a spruce fir tree, she covers the outside with green moss, which of all the substances she could select is the one most resembling the foliage of the spruce: the interior of the wren's nest is a perfect mass of feathers and soft substances.

The chaffinch builds usually in the apple-trees, whose lichen-covered branches she imitates closely, by covering her nest with the lichens and moss of a similar colour. Even her eggs are much of the same hue. Sometimes this bird builds in the wall fruit trees, when she collects substances of exactly the same colour as the wall itself.

The greenfinch, building amongst the green foliage of trees, covers her nest with green moss, while her eggs resemble in colour the lining on which they are laid. The yellow-hammer, again, builds on or near the ground, and forming her nest outwardly of dried grass and fibres, like those by which it is surrounded, lines it with horsehair; her eggs too are not unlike in colour to her nest—while the greenish-brown of the bird herself closely resembles the colour of the grass and twigs about her.

The robin's eggs being of a reddish-brown, she makes use of dried grass and similar substances. The prevailing colour of the hedge-sparrow's nest is green, and her eggs are of a greenish-blue; and in the same manner all our common and unregarded birds adapt both the outside and the lining of their nests to the colour of the surrounding substances and that of their own eggs respectively.

The little whitethroat builds her nest on the ground, at the root of a tree or in long withered grass, and carefully arches it over with the surrounding herbage, and to hide her little white eggs, places a leaf in front of the entrance whenever she leaves her nest. When the partridge quits her eggs for the purpose of feeding, she covers them in the most careful manner, and even closes up her run by which she goes to and fro through the surrounding grass. The same plan is adopted by the wild duck, who hides her eggs and nest by covering them with dead leaves, sticks, and other substances, which she afterwards smooths carefully over so as entirely to conceal all traces of her dwelling. There are several domesticated wild ducks, who build their nests about the flower-beds and lawn near the windows—a privilege they have usurped rather against the will of my gardener. Tame as these birds are, it is almost impossible to catch them in the act of going to or from their nests. They take every precaution to escape observation, and will wait for a long time rather than go to their nests if people are about the place.

The peewits, who lay their eggs on the open fields with scarcely any nest, always manage to choose a spot where loose stones or other substances of the same colour as their eggs are scattered about. The terns lay their eggs in the same manner amongst the shingle and gravel. So do the ring-dotterel, the oyster-catcher, and several other birds of the same description: all of them selecting spots where the gravel resembles their eggs in size and colour. Without these precautions, the grey crows and other egg-eating birds would leave but few to be hatched.

The larger birds, the size of whose nests does not admit of their concealment, generally take some precautions to add to their safety. A raven, which builds in a tree, invariably fixes on the one that is most difficult to climb. She takes up her abode in one whose large size and smooth trunk, devoid of branches, set at defiance the utmost efforts of the most expert climbers of the village school. When she builds on a cliff, she fixes on a niche protected by some projection of the rock from all attacks both from above and below, at the same time choosing the most inaccessible part of the precipice. The falcon and eagle do the same. The magpie seems to depend more on the fortification of brambles and thorns with which she surrounds her nest than the situation which she fixes upon. There is one kind of swallow which breeds very frequently about the caves and rocks on the sea-shore here. It is almost impossible to distinguish the nest of this bird, owing to her choosing some inequality of the rock to hide the outline of her building, which is composed of mud and clay of exactly the same colour as the rock itself.

In fine, though some birds build a more simple and exposed nest than others, there are very few which do not take some precaution for their safety, or whose eggs and young do not resemble in colour the substances by which they are surrounded. The care of the common rabbit, in concealing and smoothing over the entrance of the hole where her young are deposited, is very remarkable, and doubtless saves them from the attacks of almost all their enemies, with the exception of the wily fox, whose fine scent enables him to discover their exact situation, and who in digging them out, instead of following the hole in his excavations, discovers the exact spot under which they are, and then digs down directly on them, thus saving himself a great deal of labour.

The fox chooses the most unlikely places and holes to produce her young cubs in; generally in some deep and inaccessible earth, where no digging can get at them, owing to the intervention of rocks or roots of trees. I once, however, two years ago, found three young foxes about two days old, laid in a comfortable nest in some long heather, instead of the usual subterraneous situation which the old one generally makes choice of. Deer and roe fix upon the most lonely parts of the mountain or forest for the habitation of their fawns, before they have strength to follow their parents. I one day, some time ago, was watching a red-deer hind with my glass, whose proceedings I did not understand, till I saw that she was engaged in licking a newly-born calf. I walked up to the place, and as soon as the old deer saw me she gave her young one a slight tap with her hoof. The little creature immediately laid itself down; and when I came up I found it lying with its head flat on the ground, its ears closely laid back, and with all the attempts at concealment that one sees in animals which have passed an apprenticeship to danger of some years, whereas it had evidently not known the world for more than an hour, being unable to run or escape.

I lifted up the little creature, being half inclined to carry it home in order to rear it. The mother stood at the distance of two hundred yards, stamping with her foot, exactly as a sheep would have done in a similar situation. I, however, remembering the distance I had to carry it, and fearing that it might get hurt on the way, laid it down again, and went on my way, to the great delight of its mother, who almost immediately

trotted up, and examined her progeny carefully all over, appearing, like most other wild animals, to be confident that her young and helpless offspring would be a safeguard to herself against the attacks of her otherwise worst enemy. I have seen roe throw themselves in the way of danger, in order to take my attention from their young.

No animal is more inclined to do battle for her young ones than the otter; and I have known an instance of an old female otter following a man who was carrying off her young for a considerable distance, almost disputing the way with him; leaving the water, and blowing at him in their peculiar manner; till at last, having no stick or other means of defence, he actually got so frightened at her threats that he laid down the two young ones and went his way. He returned presently with a stick he had found, but both old and young had disappeared. Even a partridge will do battle for her young. A hen partridge one day surprised me by rushing out of some cover (through which I was passing by a narrow path) and flying at a large dog which accompanied me; she actually spurred and pecked him, driving him several yards along the road; and this done, she ran at my heels like a barn-door hen. As I passed, I saw her newly-hatched brood along the edge of the path. I have known a pheasant do exactly the same thing. Wild ducks, snipes, woodcocks, and many other shy birds, will also throw themselves boldly within the reach of destruction in defence of their young. In the same manner they all have bills adapted to the food on which they live—the grain-feeding birds have short, strong mandibles, while those of the insectivorous birds are longer and more slender, and as perfectly adapted for searching in crannies and corners for the insects and eggs that may be hidden there, as the former are for cutting and shelling the seeds and grain on which they feed.

Look also at the birds whose residence and food are placed in the marshes and swamps—the woodcocks and snipes, for example, which feed by thrusting their bills into the soft mud for the purpose of picking out the minute red worms and animalcules which abound in it, have the bill peculiarly adapted for this purpose. The upper mandible has a kind

of knob at the end, which overlaps the under mandible, and not only prevents its being injured, but makes it quite easy for the bird to pass its bill both into and out of the ground without obstruction. How peculiarly well the bill of these birds is adapted for this purpose is perceived at once by drawing it through the fingers. The end of the mandible, too, is full of nerves, which enables the bird to distinguish the soft and minute substances on which it feeds without seeing them. The oyster-catcher, which feeds on shell-fish and similar food, has a bill with hard, sharp points, with which it can dig into and break the strong coverings of its prey; no tool could be made to answer the purpose better. The curlew's long curved bill is also a perfect implement for worming out the sea-slugs, which it extracts from the wet sands. The birds that live chiefly on the insects and water-plants which are found in swamps and muddy places have their feet of great size and length, which enables them to walk and run over muddy and soft places without sinking. The water-hen and water-rail, indeed, often run along the floating leaves of the water-plants without bearing them down by their weight. The bald coot, too, a bird that lives almost wholly in muddy places, has its feet and toes formed purposely for running on a soft surface. How different from the strongly retractile talons of the hawk and owl, made purposely to seize and hold their struggling prey.

Thus also the beak of these carnivorous birds is formed for tearing and rending, while the strong wedge-shaped mandibles of the raven and carrion-crow are the best possible implements for the half-digging, half-cutting work which they are called upon to perform in devouring the dead carcasses of large animals. The goosander and merganser, which feed principally on small eels and fish, have a row of teeth-like projections inside their bill, which, slanting inwards, admits of the easy entrance of their slippery prey, but effectually prevents its escape; while the cormorant, whose food consists of larger fish, instead of these numerous teeth has a strong curved beak, well fitted for holding the strongest sea-trout or haddock. Put your finger into the bill of a common duck, and you will see how easily it goes in, but how difficult it is to draw it out again, in consequence of the sloping projections, by means of which the bird is enabled to hold worms and snails.

No bill but that of a crossbill could cut and divide the strong fir-cones from which it extracts its food. The common woodpecker bores holes with its strongly-tipped wedge-shaped bill in the hard beech-trees, with a precision and regularity not to be excelled by the best carpenter; while with its long worm-like tongue it darts upon and catches the small insects which take refuge in the chinks and crevices of the bark. The swallows, which catch their insect prey while flying at speed in the air, are provided with large wide-opening mouths, which enables them to capture the swiftest-flying moth or midge. In fact, if we take the trouble to examine the manner of feeding and the structure of the commonest birds, which we pass over without observation in consequence of their want of rarity, we see that the Providence that has made them has also adapted each in the most perfect manner for acquiring with facility the food on which it is designed to live. The owl, that preys mostly on the quick-eared mouse, has its wings edged with a kind of downy fringe, which makes its flight silent and inaudible in the still evening air.

The heron has also a quantity of downy plumage about its wings, which are also of a very concave form, and the bird alights in the calm pool without making a ripple, and whilst standing motionless, knee-deep in the water, it is almost invisible in the gloom of evening, owing to its grey shadowy colour. So also is the colour of the wild duck, partridge, and other birds which hatch on the ground, exactly similar in its shade to the dry foliage among which they sit—insomuch so, that even when they are pointed out to one by another person it is very difficult to distinguish these birds.

The feet and claws of different kinds of hawks vary very much, being beautifully adapted to the manner in which each bird strikes its prey. If we examine the claws and feet of the peregrine falcon, the merlin, or any of the other long-winged hawks, including the varieties of those noble birds, all of which I believe were called in the age of falconry the "Ger Falcon," such as the Iceland, the Greenland, and the Norwegian falcon, we find that their power consists rather in their strength of talon and foot, so different from the sharp needle-like claws of the hen-harrier, the sparrowhawk, the goshawk, etc. The rationale of this difference seems to be that the falcons strike their prey by main force to the ground in the midst of their flight; whilst the other hawks usually pounce on the animals on which they feed, and take them unawares on the ground instead of by fair pursuit and swiftness of wing. The sparrowhawk and hen-harrier seldom chase a bird to any distance on the wing.

The rough and strong feet of the osprey are perfectly adapted to the use which they are put to, that is, catching and holding the slippery and strong sea-trout or grilse. The fact of a bird darting down from a height in the air, and securing a fish in deep water, seems almost incredible, especially when we consider the rapidity with which a fish, and particularly a sea-trout, darts away at the slightest shadow of danger, and also when we consider that the bird who catches it is not even able to swim, but must secure its prey by one single dash made from a height of perhaps fifty feet.

The swiftest little creature in the whole sea is the sand-eel; and yet the terns catch thousands of these fish in the same way as the osprey catches the trout, excepting that the tern uses its sharp-pointed bill, instead of its feet. I have often taken up the sand-eels which the terns have dropped on being alarmed, and have invariably found that the little fish had but one small wound immediately behind the head. That a bird should catch such a little slippery active fish as a sand-eel, in the manner in which a tern catches it, seems almost inconceivable; and yet every dweller on the sea-coast sees it done every hour during the period that these birds frequent our shores. In nature nothing is impossible; and when we are talking of habits and instincts, no such word as impossibility should be used.

I could give numberless instances of birds and other animals performing actions and adopting habits which to all appearance must be most difficult and most unsuited for them; all these prove that we are not to judge of nature by any fixed and arbitrary rules, and still less should we attempt to bring all the countless varieties of animal life into any system of probabilities of our own devising. The more we investigate the capabilities of living animals of every description, the more our powers of belief extend. For my own part indeed, having devoted many happy years to wandering in the woods and fields, at all hours and at all seasons, I have seen so many strange and unaccountable things connected with animal life, that now nothing appears to me too wonderful to be believed.

The feet of ducks are peculiarly ill adapted for perching on trees; nevertheless, the golden-eye generally breeds in hollow trees, not only in broken recesses of the trunk, easy of access, but even in situations where, after having entered at a narrow round aperture, the bird has to descend for nearly an arm's length, almost perpendicularly, to reach the nest. Through this same entrance also has she to take her young ones when hatched, before they can be launched on their natural element.

The foot of the heron, as well as its general figure, seems but little adapted for perching on trees, and yet whoever visits a heronry will see numbers of these birds perched in every attitude, on the very topmost branches of the trees. The water-ouzel manages to run on the ground at the bottom of the water, in search of its food. All these actions of birds seem not only difficult, but would almost appear to be impossible. Nevertheless the birds perform them with ease, as well as many others equally curious and apparently equally difficult.

How curiously quick is the instinct of birds in finding out their food. Where peas or other favourite grain is sown, wood-pigeons and tame pigeons immediately congregate. It is not easy to ascertain from whence the former come, but the house-pigeons have often been known to arrive in numbers on a new-sown field the very morning after the grain is laid down; although no pigeon-house from which they could come exists within several miles of the place.

Put down a handful or two of unthrashed oat straw, in almost any

situation near the sea-coast where there are wild ducks, and they are sure to find it out the first or second night after it has been left there.

There are many almost incredible stories of the acuteness of the raven's instinct in guiding it to the dead carcass of any large animal, or even in leading it to the neighbourhood on the near approach of death. I myself have known several instances of the raven finding out dead bodies of animals in a very short space of time.

When a whale, or other large fish, is driven ashore on the coast of any of the northern islands, the ravens collect in amazing numbers, almost immediately coming from all directions, and from all distances, led by the unerring instinct which tells them that a feast is to be found in a particular spot.

Ducks go out to the grass-fields to search for the snails which they know will be found before the coming shower; the field-mouse covers up her hole in due time before the setting in of cold weather. Fish have the strongest instinct with regard to changes of the weather, refusing obstinately to rise at the most tempting baits or flies when clouds charged with thunder or rain are passing through the air. Indeed most birds and animals have a singular foreknowledge of changes in the weather; shifting their quarters according as the coming rain or the dryness of the atmosphere warns them.

The grouse foretell the approaching rains before the most weather-wise shepherd can do so, by betaking themselves to the dry heights, where they sit or walk about with erect heads and necks, in quite a different manner from their usual gait. So do the mountain sheep change their feeding-ground to the lee side of the hills before severe blasts of wind and rain. I have often been warned of an approaching change in the weather by the proceedings of the wild fowl in the bay; and before changes of wind these birds betake themselves to those places which will afford them the best shelter during the coming storm.

There are few animals which do not afford timely and sure prognostications of changes in the weather. It is proverbial that pigs see the wind; and they undoubtedly become restless, and prepare their straw beds prior to a severe storm, some hours before human organs are aware of its approach.

In fine, there is matter not only for amusement but for admiration in the actions and habits of every animal that we see, even down to the most common small birds and quadrupeds: and the unoccupied man may always find wherewithal to amuse himself profitably in watching the instinct which prompts the everyday proceedings of the animals which are always around us.

DECEMBER

Courage of the Water-rail—Owls and Frogs—Frogs and Snakes—Blackcocks—Loch of Spynie—A Snowstorm—Cunning of the Fox—Immigration of Larks—My Peregrine Falcon

December 3rd, 1847. I had occasion to remark the courage of the water-rail; one rose from a ditch when the ground was covered with snow. He flew for a hundred yards and pitched in the snow in an adjoining field, and immediately set off to return to the water from which he had been flushed; a large black gull seeing the little black bird in the snow, made a dart at it to carry it off, but the little rail flung himself on his back, and whenever the gull flew at him, struck out manfully with bill and claws, springing up and pulling feathers out of his gigantic enemy and keeping him off. Afraid, however, that the little rail would be killed, I went and drove away the gull, and allowed him to run back to the water.

During the clear frosty nights of this month we hear the owls hooting for hours together in the old ash-trees around the house. Sometimes an owl, either the common brown one or else one of the long-eared kind, posts himself all day long bolt upright in one of the evergreens near the house. The small birds first point out his whereabouts, by their clamour and fluttering round him; but the owl sits quite unconcerned in the midst of the uproar, blinking his eyes and nodding his head as quietly as if in his accustomed sequestered thicket or hollow tree.

The chief food of owls is mice and birds, but they are also very fond of frogs. When an owl catches a frog, instead of swallowing it whole, as he does a mouse, he tears it to pieces, while still alive, in the most cruel manner, regardless of its shrill cries.

[189]

I have no doubt that were it not for their numerous enemies, such as birds of prey, crows, ravens, rats, etc., frogs would increase to such a degree as to become a serious nuisance. The snake is another of the frog's devourers. It is a curious, although I cannot say a pleasant, sight to see one of these reptiles attack and swallow a living frog, of a diameter four times as large as its own. After a frog has been pursued for a short time by a snake, it suddenly seems to be fascinated by the bright sparkling eye of its enemy, and gives up all attempt at escape; then the snake with a motion so rapid that the eye cannot keep pace with it, darts on its unhappy prey, generally seizing it by the hind-leg. Now commences a struggle for life and death, the frog clinging pertinaciously to any branch or projection which it can reach with his fore-legs; but all in vain; for the snake quietly but surely, by a kind of muscular contraction, or suction, gradually draws the frog into its mouth, its jaws expanding and stretching in the most extraordinary and inconceivable manner, in order to admit of the disproportioned mouthful.

I have little doubt that many birds and other animals are in reality fascinated by the fixed gaze of a snake, when they once come under the immediate influence of his eye. Their presence of mind and power of escape, or even of moving, seem entirely to desert them when their enemy is near them, and they become so paralysed with fear, that the snake has nothing to do but to seize them. Any person who has seen one of our common snakes swallow a large frog will readily believe all accounts of deer being swallowed by the giant serpent of the East.

December 7th, 1852. Both yesterday and to-day it happened that I wounded a partridge not far from the Quarry Road, and on both occasions a peregrine falcon struck the bird in the air, and carried it away before my eyes.

Early in December the roebucks lose their horns. The roe being very much disturbed by wood-cutters in most of our woods, keep to the wild, rough cover, too young for the axe, which lies between the upper country and the shore; there they live in tolerable security, in company with the foxes, black game, and wild-fowl, which tenant the woods and swamps of that district.

The blackcocks, like other birds, are very fond of catching the last evening rays of a winter's sun, and are always to be found in the afternoon on banks facing the west, or swinging, if there is no wind, on the topmost branch of the small fir-trees. On the mountains, too, all birds, as the sun gets low, take to the slopes which face the west; whilst in the morning they betake themselves to the eastern banks and slopes to meet his rays. No bird or animal is to be found in the shade during winter, unless it has flown there for shelter from some imminent danger.

There is no fresh-water lake which has so large a quantity of wild-fowl on it as the Loch of Spynie; and I do not know a more amusing sight than the movements and proceedings of the thousands of birds collected there during this season. On the approach of night, however, the whole community becomes restless and on the move, and the place is alive with the flocks flying to and fro, uttering their peculiar notes, and calling to each other, as they pass from one part of the loch to another. The mallards for the most part take to the fields in search of food, flying either in pairs or in small flocks of five or six. The widgeon keep in companies of ten or twelve, whistling constantly to each other as they fly to feed on the grassy edges of the lochs. The teal and some other birds feed chiefly on the mud-banks and shallows which abound in parts of this half-drained lake; and amongst the loose stones of the old castle of Spynie, which overlooks it, and where formerly proud ecclesiastics trod, the badger has now taken up his solitary dwelling.

December 11th, 1846. Severe snowstorm; widgeon are driven to the open ditches and are very tame. The long-tailed ducks are in every open pool and ditch, and are so tame that they will rather dive than fly, however near I approach.

12th and 13th. The snipes begin to come in great numbers to every open ditch, but they are very wild, in consequence of all their cover being beaten down by the snow, which makes them unable to conceal themselves.

December 13th, 1852. I see peregrines nearly every day. Yesterday the largest peregrine I ever saw passed me with a pigeon in her feet; she was not eighty yards off, and her bright feet holding the bird were quite visible; she was dark slate colour above and nearly white below.

14th and 15th. The redwings, thrushes, linnets, and other small birds, become very tame and distressed for want of food; a tawny bunting, a rare bird here, came into the house.

In the snow I constantly see the tracks of weasels and stoats going for considerable distances along the edges of open ditches and streams, where they search not only for any birds which may be roosting on the grassy banks of the ditches, but also for eels and whatever fish they can make prey of.

The otters, too, puzzled by the accumulation of ice and frozen snow on the shallows, and about the mouth of the river, go for miles up any open ditch they can find; turning up the unfrozen mud in search of eels, and then rolling on the snow to clean themselves.

In the low parts of Morayshire the snow seldom lies long, and consequently after every lengthened snowstorm there is a migration not only of wild-fowl of all kinds, but also of partridges and other game, who come down to the bay and shore from the higher parts of the district, where the ground is more completely covered with snow, the depth of which increases gradually as one recedes from the shore.

If a fox finds a rabbit at a sufficient distance from the cover, he catches it by fair running; but most of his prey he obtains by dint of the numberless stratagems which have earned for him a famous, or rather an infamous, reputation from time immemorial. From what I have myself seen of the cunning of the fox, I can believe almost any story of his power of deceiving and inveigling animals into his clutches. Nor does his countenance belie him; for, handsome animal as he certainly is, his face is the very type and personification of cunning.

The cottagers who live near the woods are constantly complaining of the foxes, who steal their fowls frequently in broad daylight, carrying them off before the faces of the women, but never committing themselves in this way when the men are at home. From the quantity of débris of fowls, ducks, etc., which are strewed here and there near the abodes of these animals, the mischief they do in this way must be very great.

December, in this part of the island, is seldom a very cold or boisterous month; our principal storms of snow and wind come with the new year. Frequently indeed there is no covering of snow on that part of the country which lies within the influence of the sea-air till February.

December 19th, 1847. Robins are very carnivorous, devouring raw meat most voraciously;—so do tomtits.

During the first days of snow and storm a constant immigration of larks takes place; these birds continuing to arrive from seaward during the whole day, and frequently they may be heard flying in after it is dark. They come flitting over in a constant straggling stream, not in compact flocks; and pitching on the first piece of ground which they find uncovered with snow, immediately begin searching for food; feeding indiscriminately on insects, small seeds, and even on turnip leaves when nothing else can be found.

The wagtails frequent the sheepfolds near the shore, and keep up an active search for the insects which are found about sheep.

December 31st. My falcon got loose three days ago, and I had not seen her since then, but this morning I saw a hawk in full pursuit of a magpie, and, thinking it was her, I called in the manner I used to call her, and she immediately left her chase, and after wheeling round and round for a short time, came down on my arm, and began to caress me.